The Nethercutt Collection

The Cars of San Sylmar

Written & Photographed by Dennis Adler

Foreword by Phil Hill

The Nethercutt Collection
A California Nonprofit Public Benefit Corporation

PRINCIPAL OFFICERS

J.B. Nethercutt
Chairman of the Board
Chief Curator

Richard Nolind
President

Byron Matson
Curator

The Nethercutt Collection is dedicated to the preservation
and perpetuation of historical vehicles and memorabilia
for public viewing and education

The Nethercutt Collection
Written & Photographed by Dennis Adler
Published by The Nethercutt Collection
and Blue Book Publications, Inc. ©1999 All rights reserved.

ISBN: 1-886768-14-5
Library of Congress Catalog Card Number: 99-64948

CREDITS:
Photography - Dennis Adler
Layout, Design, & Styling - Thomas D. Heller, Art Director
Cover Photography - Dennis Adler
Cover Design & Layout - Thomas D. Heller
Printing and binding - Sung In Printing, Inc., Korea
U.S. printing representative - Petrice M. Dahl, Pacifica Communications

DEDICATION

To J.B. and Dorothy Nethercutt - for their lifelong commitment to the preservation of
the world's greatest automobiles.

Contents

Foreword
by Phil Hill

Over the many decades that J.B. has been an ardent car collector, I have come to understand and share his passion for great automobiles, whether of antique, classic, or postwar vintage.

Even before I became a race driver in the 1950s and 1960s, I had grown to appreciate fine mechanical engineering, not only in race cars but all automobiles, and particularly twelve-cylinder Packards which have been in my family for as long as I can recall. The car in which my mother brought me home from the hospital, was my aunt's 1918 Twin Six Fleetwood Cabriolet. It is still in my family, as is the 1938 Packard Brunn All-Weather Cabriolet that my wife and I drove to our wedding in 1971. Keeping up a family tradition, this was the car that our children came home in when they were born, and our oldest daughter used in her wedding.

In later years as an automotive restorer and partner in Hill & Vaughn, I also came to understand and appreciate the complexities of restoring automobiles that are better than half a century old. J.B. Nethercutt has shared many of these same experiences with me, and over the years has built one of the finest, if not the finest, restoration shops in the country. The cars of San Sylmar have been among the best restored and most superbly maintained of any in the world, and J.B. has the awards to prove it. He has won Best of Show at the prestigious Pebble Beach Concours d'Elegance six times in the past 35 years, more than any other car collector in history.

It is an honor for me to introduce you to this magnificent collection of the world's greatest automobiles. The cars you will see in this book and at the two Nethercutt museums represent the most important achievements in the history of the motorcar, eras when every improvement in automotive design and engineering was a technological breakthrough. Throughout the collection you will see firsthand, legendary cars which have set the standards in design, engineering, and styling since the late 1890s.

Today, modern automotive technology can do very little to equal, let alone surpass the magnificence of celebrated automobiles like the Rolls-Royce Phantoms, Packard Twelves, and Sixteen-Cylinder Cadillacs, cars that have become far more than mere machines. Over the years since these rolling steel masterpieces were first created, they have ascended to the stature of cultural icons that illustrate and define the greatest decades of the 20th century.

The body design, engineering, and performance of an automobile speaks volumes about the men and women and the very nature of the culture which existed at the time it was built. Nothing says Roaring Twenties like a Packard Eight, defines the dynamics of the 1930s with more clarity than a supercharged 320 horsepower Model SJ Duesenberg, or leaves us in awe of the achievements in automotive design pioneered throughout the Postwar Fifties by cars like the Mercedes-Benz 300SL Gullwing coupe.

As we reach the turn of another century, we can be thankful for men of vision and passion like J.B. Nethercutt, who have preserved the past so that future generations may come to know the great achievements man has made in the pursuit of personal transportation.

Let me be the first to welcome you to San Sylmar and The Nethercutt Collection.

have had the privilege of knowing J.B. and Dorothy Nethercutt for more than 45 years, and of visiting their magnificent automobile museum more times than I can remember.

Phil Hill was America's first Formula I Grand Prix motor racing champion. He is also a well-known car collector and former partner and founder of Hill & Vaughn Restorations.

Introduction

J.B. NETHERCUTT AND THE PRESERVATION OF FUNCTIONAL FINE ART

by Dennis Adler

here is a whimsical quality about J.B. Nethercutt. The man has a perpetual twinkle in his gentle brown eyes and an engaging cherub-like smile accentuated by a pencil thin mustache. It is impossible to look at J.B. Nethercutt and not smile back, not feel comfortable, and yet just a bit apprehensive, as a student might feel in the presence of an esteemed scholar. In the world of car collecting, Jack Boison Nethercutt is the dean, the grand old man, who at age 86 still rattles off specifications, makes, models and production dates of cars built more than half a century ago as though they were scripture. He is a man possessed with a sense of revelry over his lifelong pursuit of great automobiles, what he calls, "functional fine art," an aesthetic rather than pragmatic definition of these otherwise historic monuments to man's mechanical ingenuity.

Today, the Nethercutt automobile collection is considered among the finest in the world, the realization of a vision that began more than 65 years ago with a simple desire to fulfill the dreams of a young couple.

"The first car I owned was in the very early days of my courtship with my wife Dorothy," recalls J.B. Nethercutt. "We've been married 66 years and we were sweethearts for five years before that, and somehow automobiles always played a part in our life together. That first car was a 1923 Chevrolet touring, in very poor condition. It had a loose piston in the engine, there were no floorboards in the front, and the running boards were gone. But since I'd only paid $12 and a .22 pump rifle for it, it really wasn't too bad of a deal!"

The Chevy was J.B. and Dorothy Nethercutt's getaway car in their early years. "Dorothy and I used to take long rides in this old car, which terrified her, especially in the rain because of the missing floorboards, so I borrowed $10 from her mother and bought a used sedan body, which was in pretty good condition. We drove the car with that body on it for many more years."

It was during the early part of their life together that J.B. and Dorothy Nethercutt began their love affair with old cars, of course, back then, they were new cars.

"When we were out driving we would see these gleaming monsters that we call Classics today, and we studied them, visited the automobile showrooms, we bugged the salesmen to death," he says with a mischievous smile, "until finally we got to the point where we could identify a car two blocks away and pretty well quote the specifications on it. Of course, we never in the world thought that we could own one because they were so horribly beyond our reach. Years later when I became successful in a business I had started, and we were affluent enough to afford one of those gleaming monsters we remembered so well, we found that most of them were in dreadful condition."

That was the beginning of a life-long passion to preserve the cars from their youth. In 1956, J.B. and Dorothy decided that the only way they could get one of the cars they had so admired in the 1930s was to buy the best example they could find and have it restored.

It was around this same time that J.B. met a used car dealer named Marshall Merkes. "He had some Duesenbergs for sale in Glendale, California. I visited him and on the spot bought a 1936 Model JN convertible coupe. That car is still in our collection at San Sylmar. At the time, Merkes said he couldn't let me take delivery for about three weeks because he had to replace some items that had been taken off to fix up another car. I'm not sure if it wasn't the other way around, though. Needless to say, I was very disappointed in not being able to take the car with me to show Dorothy, so on the way home I saw a big,

black, hulking monster of a car parked at a corner filling station." Curiosity got the better of J.B. and he stopped to inquire. It was a 1930 DuPont town car. And it was in awful shape. Recalls J.B. as though the event only happened a few days ago, "Its bumpers were missing and the interior fabric was flapping out the window in the breeze," he says with a waving gesture to punctuate the car's windblown upholstery. "I bought it for $500 and thought that I could restore it in the three weeks that Merkes needed to put the Duesenberg back together. I miscalculated slightly. Nineteen months and $65,000 later I finished the DuPont!"

Proud of their effort, J.B. and Dorothy transported the DuPont on a truck to the mid-winter meet of the Classic Car Club of America, which was held that year in Skytop, Pennsylvania. It was judged at 99-3/4 points. "I lost a quarter of a point because the horn didn't blow the first time I pressed the button, but it was still the highest point car the club had ever had up to that time."

Later in 1957, the Nethercutts entered the DuPont in the Pebble Beach Concours d'Elegance. Recalls J.B., "We decided to drive it to the Monterey Peninsula from Santa Monica. In doing so we went over a freshly-oiled road which threw oil all over the undercarriage and the back of the car. Made a pretty bad mess. Dorothy and I had no help with us, so in order to put the car into the Concours we cleaned it up ourselves. It was at that time I discovered floating a thin film of kerosine in the wash water helped to get rid of road film and oil. It worked out beautifully, we repolished the car, went through the judging and took Best of Show."

Looking back on his first misadventure with the DuPont, he remembers that it was not a very good car. "It was poorly engineered, but it gave me a taste of classic car collecting, particularly since I had seen so many beautiful cars at the Pebble Beach Concours, and I gradually accumulated many of the cars of our courtship." That accumulation totals slightly more

than 200 cars today, among them some of the finest classic and antique models from the world over.

Like most people caught up in the enthusiasm of a new hobby, J.B. Nethercutt hadn't considered that he was building a collection when he purchased his first few cars. "At the time I never had it in my mind that there was a car collection in the making, I just owned cars that I liked." That interest continued to expand over the years and in the early 1960s he acquired a taste for antique motor cars, as well.

"My interest in antique and vintage cars began long after I had started collecting Classic Era cars. I became seriously interested in the horseless carriages and early antiques through a really good friend of mine, Roger Morrison, who had told me about a car tour in the little Northern California town of Alturas. It was run by a gentlemen named Rodney Flornoy. Most of the cars on the tour had been built in the 1910s, and this intrigued me." This was the first time J.B. Nethercutt had seen any of the older models actually running on the road. "I was amazed at the way they performed, and how well they were built. I discovered that people back in those very old days, 1908 and so on, thought that when they bought a car it was for a lifetime. They didn't anticipate that there would be a model change every year as we have today. The cars were made substantially so that they would last, and they lasted long enough to become out of date."

Today, The Nethercutt Collection consists of some of the rarest cars from the turn of the century and early 1900s. Says Mr. Nethercutt of the somewhat eclectic mixture of horseless carriages and vintage makes he has accumulated over the last 30 years, "I never had any trouble finding them, they found me," he says, pausing to chuckle over his unusual array of rolling antiquity. "Somehow or other word got out that there was a sucker loose with money."

Since he first displayed his DuPont at Pebble Beach in 1957, J.B. Nethercutt has won Best of Show six times, and has shown at least one car each year for the past 43 years, except in 1966 when he was unable to attend. While that may sound like a staggering number of cars, cars restored to the rigorous standards of the world's most prestigious Concours d'Elegance, it represents less than one quarter of the automobiles in The Nethercutt Collection today!

One of the true founding fathers of the collector car hobby, J.B. Nethercutt is a man who has not only recognized the importance of these once grand automobiles, but put forth the time, effort, and the money to see that they are restored to their original condition.

"I am by nature a perfectionist," he admits, "and in my restoration of cars nothing short of perfection has ever suited me."

"J.B. is a perfectionist," says Dick Nolind, President of The Nethercutt Collection. "He used to say, we can't get away with a thing, and he developed us all into perfectionists, to ensure that every car is restored in exacting detail." The mechanics, fabricators, and artisans employed by The Nethercutt Collection are indeed among the finest in the world, a fact that is reflected in the magnificent cars on display at San Sylmar, and in the countless Best of Show and class awards which have been received by Nethercutt cars in AACA, CCCA and Concours d'Elegance competition for more than 40 years. "That's the way I have always restored my cars," says Mr. Nethercutt, "and in order to compete with me other people have had to match that standard." It has come to be known as a "Pebble Beach quality restoration," says Dick Nolind, "and the Nethercutt cars really established the gold standard for automobile restoration."

While at first glance appearing to be comprised almost entirely of American-made cars, the Nethercutt Collection is uniquely balanced between models designed and built in the United States, Great Britain and Europe during the first half of the 20th century.

Explains J.B. Nethercutt, "The collection is comprised of cars from the world over. Now true, the very finest cars in the world, such as Lincolns, Cadillacs, Packards, Pierce-Arrows, and Duesenbergs, are absolutely necessary in any worthwhile collection, but so too, are the great European marques such as Isotta-Fraschini, Hispano-Suiza, Mercedes-Benz, and Rolls-Royce. In studying any make of car, I've tried to find the best example of the marque in year, body style, and in some cases, body builder."

The collection also consists of some of the most unusual motor cars ever built, a handful of which are the sole surviving examples of the marque, such as the Nethercutt's 1907 Westinghouse, the 1909 Gobron Brille, and the 1904 Cameron.

There are cars in the collection made famous by the celebrity of their original owners, such as film star Rudolph Valentino's 1923 Voisin, Fatty Arbuckle's 1923 McFarlan, and Constance Bennett's stunning 1930 Rolls-Royce Phantom II Town Car, featured in such films as the 1937 MGM classic, The King and the Chorus Girl, starring Jane Wyman, Edward Everett Horton, and Joan Blondell.

With so many remarkable cars in the collection, one might wonder if J.B. Nethercutt has a favorite, and his response to that question is just as imaginative as the collection. Says Mr. Nethercutt without a moment's hesitation, "I have no favorite car because every one is a favorite for some reason, otherwise it wouldn't be in the collection. Some of the cars are in the collection because of their beauty, others because of their performance, and some for their mechanical detail or advance in automotive engineering." There are many reasons why each car is a favorite.

Housing and preserving so many automobiles led to a decision in the early 1960s to establish a museum which could maintain and display the collection. At the time, Mr. Nethercutt recalls that the cars were being stored in various parking lots and just covered with canvas. "I spoke with my friend Tony Heinsbergen, who was gracious enough to let me use his abilities as a designer and decorator to create a very nice building which would include a grand showroom that could display about 30 cars, and was suitable for viewing by the public. That building has become known as San Sylmar, and has been visited by over 1 million people to date."

The stunning six story structure also houses Dorothy and J.B. Nethercutt's magnificent collection of rare musical instruments, player pianos, Orchestrions, and the second largest Grand Wurlitzer theater organ in the world, all beautifully complemented by fine art, antique furniture, automotive memorabilia, and one of the finest restoration shops in the world.

In the year 2000, the second Nethercutt museum opens its doors across the street from the famed Tower of Beauty, displaying another 200 cars from the collection as well as an open view of the most modern automotive restoration facility in the world.

To ensure the future of the collection and the museums, which, as in the past, are open to the public free of charge, J.B. Nethercutt has established a perpetual endowment for the museums. "Collecting and restoring old cars is more than a hobby, it goes far beyond that," he says. "It is a commitment to preserving the past for future generations."

Over the past 40 years The Nethercutt Collection has become what J.B. Nethercutt best describes as "part of a lifestyle," one that has made him the caretaker and preservationist for one of mankind's greatest and longest lived engineering achievements. "It is my intention that this collection will be available for the public, that it shall be preserved and perpetuated as far as the human mind can conceive."

Preface

The San Sylmar Collection

by Byron Matson, Curator

Welcome to the Nethercutt Collection. Throughout the pages of this book you will be viewing the collections assembled by J.B. and Dorothy Nethercutt. You will be seeing the same renowned American and European cars, artifacts, and remarkable musical instruments that more than a million visitors to San Sylmar have enjoyed for over a quarter of a century. You will also get a look "behind the scenes" that few people have ever had the privilege of experiencing.

The Nethercutts began their collections in 1956 with the purchase of a 1936 Model J Duesenberg, the car which started them on the road to acquiring a world-class collection of over 200 antique and classic cars.

With the presentation of an antique music box as an anniversary gift to Dorothy, a collection of disc and cylinder music boxes, player and reproducing pianos, nickelodeons, giant Orchestrions, and one of the world's largest and finest concert theater organs were assembled. They surprise and delight those who see and hear them on the tours.

In looking for an antique desk from which to conduct operations, a 19th century copy of the first roll-top desk built for King Louis XV, led to a collection of pieces in that famous style. These with other of the decorative arts make a whole that is at once breathtaking and yet inviting.

The renowned design studio of Tony Heinsbergen, which created some of the grandest interiors of public and private edifices throughout the United States, Canada, and Mexico, designed the sumptuous building to house and display these treasures. While the collections encompass what generally would be termed "applied and mechanical art," the collections are restored to perfection and everything is in perfect operating condition. The automobiles are prize-winning showpieces and every one starts and drives as it did when new. The automatic musical instruments all play as they did when they entertained their original listeners generations ago. Everything is indeed, "functional."

Ground was broken for the original Tower of Beauty in June 1969, and gradually a huge steel and concrete shell grew on the site in Sylmar, California. Then disaster struck at 6:01 am on February 9, 1971. The Sylmar earthquake damaged the new construction and months were spent strengthening the structure to make it even more resistant to the earth's tremors. In December 1973 the building was completed and the following January the Nethercutts opened San Sylmar to the public for free tours.

Mother Nature once again shook the ground in January 1994, and the force of this great quake closed the collection for 14 months. Again, along with repair and restoration, the structure was thoroughly and seismically upgraded to rigorous new standards. Since reopening in 1995, the collection has been further improved with the addition of more cars and an increase in the size of the Wurlitzer theater organ, which now has more than 5000 pipes!

With the grand opening of the second Nethercutt Collection building in 2000, more than 200 antique, vintage and classic American and European automobiles can be seen on display, along with the world's finest collection of mechanical musical instruments.

The Nethercutts have enjoyed the years spent in collecting and planning the display of their treasures, and that enjoyment is all the more enhanced in sharing them with you!

Acknowledgements

by Dennis Adler

It has been my pleasure to know J.B. Nethercutt for more than 20 years, to have had the privilege of visiting his museum countless times, and of being allowed to drive many of the cars in the collection. To truly appreciate the craftsmanship that has gone into the restoration of the Cars of San Sylmar, a seat behind the steering wheel drives home the hundreds, often thousands of man hours that go into a restoration. This truly is one of the world's great automobile collections.

In the production of this book more than 100 cars from the collection were taken on location around Southern California, particularly to Pasadena, where some of the grandest homes in America can be found, great, sprawling estates built in the 1920s and 1930s, the same time as many of the cars in the collection. It was our desire to place these vintage automobiles in proper, historical surroundings for the photography, and we owe a great debt of gratitude to the many homeowners who allowed us to invade their personal sanctuaries with our cars and crew.

Our sincere appreciation also goes to Carol Mailloux, Executive Director of the Santa Paula Chamber of Commerce for her help securing locations in the historic Santa Paula valley. Recognition is also due the Los Angeles County Department of Parks and Recreation for their patience and cooperation, the city of Fillmore, Stan Garner and the Fillmore and Western Railroad, George Lewis of Ronnie's Automotive Service, Edward and Patty Turrintine, Bob Langton, Sandy Snyder and the L.A. Arboretum, Steve English, Dr. Val Clark, Mrs. Bernice Harbers, Johnny Mountain, Dennis Lowe, Dolores Kroop, Mr. & Mrs. Keneth Grobeker, Tony Heinsbergen, Jim Zoleski, Bruce Meyer, Winston Millet, David Sydorick, Regina Drucker, and the City of Beverly Hills, for providing additional locations.

Needless to say, it takes the efforts of many people to produce a book such as this. As author and photographer I am but one part of a team which performed like a well restored car. My personal thanks to Dick Nolind, President of The Nethercutt Collection, Curator/Archivist Skip Marketti, the restoration department staff, Jim Shewbert, Skip Gackstetter, Roger Morrison, Arnold Schmidt, Toby Allison, Dave Ritter, Don Rudd, Lou Keer,

A moment's rest on location with Collection Archivist Skip Marketti, Restorer Dave Ritter, and Transportation Coordinator Lou Keer.

Acknowledgements

and Nethercutt Collection Vice President Mike Regalia. Our thanks also to Music Department Director and Nethercutt Collection Vice President Gordon Belt, Gerry McCoy, and Lori Underwood. The quality of this book reflects their commitment to going the extra mile in everything they do.

Last, the best photography and writing mean nothing unless a highly-skilled and talented art department and publisher take on the task of producing the finished product. To that end, we owe our thanks and appreciation to Steve Fjestad and his staff at Blue Book Publications, Inc. for delivering the highest quality graphics, design, and printing in automotive book publishing.

To everyone who has played a role in creating this tribute to The Nethercutt Collection, my sincere and heartfelt congratulations and thanks. ◉

Publisher S.P. Fjestad (left), Nethercutt Collection President Dick Nolind, and Author Dennis Adler.

Chapter One

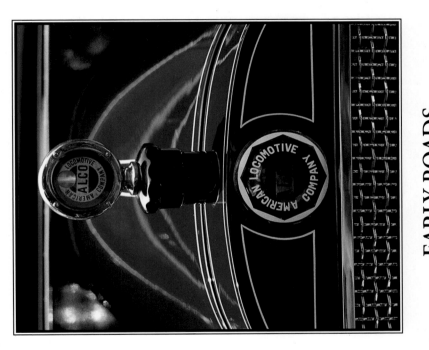

EARLY ROADS

From the Turn of the Century to 1915

Chapter One

ould it be that we've come so far in the last century that the past is beginning to fade from memory? When Indy cars draft each other today at 240 mph, can any of us even appreciate that in 1911, when the first Indianapolis 500 was run, reaching 60 mph--a mile in a minute--was considered a remarkable feat.

So much has come to pass in the last 100 years that what remains today of the American automotive industry is but a sliver of a once grand era when everything was new and fascinating. This was the world of the early 1900s, when automakers were springing up all across the country and every wagonmaker, blacksmith, and mechanic with half an idea threw caution to the wind on a crazy new idea--building a horseless carriage.

Of the thousands of automotive makes that have come and gone since the turn of the century, those that remain amount to a mere handful, and the hand is getting smaller each year with corporate mergers and consolidations. In the last 50 years alone we have seen the demise of Packard, Hudson, Nash, American Motors, Studebaker, and DeSoto, to name but a few. Chrysler is now in partnership with Daimler-Benz. Legendary marques Jaguar and Aston Martin are divisions of Ford Motor Company, and in the new millennium Rolls-Royce motorcars will be built by BMW.

The times they are a changin', but they always have been.

By the end of the 1930s, the Great Depression and an emerging shift in the automotive tastes of American consumers had sidelined such legendary companies as Pierce-Arrow, Marmon, Franklin, Auburn, Cord, and Duesenberg. A generation before, in the years from 1899 to 1915, companies whose names are barely remembered today, such as Alco, Cameron, Columbia, Chalmers, Knox, Toledo, and Pope-Hartford, had already failed in their attempts to bring the motorcar into the 20th century. Today, these earliest makes are regarded as antique automobiles, but in their time they were the greatest cars that had ever been produced. Here then, are a few examples of mankind's earliest efforts to put the cart before the horse.

1886 Benz

1886 BENZ PATENT MOTORWAGEN REPRODUCTION

The birth of the automobile can be traced back to 1885 when a German engineer named Carl Benz opened the doors of his small Mannheim workshop and rode around the yard in a three-wheeled carriage powered by a single cylinder, internal combustion engine. The gasoline engine was not a new idea in the 1880s. Large, stationary engines had been in use since the latter part of the 19th century to power industrial and farm machinery, in fact Carl Benz had pioneered the development of stationary engines. It was his conception of a small single-cylinder version that allowed Benz to create a phenomenon--the motor carriage.

The first successful model of its kind, the 1886 Benz Patent-Motorwagen was powered by a water-cooled, single-cylinder, horizontal engine. The piston and cylinder were oriented fore and aft, and displacement was 954 cc or 58 cubic inches. Output was a trifling 3/4-horse-power at 400 rpm, but it was sufficient enough to propel the light, three-wheel carriage at speeds of up to 10 mph.

On January 29, 1886, Carl Benz was granted German patent number 37435 for his invention-the Benz Patent-Motorwagen--recognized today as the first automobile and the source of all that has followed for more than a century. The example shown is one of a handful produced in 1986, using the same type of tools and materials that Carl Benz had at his disposal more than a century ago. The Motorwagens were built to commemorate the company's 100th anniversary in 1986.

1901 Toledo

1901 TOLEDO MODEL A STEAM CARRIAGE

By the turn of the century encouraging break-throughs had been made in the development of motorized transportation using three means of power--gasoline, electricity, and steam. In 1900, the American Bicycle Company reorganized its manufacturing plant in Toledo, Ohio, into the International Motor Car Company and began producing a line of steam-powered motor carriages. The first steam cars were sold under the names Toledo and Westchester, but by 1901 the entire company was simply known as Toledo.

Their first steam cars were powered by a vertical two-cylinder 56.5 cubic inch, double-acting engine developing 6-1/4 horsepower. Typical for 1901, the Toledo utilized a simple tiller steering handle and carriage-style coachwork with the steam engine positioned under the body and passenger seat. Noted Toledo advertising for the 1901 Model A: "To those desiring a carriage for pleasure driving, in

1903 Peerless

American automaker that produced an exceptional car, Peerless opened its Cleveland, Ohio, factory in 1900. One of the "Three P's," along with Pierce-Arrow and Packard, Peerless came to be regarded as one of the finest motorcars manufactured in the early part of this century. Not bad for a company that started out making clothes wringers.

By 1903 Peerless was building one of the most stylish and ingenious automobiles on the road. The Rear-Entrance Tonneau pictured, is indicative of the company's fine early efforts, not only in styling, but engineering. Powered by a front-mounted, two-cylinder, 16-horsepower engine, Peerless pioneered the use of shaft drive in the U.S. auto industry, a very innovative feature in an era when most automakers the world over were using chain or belt drive.

The Peerless was a high-quality car for its day with a frame constructed of channel steel rather than wood, very elaborate coachwork, and a reputation for durability that justified one of the most pretentious slogans of the day: "All that the name implies."

jaunts through the country, to the golf links, or sea side, it will prove a most delightful and certain means of transportation. For city and business or professional use, no type of motive power is so well adapted."

Well adapted or not, at a price of $900 (a considerable amount of money in 1901), the Toledo lasted for only three years. The steamers were dropped in 1903 when the Pope Motor Company succeeded the International Motor Car Company. This superbly restored and award-winning '01 Toledo, is one of the very few surviving examples known.

1903 PEERLESS REAR ENTRANCE TONNEAU
Another turn of the century

1903 Peerless

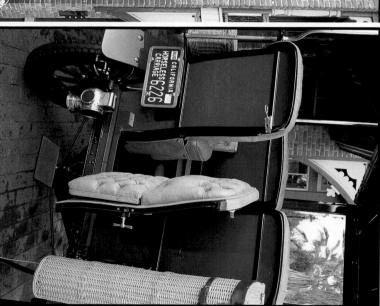

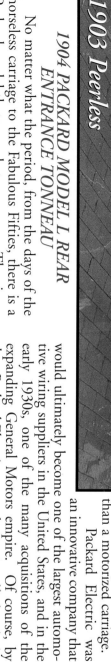

1904 PACKARD MODEL L REAR ENTRANCE TONNEAU

No matter what the period, from the days of the horseless carriage to the Fabulous Fifties, there is a Packard model that appeals to someone. That is an accomplishment few automakers can claim, especially one that has been out of business for nearly half a century!

The Packard brothers, James Ward and William Doud, opened the doors to their North Avenue assembly plant in Warren, Ohio, in the summer of 1899. The Packards were already highly successful manufacturers of incandescent lamps and electrical transformers, a flourishing enterprise in a country where the Edison electric light was far more practical than a motorized carriage.

Packard Electric was an innovative company that would ultimately become one of the largest automotive wiring suppliers in the United States, and in the early 1930s, one of the many acquisitions of the expanding General Motors empire. Of course, by then Packard Electric was no longer involved with the Packard Motor Car Company, nor were James and William Packard, who had both passed on, William in 1923 and James in 1928.

Back in the 1890s, however, James and William saw great promise in the motorcar, and being financially and technically capable of pursuing this new endeavor, proceeded to build their first production automobile just before the turn of the century. With a successful line of motorcars selling through dealerships in New York, Philadelphia, and Chicago, the brothers were approached by one of their largest stockholders, wealthy Detroit entrepreneur Henry B. Joy, who proposed moving their flowering enterprise to Michigan.

Like the Packards, Henry Joy grew up in comfortable surroundings and attended the finest schools, his father, James F. Joy, having made his fortune governing the Michigan Central and Chicago, Burlington and Quincy railroads. When the Packard board of directors issued an additional 2500 shares in the company in 1903, Joy and a group of Detroit investors purchased the entire offering.

Joy's investment group included such luminaries as dime store magnate J.J. Newberry; (who was Henry Joy's father-in-law); Truman H. Newberry; Joy's partner, financier Russell A. Alger, Jr.; brother Richard; C.A. DuCharme; D.M. Ferry, Jr.; Joseph Boyer; and Phillip H. McMillan. Altogether, Joy and his associates had invested more than a quarter of a million dollars in Packard by 1903, and in so doing had gained controlling interest in the company.

The decision to move operations to Detroit was made long before anyone in Warren was willing to concede that Packard had outgrown its Ohio-born roots. But the truth was, even if Packard hadn't run out of space to expand its operations, with its board of directors seated in Detroit, the move would have come about regardless.

In Detroit, Joy commissioned architect Albert Kahn to draw up plans for an assembly plant and executive offices. (During his career, Kahn would go on to design many of the Ford, Chrysler, and General Motors assembly plants as well, making him the most renowned industrial designer in the automotive industry.)

The site Joy chose for the new Packard factory was an open field occupied in 1903 by grazing cattle. It was on the outskirts of Detroit at the east end of what

1904 Packard

1904 Packard

was then known as Grande Boulevard. The design of the original buildings also called for a spur to be built off of the Michigan Central Railway, (which had been controlled by Joy's family), thus allowing finished cars to be taken directly from the factory and loaded into railway cars for delivery to Packard's expanding network of retailers. It was an ambitious undertaking considering that the automobile barely had a foothold in America of the early 1900s. The horse drawn carriage, wagon, and the steam locomotive were still the foremost means of transportation in this country. The automobile was at best a curiosity being championed by inventors, engineers, and venture capitalists like Ransom Eli Olds, Henry Ford, David Dunbar Buick, Henry Martyn Leland of Cadillac, and Joy, who would take Packard full speed into the 20th century.

In 1904, a year after the company moved its manufacturing operations to Detroit, Packard introduced its first contemporarily-styled motorcar, the Model L, and along with it, the distinctively shaped Packard radiator shell that would become a trademark for decades.

This magnificent Model L Rear Entrance Tonneau sold for a staggering $3,000 in 1904, and was powered by Packard's 241.7 cubic inch L-head four-cylinder engine. The body, hood and fenders are all aluminum and the molding around the seats is lead filled brass stock. The color of the car is Packard's traditional Richelieu Blue with Corona Cream Yellow wheels, undercarriage, and striping. The elegant Packard interior is upholstered in dark blue leather and all of the accessories are polished brass. This handsome Rear Entrance Tonneau is one of only two 1904 Packards still known to exist!

1905 FRANKLIN ROADSTER

The idea of using an air-cooled engine was not unique to the post World War II era, in fact, in 1902 Herbert H. Franklin brought out what was to become the most successful name in air-cooled automobiles prior to the Volkswagen.

The Franklin engine was originally conceived in 1901 by a Cornell engineering graduate named John Wilkinson. He brought the idea to former newspaper publisher and industrialist Herbert H. Franklin, and Upstate New York venture capitalist Alexander T. Brown. Wilkinson had already completed two air-cooled prototypes for the New York Automobile Company, but the because of, its unusual styling, but in the summer of 1923, a contingent of Franklin dealers led by Southern California distributor Ralph Hamlin, descended upon Franklin's Syracuse, New York, headquarters with an ultimatum: "New car, or no car."

The dealers were prepared to surrender their franchises unless Franklin started building a more conventional looking automobile. H.H. Franklin bowed to the demands of his dealers, after which, the cars looked more or less like any other on the road. In their time, however, early Franklins, such as this '05 Roadster were among the most uniquely-styled, and distinctive motorcars on the road.

firm had neither acted on the idea nor paid him for his work. Brown convinced Franklin to take a ride in one of the prototypes, which so impressed him that he decided to form the H.H. Franklin Company and get into the automobile business.

After some litigation with the New York Automobile Company, the firm was absorbed into the new Franklin Automobile Company in 1902, and the first production version of the Wilkinson design was delivered on June 23. At the rather substantial price of $1,200, a dozen more Franklins were delivered in 1902. This 1905 Franklin Roadster was the company's sportiest model, featuring a transverse-mounted engine, and although unusual in design, because the Franklin had no need for a radiator or grille, it was one of the most successful new cars sold in the country.

A robust and dependable car, Franklin built its early reputation for durability in 1904 when transcontinental driver L.L. Whitman, accompanied by Franklin representative C.S. Carris, drove a runabout from New York to San Francisco in just under 33 days, breaking the previous records held by Packard and Winton by almost a month! Although Franklins did exceptionally well in road races and endurance runs, their greatest selling point was that they never overheated, a problem which plagued most water-cooled automobiles in the early 1900s.

For years Franklin prospered, either in spite of, or

1907 PIERCE GREAT ARROW

Dusters and goggles and hats.

That was what drivers wore in the golden days of motoring, unless they wanted 40 mph winds tugging at their clothes, road dust blowing into their eyes, and hair turned into dirty twisted snarls. Almost every automobile on the road in the early 1900s was a convertible, or to be more precise, a Touring, an open car with a fabric top suspended over the driver and passenger compartment and held steadfast by leather straps. For foul weather, some models also came with side curtains which provided a blurry view of passing scenery through filmy isinglass windows, while keeping most of the rain on the outside of the passenger compartment. It was not an exact science. At the turn of the century the motor car was still a work in progress.

At the vanguard of American automakers dedicated to abating the adversities of motoring in the early 1900s, was the Buffalo, New York, firm of George Norman Pierce. Pierce had begun, as had many in the auto industry, by building bicycles, and had even been at the forefront of that industry, developing a shaft and bevel gear driven bicycle in the late 1890s. Truly diversified, the George N. Pierce Co. also built deluxe bird cages, refrigerators and ice chests! While that might not make the design and production of an automobile the next logical step, for many industry pioneers, Pierce included, the manufacturing of any type of machine was grounds for branching out into the motor trade.

While Pierce was the company's founder and president, he relied heavily on his board of directors: Henry May, Col. Charles Clifton, George K. Birge, William H. Gardner, William B. Hoyt, and Lawrence H. Gardner, as well as David Fergusson, Pierce's first chief engineer, and Herbert M. Dawley, whose job it was to design cars suited to the individual needs of Pierce-Arrow's elite clientele. His was perhaps the most difficult job at Pierce, because he had to deal directly with the some of the wealthiest and most difficult to please people in the country.

The Pierce Great Arrow was almost without a peer (unless one considers Peerless), and in 1907 when this magnificent 135-inch wheelbase Touring was built for a wealthy family in Worchester, Massachusetts, few motorcars of the day could match its performance, quality of construction, and above all else, its lofty

price, $6,500!

The mighty Pierce was powered by a enormous six-cylinder engine displacing 647.9 cubic inches, coupled to a three-speed column-mounted shift mechanism. The big six was used for the first time in 1907, making the Model 65Q Great Arrow not only one of the most elegant and exclusive motorcars of the early 1900s, but also one of the most powerful.

1909 GOBRON-BRILLIE MODEL 70/90 TOURER

In Europe, the motorcar was nearly a decade ahead of the emerging American automotive industry and automakers such as Société des Moteurs Gobron-Brillié (pronounced go-bron bree-a), in Paris, were on the leading edge of design and engineering. Gobron, perhaps was slightly over the edge with the Model 70/90, an elegant Victoria Tourer bodied by Murry Aunger, Ltd., in 1909, which was powered by a gigantic 679.6 cubic inch six-cylinder engine with dual opposed pistons! One of the most complicated and intriguing engines ever conceived, the 12-piston six had two different strokes, 110mm on the bottom set and 90mm above. The output was 90 horsepower, enough to propel a sports model to over 100 mph, making Gobron the first production automobile to break the century mark. Most of the French automaker's cars, however, were large, luxurious models like this '09 originally shipped to Australia, where it remained until coming to the United States in 1970, at which time it was purchased by J.B. Nethercutt.

The small French company manufactured automo-

1909 Gobron-Brillie

biles in Boulone-sur-Seine, on the edge of Paris, up until 1930. As far as can be determined, this is the only 1909 Gobron-Brillie left in the world.

1910 PIERCE-ARROW MODEL 48

"The man who looks at a Pierce-Arrow envies the owner for the striking individuality of the car's design. The man who rides in a Pierce-Arrow envies the owner for the car's absolute reliability under all conditions of service. The man who owns a Pierce-Arrow envies no one".

Pierce-Arrow advertisement, 1912

The first Pierce-Arrow automobiles (the Arrow portion of the name having evolved from the arrowed Pierce logo used on the bicycles), had been completed in May 1901 and shown to Pierce bicycle agents around the country. By year's end George N. Pierce was in the thick of the automobile industry building a line of sturdy, reliable motor cars, and a reputation for quality that would establish Pierce-Arrow as one of the best names in the business.

As sales increased the company outgrew its original facilities on Hanover Street, in Buffalo, and the automotive operations were moved into new buildings erected in 1906 on the former site of the 1901 Pan-American Exposition midway. The 1.5 million square foot complex allowed for engines, chassis, wheels, bodies, and other components to be built almost under one roof.

Like the new Packard plant in Detroit, the Pierce building in Buffalo was among the first in this country to be constructed of reinforced concrete. With what was considered to be one of the most modern production facilities in the world at the time, Pierce settled into a decade marked by advancements in design and engineering that would set a standard for American automobiles well into the 1910s and 1920s, and establish a reputation for building fine motor cars shared only with Packard and Peerless, the other makes that came to be known in the automotive industry as "The Three P's."

Prior to Pierce's retirement in 1909, the George N. Pierce Company officially became the Pierce-Arrow Motor Car Company. By now Pierce had distinguished itself building cars acclaimed and awarded for their reliable operation. In 1909 Pierce-Arrow won the sought-after Glidden Trophy for the fourth time, as well as the coveted Hower Trophy. Pierce had won the very first Glidden Tour in 1905 with a Great Arrow driven by George Pierce's son Percy. The Buffalo automaker won the Glidden Tour again in

1910 Royal Tourist

1906 and 1907, failing only in 1908 to make it a complete sweep for five straight years.

By 1910, when this handsome Model 48 Seven-Passenger Touring was built, the average price of a Pierce-Arrow had reached $5,000, commensurate with competitive models from Packard and Peerless. The Model 48 was powered by Pierce's proven T-head six, which had the cylinders cast in pairs. It was a massive motor displacing 453.2 cubic inches and developing 48 horsepower.

The company standardized its model lines in 1910 offering three basic chassis and engine combinations with 36 horsepower, 48 horsepower and 66 horse-power, respectively on 125, 134-1/2, and 140 inch wheelbases. The 48 was considered to be the quintessential Pierce, and according to the company, the Pierce-Arrow's chassis and engineering had been refined to such a high quality by 1910 that no major changes were needed. Indeed, the three new cars were so well engineered that they went almost unchanged for the next eight years.

The example pictured is a Model 48 built on the 134-1/2-inch chassis and powered by the mid-range engine with a bore x stroke of 4-1/2 x 4-3/4 inches. The stylish open coachwork on the touring body is made of lightweight cast aluminum and all of the trim is polished brass, a handsome, if not conservative design. The 1910 models were all right-hand-drive, with the driver required to enter from the left side of the vehicle and slide across the seat. The right side was usually blocked by the spare tires.

Seating was exceptional in the Pierce, with enough room in the rear compartment for five passengers (two in the fold out jump seats) and the wide front seat allowed ample room for driver and passenger. The deeply padded seats were upholstered in heavy duty pleated leather. These cars were designed to last for many years, and in 1910 when someone purchased a motor car they believed it was likely the only one they would ever need.

1910 ROYAL TOURIST
MODEL M ROADSTER

The Royal Motor Car Company of Cleveland, Ohio, was one of the more short-lived success stories in the American automotive industry. Founded in

1904, Royal was gone by 1911, just one year after this sporty Model M Roadster was introduced. Royal produced a handful of exceptionally well-made medium-priced motorcars, the 1910 Tourist selling for $3,500.

Among features introduced by Royal to the American automotive industry was the very first steering wheel hub horn button, with the horn itself mounted beneath the hood. Not exactly a claim to fame, but up until the Royal, externally-mounted bulb horns had been the order of the day.

The sporty Royal Tourist M Series models were powered by a four-cylinder T-head engine of the company's own manufacture, dispensing a generous 65-horsepower at 1800 rpm, and capable of delivering the cars to a top speed of 65 mph. Pretty heady stuff for 1910.

The two-passenger bodywork was Royal's own design, and for adventurous sorts, an additional third seat was available, mounted atop the spare tires! Built on a 126-inch wheelbase chassis, with a purposefully short front and rear overhang, "...to permit the car to turn in a much shorter space than cars of equal wheelbase," the Royal Tourist could be considered one of America's first true sports cars.

This striking example is one of only 16 known surviving examples from the 1910 model year.

1911 OLDSMOBILE
LIMITED LIMOUSINE

When the American automotive industry was developing in the early 1910s, the Oldsmobile Limited was literally the biggest thing to come out of Detroit, a car so impressive in size and power that it was virtually in a class by itself.

Produced for just three years, 1910 to 1912, the Limited was built on a 138-inch wheelbase frame riding on colossal 43-inch diameter wheels. Under the hood was a massive six-cylinder engine displacing 706 cubic inches (cylinders the size of paint cans) with a bore and stroke of 5 x 6 inches. Developing 60 horse-power delivered through a 4-speed transmission, Olds Limiteds could attain an impressive top speed of 70 mph. Equally awe-inspiring was the car's price, beginning at $5,160. The limousine model pictured sold for an astounding $7,000 in 1911, enough to have paid for several nice homes in the early 1900s.

Ransom Eli Olds was one of America's first automakers. He built his first gas engine motor carriage in 1896, and had half a dozen experimental models on the road when he formed the Olds Motor

Works in May 1899. The first models to bear the Oldsmobile name featured a simple carriage-style body curved up to form the dashboard, which led to the nickname "Curved Dash Olds." The success of the Curved Dash, one of the most popular cars in turn of the century America, led to a decision by the Olds Board of Directors to produce a more elaborate and expensive car, this against the advice of R.E. Olds who finally resigned from the company in January 1904, rather than take part in what he believed would be a disaster. He went on to form the REO Motor Car Company, using his initials to skirt around the use of his name on a competitive product. Meanwhile, the Olds Motor Works continued under the direction of the Smith brothers, Frederick and Angus, whose father, lumber millionaire Samuel L. Smith, had invested nearly $200,000 in the company and gained controlling interest. Just as Ransom Olds had feared, the Smiths moved too quickly, abandoning a ready market for the affordable $650 Curved Dash and replacing it with a new model priced at $2,750. Within a year Olds was awash in red ink. It was the fatal error of all too many overzealous automakers in the early 1900s. Facing receivership in November 1908, the Smiths sold out to William C. Durant for just over $3 million in General Motors stock and a mere $17,279 in cash.

Billy Durant had a knack for purchasing troubled companies and turning them around. In 1904 he had taken over another financially bereft firm, Buick, upon which he had built the foundation for General Motors. Oldsmobile turned out to be another of his success stories and since Durant had the capability of executing the very plan that had felled the Smiths, he quickly expanded the model line to include a $4,500 six-cylinder Olds (introduced for 1908), a $2,750 four-cylinder version, and a new, smaller four, the Model 20, which was based on the Buick Model 10, and priced at just $1,250.

Durant cleverly produced the Model 20 for only one year to bring in some fast cash and bolster Oldsmobile, which is exactly what it did, posting a total of 5,325 sales for the 1909 model year. With his profits, Durant turned Oldsmobile into an all-luxury car line in 1910 with the introduction of the magnificent Olds Limited.

With the luxurious and imposing Limited limousines and tourers towering better than eight feet at

their rooflines, Oldsmobile captured the imagination of a nation just beginning to embrace the automobile, and in just three years achieved Durant's goal of establishing Oldsmobile as one of America's premier automotive marques.

In 1911, Durant's advertising staff wrote of the Oldsmobile: "In the Limited we offer a car which leaves nothing to be desired in design, construction, finish, power or equipment. It stands in the front rank of high grade cars, the greatest of a line universally recognized and ranked among leaders." Although its total production was well under 1000 cars, by 1913, when a less formidable six-cylinder model replaced the Limited, the future of Oldsmobile as a builder of quality automobiles was assured.

1911 POPE-HARTFORD
7-PASSENGER TOURING

One of the most complex stories of the early motor industry in the United States was the rise and fall of Colonel Albert A. Pope's empire, which included Pope-Toledo, Pope-Hartford and lower-priced Pope-Tribune gasoline cars, as well as production of an electric car known as the Columbia.

Associated with Pope was the Electric Vehicle Company of Hartford, headed by former US Naval Secretary W. C. Whitney, who used the Pope plants for most of his requirements, including an order for 1600 electric taxis in 1899 produced by the Columbia Automobile Company. By 1907 more than 9000 electric taxis were combing the hard-packed dirt roads of the eastern United States, and Albert Pope had built them all.

Pope's financial success, however, was not based solely on sales. Among other things, Whitney and Electric Vehicle, which owned Columbia and was in partnership with Pope, held the rights to the Golden Fleece of automotive patents, the Selden patent, which required every automaker to pay a royalty of 1.25 percent on every car sold in the United States to Whitney and Electric Vehicle. This helped fill Pope's coffers until the patent was finally broken by Henry Ford in 1911, ending one of the most controversial patent battles of the 20th century.

As an automaker Pope-Hartford built some impressive cars, particularly in the 1910s, when models such as this tall and stately 7-passenger Touring, were regarded among the most opulent of American motorcars. The Pope-Hartford sales brochure noted that "...a wide range is offered the prospective purchaser in the matter of body styles and the choice offered in finish and upholstering is almost unlimited. We lay great stress upon the fact that the complete car, including the motor, carburetor, bodies, transmission, crank shaft, radiator, axles and other important members, is made in the Pope shops at Hartford."

Despite the quality of its cars and the diversity of products and model lines under the control of Col. Pope and his family, the entire enterprise had collapsed by 1914.

It began with Columbia which became embroiled in the ill-fated United States Motors Corporation debacle that not only brought an end to Columbia, but Brush, Stoddard-Dayton and Maxwell-Brisco as well. The whole affair was survived by Maxwell-Chalmers, which ultimately became the Chrysler Corporation. Pope-Tribune ended production in 1908, Toledo followed a year later, and with rapidly declining sales, Pope-Hartford finally closed its doors in 1914, selling its main plant in Hartford, Connecticut, to Pratt & Whitney.

1912 ALCO

1912 ALCO
7-PASSENGER TOURING

Odd as it may sound, Alco's claim to fame was boasting that it built the most expensive car in America! The Model 9-60 Touring shown sold for $6,000 in 1912. In all truth, it wasn't the most expensive car available, but it was priced high enough to eliminate itself from consideration by about 95% of new car buyers. The remaining 5% were drawn to more recognized makes such as Oldsmobile, Packard, and Cadillac. Still, Alco sold enough cars to remain in business from 1905 to 1913. They were produced by the American Locomotive Company, which came about through the 1901 merger of eight railway locomotive builders, and eventually expanded into the automotive arena in 1905. Virtually hand built, the cars were made to order in Providence, Rhode Island, at an exhaustingly slow pace. In 1909 and again in 1910 the mighty Alcos won the prestigious Vanderbilt Cup, but it did little to increase sales, since it took an average of 19 months to build an Alco!

Built atop a chassis of vanadium steel, described as the "anti-fatigue metal," and fitted with a live rear axle forged in one piece by the largest drop hammer in the world, the Alco 9-60 Series was powered by a 579.5 cubic inch T-head six-cylinder engine developing 70 horsepower. Beautifully finished and handsomely styled automobiles, Alco claimed that they lost $460 on every car they built, which no doubt contributed to the company's decision in 1913 to throw in the towel and concentrate all of its efforts on building steam and diesel locomotives. The car pictured is one of only two or three still known to exist.

1912 CADILLAC
FOUR-PASSENGER COUPE

In 1901, Henry Martyn Leland was contracted to produce engines for automaker Ransom Eli Olds. The long established firm of Leland, Faulconer and Norton supplied 2,000 engines for the curved-dash Oldsmobile, America's first mass-produced automobile. The following year, Leland became part of the first Henry Ford Company, (Ford having been asked to resign by his partners in 1901) and on August 22, 1902, the business was reorganized as the Cadillac Automobile Company, a name chosen in honor of Le Sieur Antoine de la Mothe Cadillac, the French explorer who had founded Detroit in the early eigh-

teenth century.

Leland supplied engines, transmissions and steering gears for the new Detroit-built luxury cars, and was granted a small block of stock and then appointed company director.

Much to Leland's fetish for thousandths-of-an-inch precision, an idiosyncrasy rooted to his youth working with Connecticut firearms manufacturer Samuel Colt in the 1860s, Cadillac became the best built car produced in America. In 1908 the company was presented the coveted British Dewar Trophy for

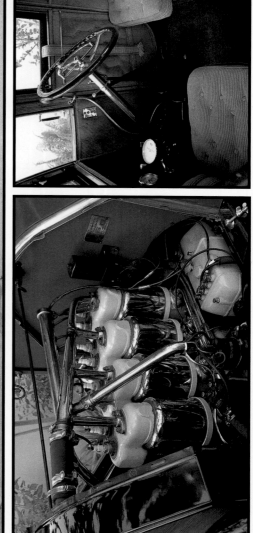

engineering excellence. To achieve this distinction, three Model K Cadillacs were torn completely down, their parts mixed, and the cars reassembled under the scrutiny of the Royal Automobile Club of Great Britain. Not only did the trio of Cadillacs go back together without any filing or hand-fitting, they were immediately sent off on a 500-mile endurance run on the Brooklands track where they ran at full throttle without a single mechanical failure!

By 1910, Cadillac had earned its "Standard of the World" reputation, and regard as one of the most prestigious automobiles built in America. Along with Buick, Oakland, and Oldsmobile, Cadillac had also become part of William C. Durant's General Motors conglomerate, giving GM four of the most distinguished names in the automotive industry.

With Cadillac as the crown jewel of the General Motors empire, the standards for engineering, design, and production increased each year, and in 1912 when this regal Model Thirty Coupe was built, Cadillac had ascended to the top rung of automotive hierarchy producing the best selling luxury cars on the American road. GM closed the model year with 13,995 Cadillac deliveries. More than any other luxury car produced. This was also the year Cadillac introduced the electric self-starter, an unprecedented breakthrough in automobile engineering. No longer would one have to hand crank an engine to get it started. Ford may have put America on wheels, but Cadillac had made it easier to get those wheels rolling, and boldly told the American public with ads that read: "The Car That Has No Crank." Overnight, every other car on the road seemed obsolete compared to a luxurious, self-starting Cadillac.

The 1912 Cadillac line consisted of six standard body styles including the stately four-passenger coupe, one of the year's most expensive models. At this point in history, closed cars were relatively rare, Cadillac having introduced one the world's first in 1906. Half a dozen years later, the exquisitely-finished coupe for four passengers commanded a base price of $2,250. One had to order a Cadillac seven-passenger limousine to spend more.

Built on a 116-inch wheelbase, the high, angular coupe towered at almost seven feet and was powered by a 286.3 cubic inch four-cylinder engine developing a near silent 30 horsepower. For the early 1910s, a Cadillac coupe was the last word in individual luxury.

1912 WHITE
SEVEN-PASSENGER TOURING

Automakers came from every corner of industry, and White's corner in Cleveland, Ohio, concerned the manufacturing of sewing machines, at which White was eminently successful producing as many as 8,000 a month in the late 1880s. A decade later, Rollin White, a younger member of the wealthy industrial family, developed a steam car which went into production in 1900. Like their sewing machines, White steam cars were a resounding success and production climbed to more than 1500 a year by 1906.

As the decade of the 1910s unfolded the sale of steam cars began to lose... well, steam, and White expanded into the internal combustion engine arena in 1912, adding a 489 cubic inch monoblock 60-horsepower, six-cylinder engine to the line. Known as the GF Sixty, models such as this enchanting white and green Touring, which came with a factory-supplied chauffeur, were gaining popularity among the well-to-do, just as World War I brought an abrupt end to automobile their manufacturing in 1917. Only 432 White GF Sixtys were produced at a base price of $5,000 f.o.b. Cleveland.

This car was purchased by the Halstead family of Rye, New York, but at the time, the roads outside of New York City were so bad that the White could barely be driven, (it came to be known as "Mama's folly" because it was Mrs. Halstead's idea to purchase the car), and after only 3000 miles, the great White Touring was put up in the family barn. Undriven for the next ten years, the White Co. still sent a factory mechanic to the Halstead estate once each year through 1924 to change the oil and turn over the engine so as to prevent it from becoming corroded!

When J.B. Nethercutt purchased the White from the Harrah Collection in 1986, the car was still in excellent original condition!

1913 MERCEDES 37/95 TOURER

"Thus the Mercedes Comes,
O she comes, This astonishing
device, 'The amazing Mercedes
With Speed.'"

--William Ernest Henley,
"A Song Of Speed"

The 1901 Mercedes had redefined the motorcar, setting into motion a machine that would change the very nature of personal transportation. Over the next dozen years Mercedes automobiles would lead the world in design and engineering, Mercedes, or rather Daimler, still quite independent of crosstown competitor Benz. The two would eventually merge in 1926 to create Mercedes-Benz.

By 1913, when this majestic 37/95 Tourer was built, the Mighty Mercedes was regarded as the most powerful production automobile in the world. The Mercedes engine had two blocks of two cylinders each with three overhead valves--one intake, two exhaust--per cylinder, and a single camshaft mounted high in the crankcase. The fuel was delivered by a single Mercedes-design sliding piston carburetor. A four-speed gearbox, with a gate change shifter mounted to the outside the body, delivered the engine's puissance to the dual chain-driven rear axle. The car's estimated top speed was 115 km/h--roughly 70 mph--although it was reported that with light-weight coachwork a 37/95 could almost attain the coveted 100 mph. In 1913, few vehicles could achieve such speeds unless fitted with weightless coachwork best suited for racing.

Produced from 1910 through 1914, the Mercedes 37/95 chassis was replaced in 1915 by an even more powerful 38/100 horsepower model. The actual output of the engines, incidentally, was always the second figure shown, the first was nominal output used solely for taxation purposes in Germany.

In the early 1910s, Mercedes models were available either with shaft-drive, designed by Paul Daimler in 1907, or the original chain-drive, and while the latter was being phased out, in 1910 the factory introduced a new series of chain-driven cars, including the 37/90, 37/95 models. The justification was simply that chain-drive had proven more durable in cars equipped with higher powered engines such as the 37/95. Daimler offered a total of 12 different chassis, four

1913 Mercedes

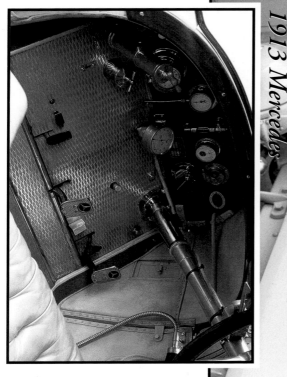

with conventional chain-driven rear axles and eight with shaft drive. Still, the most powerful car in the line was the chain-driven 37/95, such as this custom-bodied Tourer.

In the early 1900s, Mercedes styling ran the gamut from conservative formal Limousines and Landaulettes to dashing Phaetons and high-spirited sport two-seaters. Tourer designs, however, were among the most preferred of the period.

Built on chassis number 13294, this graceful French-bodied model was commissioned in 1913 by Mercedes Société in Paris and built by Carrossier Rothschild et Fils. The car was subsequently sold to a Monsieur Beeche of 45 Avenue Hoche, Paris, on September 6, 1913, for 21,000 francs and the trade of a 45 HP chain-driven chassis with a Rothschild phaeton body. Beeche kept the Mercedes until 1930 and then sold it to a Monsieur I. Grossman, of 21 Boulevard Mariette, Boulogne, Sur. - Mer., on March 19, 1930.

The car's history throughout the 1930s and on into the postwar era is unknown, except that it is one of the few 37/95 examples to survive in tact for more than 85 years. It was restored in the 1970s by James A. Conant of Cleveland, Ohio.

According to records kept at the Nethercutt Collection, it was in good original condition when Conant purchased it. Restored as it is today with the distinctive body-mounted nickel-plated spotlight, dark-white exterior paint, two-tone cream leather upholstery and tan canvas top, it represents one of the benchmarks in pre World War 1 automotive engineering and body design.

1913 WINTON MODEL 17-D TOURING

Following contemporary motor carriage design and utilizing chain drive and tiller steering, a Scottish emigrant and bicycle-maker named Alexander Winton put a one-cylinder engine in the rear of what for all intents and purposes was a two-seat wagon, and in 1897 launched himself into the automotive trade from his new American home in Cleveland, Ohio.

Winton built his first motorcar with exceptional durability and powered it with a 10-horsepower engine capable of propelling the carriage to a then breathtaking speed of 33.64 mph. In a new two-cylinder, model Winton drove from Cleveland to New York City, a feat which earned him headlines in the Cleveland Plain Dealer and clinched the sale of his

tors shown any superiority over it. It is an up-to-the-minute car. To change such a car as the Winton Six, except to refine details, would be high folly."

It was a bit pompous, as was Alexander Winton, and such thinking eventually began to cut into Winton sales. He raised prices in the early 1920s, believing that there should not be a cheap Winton, and sales plummeted in 1922. The following year he admitted to being "financially embarrassed." A year later there was talk of a merger with Haynes and Dorris, but in the end the feisty Scotsmen chose instead to get out of the car business and concentrate on the production of diesel engines. The Winton Motor Carriage Company eventually became the Cleveland Diesel Engine Division of General Motors. The last Winton motorcar was built in 1924.

permitted such speeds.

Much to his own detriment, Alexander Winton hated to make changes, and in 1913 the sales brochure even bragged that the 48 H.P. Winton Six had not undergone a single radical change since its introduction in January 1907! "The Winton Six is a proven success...steadily increasing its popularity, and winning new and enlarged numbers of enthusiastic owners. In five consecutive years of success it has developed no weaknesses and no short-comings that needed to be remedied, nor have its competi-

first car on March 24, 1898. Within a year Winton had built and sold more than 100 motor carriages.

Wintons produced after 1901 were the first to feature a new invention...the steering wheel, an idea shared with fellow Ohio automakers James and William Packard, who were to become Winton's arch rivals in the early years of the American motorcar industry.

In the 1910s, Winton models like this immense 1913 Touring roamed the rough hewn roads of America along with countless other upstart makes and models. Wintons, however, had a long-standing reputation for durability and style, albeit rather conservative style. Priced competitively for the era, the cost of this handsome maroon Winton Six was just $3,000.

Powered by a 477 cubic inch six-cylinder engine of Winton's own design, the Model 17-D had an output of 48-horsepower delivered via a 4-speed gearbox, and sufficient brawn to get the lengthy Tourer up to better than 65 mph, if one could find a road that

1914 American

1914 MODEL 644 AMERICAN UNDERSLUNG TOURING

While Ransom E. Olds and Henry Ford were developing affordable, mass produced cars between 1900 and 1914–cars which were to drive the price of most automobiles below $1000–the affluent were privileged to such costly voitures as the American Underslung,

considered among the sportiest cars on the road.

Even with its lowered chassis it was quite a step up into the American, due to the use of immense 38-inch wooden-spoke wheels, chosen to bring ground clearance to an even foot, increase stability, and allow the cars to chug through muddied roads that would bog down lesser cars.

American's chief engineer became intrigued with the juxtaposition and had the axles and springs mounted above the frame to see how it would turn out. The answer was quite well. The early Underslung Roadsters introduced in 1907 were the first American sports cars. Larger models, like this 132-inch wheelbase 1914 Touring, were still

selling for upwards of $4,000.

The Underslung was a radical departure from the canons of conventional automotive engineering in the early years of the 20th century. The main frame, instead of being carried above the axles, was hung below them on half-elliptic springs, thus reducing the overall height of the car and lowering the center of gravity. Quite an ingenious idea for the early 1900s.

Exactly how this came about has been the subject of much speculation over the years, but the popular belief is that the innovative design was an accident. A chassis being brought into the workshop by movers was inadvertently set atop the assembly horses upside down. Fred Tone,

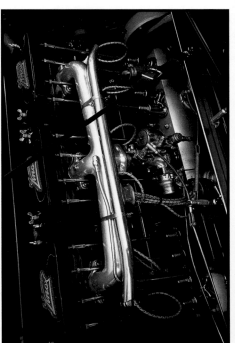

American Underslung owners had at their control a 571 cubic inch, six-cylinder, 60-horsepower engine, one of the most powerful available at the time, electric starting, and one of the easiest to control automobiles on the road, guaranteed by virtue of its low slung design to be almost impossible to overturn. With luxurious upholstery and fastidious attention to every detail of construction, this was truly one of the greatest automobiles produced in the early 1900s. It was also one of the most expensive to build, and American, like so many companies in the early 1900s, over extended itself, and was eventually was pushed into receivership by creditors. This 1914 Model 644 Touring was one of the very last cars to be built by the Indianapolis, Indiana, company.

1914 KNOX MODEL 46
LITTLE SIX TOURING

In the early 1900s every automaker was a pioneer, but Harry A. Knox truly was one of the first, building an experimental four-cylinder opposed internal combustion engine in 1895. After a brief stint with Duryea, he organized his own company in 1898 in Springfield, Massachusetts, producing air-cooled three-wheelers. The Knox design evolved into a more substantial line of four wheel tourers in 1901, and the company continued to improve its cars throughout the 1900s, introducing a handsome line of water-cooled six-cylinder models in 1911.

From around 1907 on, Knox had also begun to build large and expensive luxury cars like this stately Model 46 Little Six Touring model, which was produced in 1914, the year Knox ceased automobile production. It was ironic, because the company had gone to such great lengths to build what it believed was the ideal mid-priced luxury car for the American market. Knox literature stated that, "Our aim in the design of the Model 46 has been to fulfill the requirements of that large number of automobile enthusiasts who desire a trim, handsome six of reasonable capacity, designed with an efficient motor of sufficient power and flexibility to meet the

1914 Peerless

requirements of both town and country service.

"We believe a car has been given the American motoring public in the Knox Model 46 which marks a new epoch in high-grade motor car design and refinement and one which successfully meets every need of the discriminating motorist."

The Model 46 offered a lot of car for the money, priced at $4,350 with a 46-horsepower 496 cubic inch overhead valve six-cylinder engine, but it was too little, too late. By 1914 the company was deep in debt, mostly in the hands of its creditors, and reorganized at the end of year to specialize in the manufacturing of tractor-trailer and fire apparatus units, a spin-off of Knox Motor Truck/Atlas Motor Car Co. also started by Harry Knox in 1904, which, in the long run, proved itself more successful than the automobile venture ever had. In 1916 the new enterprise, operating under the name Martin Rocking Fifth Wheel Co. (named after the innovative direct coupling device it had invented) merged with Militor Motors Co. to form Knox Motors Associates, in Springfield. The new concern produced winch tractors and articulated vehicles under the Knox-Martin name. The whole venture finally collapsed during the post World War I recession, and that was the end of Knox. The automotive branch, did, however, go out on a positive note in 1914. The Model 46 Little Six was the best car Knox ever built.

1914 PEERLESS MODEL 48-SIX TOURING

Peerless had entered the 20th century producing a single-cylinder model in 1900, but was one of the first American automakers to introduce four and six-cylinder models of exceptional quality, the four in 1904 and its first six in 1907. The Peerless slogan, "All That the Name Implies," unabashedly proclaimed the car's quality and high standing within the automotive world. Peerless was always on the cutting edge, keeping pace with engineering advances at Packard and Cadillac, its two closest competitors. This was always a great financial burden on the company and there were numerous changes in management and ownership over the years, with the company often under the guiding hand of former General Motors executives.

In 1914, the Cleveland, Ohio, automaker offered a total of three Series and seven different body styles, the most popular being the Model 48-Six Touring,

The 48-Six was the mid-priced Peerless model, positioned between the 38-Six and 60-Six, the model numbers designating the actual horsepower of each Series. The Model 48 was built on a 137-inch wheelbase chassis and available in five different body styles, the Seven-Passenger Touring, pictured, Torpedo, Landaulette, Limousine, and Berline-Limousine.

Peerless body styling was refined for 1914 with straight unbroken lines from the radiator to the gentle upward curve of the parapet at the rear seat. The new, lower appearance endowed the 1914 models with an air of genteel strength and lithe energy. Peerless called the look "dignity and racy grace."

To streamline the cars traditional side-mount spares were done away with and relocated to a rack at the rear of the body, thus permitting easy entry to the driver's compartment from either side of the car, and the fuel tank was rehung under the back of the frame, affording it better protection. The fully-equipped Peerless models came with electric interior lighting, leather upholstery and the finest wool carpeting. Peerless described the 1914 Model 48-Six as "a worthy culmination of 14 years of unrelenting effort to produce the most perfect motor car." At $5,000 it truly was the best that money could buy.

1914 RAUCH & LANG B4 ELECTRIC BROUGHAM

History has an odd way of changing facts. Fact. Carl Benz patented the motorwagen in 1886, and this is regarded as the first automobile, historically speaking. However, at the time Benz was manufacturing motor-cars powered by an internal combustion engine, the automobile was perceived by most people as something altogether different, and vastly superior to the stinking, vibrating, obstreperous gas-engined "horseless carriages" being offered as an alternative to the almost silent and more gracefully styled electric car.

By the turn of the century, the majority of automo-biles on the road were either powered by batteries or steam. The internal combustion engine was not yet king of the road.

The first Rauch & Lang electric was completed in 1904, and production started in 1905 when 50 cars were built. In 1907, capital stock in the Cleveland, Ohio, company was increased from $75,000 to $250,000 and by 1909 to $1 million. The Hertner Electric Co, which supplied motors to Rauch & Lang, was bought in 1907 and John H. Hertner became the company's chief engineer. Two years later production was running at 1000 cars annually and sales agencies had been appointed in 20 cities, some as far afield as Manchester, New Hampshire, and Denver, Colorado. Success, however, was fleeting. In 1920 Rauch & Lang sold its passenger car business to the Stevens Duryea Co. of Chicopee Falls, Massachusetts, which built a new fac-tory adjacent to its existing plant. There, a dwindling number of electric passenger cars were produced along with a line of taxicabs. The era of the electric car as a means of personal transportation had come to an end.

What had begun as one of the most successful indus-tries in the world at the turn of the century, simply went out like a light. One can only imagine how far electric car technology would be today if the original companies like Rauch & Lang, Baker, and Detroit Electric had sur-vived.

The regal 1914 Brougham in the Nethercutt Collection was built during the glory days of the elec-tric car, and is perhaps the finest example extant of the luxurious Rauch & Lang Brougham. It is elegantly upholstered in plush red velvet, and comfortably seats four with remarkable all-around visibility for passen-gers and driver, who, incidentally, controls the car from a rear seat.

Driving the Rauch & Lang wasn't too different from today's electric golf carts, there was a forward and reverse lever, and the more power that was applied, the faster the car went, although speed was not of the essence, since the Brougham was just a bit top heavy, and with tiller steering, not that easy to maneuver at anything above 30 mph. Driven by an 80 volt electric motor and a cache of rechargeable batteries, the Rauch & Lang was virtually silent. The only noise generated was the sound of the tires rolling over the road!

1915 PACKARD MODEL 5-48 TOURING

It came to be known as "The Dominant Six," but around Packard's East Grand Boulevard factory, everyone called the Model 5-48 "Jesse Vincent's Hot Rod."

It wasn't intended to be a car known for its unsurpassed speed, but it turned out that way just the same. In a 1915 Packard advertisement, East Grand's chief engineer, Jesse Vincent, was quoted as

saying, "Be careful how you step on this car. It leaps like a projectile."

The Packard Six had a massive engine with a swept volume of 525 cubic inches, (4-1/2 x 5-1/2 bore x stroke), and an output of 80 horsepower, giving the car what Packard called "The Fastest Getaway--60 Miles an Hour in 30 Seconds from a Standing Start." While that may not sound very impressive today, in 1915 it was a startling speed for anything that wasn't built for racing. The last of the series, the 5-48 or Fifth 48, as it was also known, set a record at the Indianapolis Speedway, clocking 70 miles in just one hour. Packard noted this feat in their advertising, proclaiming the Dominant Six as "Boss of the Road."

The Packard's high speed capability became so well known that by 1915 it was practically adopted as the official getaway car of the underworld, one that could easily outrun the lower-priced automobiles used by local and state law enforcement agencies. As early as 1913, The Packard, East Grand's official publication, noted that "No longer may we ignore the ironical suggestions that have poured in since homicide by motor car has come into prominence in New York."

1915 Pierce-Arrow

Newspaper pictures of the 'gray murder car' show unmistakably that it is a Packard, an unknowing and innocent accomplice of 'Lefty' Louis, 'Dago Frank' and the rest. Our friends intimate that the lightening like getaway has recommended the Packard to the dark uses of the powers that prey. Jesse James, Dick Turpin and other outlaws of yesterday and the day before used the best horses obtainable...The selection of the Packard by the gun men of New York is, we insist, a matter of evolution and no reflection on the integrity of the car." Still, the notoriety didn't hurt.

In 1914, Packard sixes were available in a total of 20 different body styles and in both "38" and "48" series, the "38" having been added as a lower-priced model (replacing the four-cylinder Model Eighteen). Mechanical improvements to the driveline, engine, and suspension on all Packards made 1914 models the best riding and handling cars that had yet come from East Grand Boulevard.

The new Fourth Series 4-48 was powered by an L-head engine developing 82 horsepower. The engine was further refined by having the cylinders cast in two blocks of three (previously they had been cast in three blocks of two).

The Packard transmission was equipped with a new rear axle ratio of 3.58 and an optional 3.28 gearset. Brakes were increased from 15-inch to 17-inch drums, and only one wheelbase was available for all body styles, a massive 144-inch frame.

Having reached what many considered to be the epitome of design and engineering for the era, Packard's 4-48 models were virtually unchanged and carried over as the 5-48 in 1915, the year a Packard Six Touring was chosen as pacesetter for the fifth Indianapolis 500 Mile Memorial Day Race. The crowning achievement for the mighty Dominant Six.

This elegant 1915 Model 5-48 seven-passenger Touring is painted traditional Packard colors: Richelieu Blue and black with yellow trim, and upholstered in black leather. The 1915 Packard Six radiator cap, a tall stack with an enamel finish and bright red "48" emblem, indicated that this was a six-cylinder model. And if the latch used by Packard for the radiator cap looks oddly familiar, that's because the design was inspired by the Mason jar!

This stunning open car originally sold for $4,850.

1915 PIERCE-ARROW
FIVE-PASSENGER TOURING

Pierce-Arrow had solidly established itself as one of America's preeminent automakers by 1915, going from strength to strength each year, and never shying away from letting its exclusive clientele know about it. The 1915 sales brochure stated that "Discriminating men

and women have little patience with compromise. They want the best, always, whether it's food or clothing, a room in a hotel, a cabin on a ship, a horse, or a motor car. Motor cars are of three kinds: cheap cars, cars of compromise, and cars of quality." Needless to say where Pierce-Arrow placed itself.

The 1915 model line consisted of no less than 13 different body styles from a sporty two-passenger Runabout to a regal Vestibule Suburban Landau. All models, regardless of style or wheelbase in the 1915 Series 36C, 48B and 66A, featured the exclusive Pierce-Arrow fender design with integrated headlamps, a Pierce trademark established in 1913 that was literally decades ahead of any other automaker.

The 1910s were Pierce-Arrows best years, when the New York automaker was regarded as an industry leader. That would change in the 1920s, and by 1938, Pierce-Arrow would be another of the great early American automotive names left behind in the path of progress.

This imposing 1915 Model 48B Five-Passenger Touring was one of Pierce-Arrow's most popular body styles, selling for $4,900. Pierce coachwork for 1915 was highlighted by a trend toward more rounded bodylines, larger fenders, and a cowl that flowed from the hood up to the body. To give the cars a more streamlined appearance the frames were dropped between the axles and the entire body lowered by three-inches. The famous headlights also received a facelift, the housings redesigned into a concave silhouette that would remain unchanged for the next 18 years.

1915 STEVENS-DURYEA SEVEN-PASSENGER TOURING

The Duryea Brothers, Charles E. and J. Frank had put America on wheels in 1896 with the first production car built in the United States, but the brothers soon went their separate ways, Charles building Duryea cars in Reading, Pennsylvania, and J. Frank moving to Massachusetts, where he joined the Stevens Company, a well-known armaments firm with automotive aspirations. In 1901 they introduced the first Stevens-Duryea motorcar. Charles venture failed in Reading and most of his further attempts followed suit. It was J. Frank who would eventually get all the credit for building the first American production car, and for the Stevens-Duryea, which became one of the most successful motor cars of the early 1900s.

By 1915, when the Chicopee Falls, Massachusetts, firm built this stylish Seven-Passenger Touring, there were already more than 14,000 Stevens-Duryeas on the road!

Although there was nothing exceptional about Stevens Duryea body styling, other than that the coachwork was all aluminum, the cars were well appointed and upholstered throughout with hand-buffed black leather. Powered by a 518.8 cubic inch L-head six-cylinder engine, the 138-inch wheelbase cars could easily reach speeds in excess of 60 mph. The 1915 models were the first to offer a Delco-electric starter and left-hand drive, which was still a relatively new idea in America where right-hand-drive had been the accepted standard since the turn of the century. Moving to the left side of the car wouldn't become de rigueur until the 1920s.

Well made, and competitively priced at $4,800, it seemed as though the Stevens-Duryea would continue long into the coming decade, but to everyone's surprise, 1915 was the last year the company would build cars until after World War I.

Production ceased when J. Frank, who had gained control of the company in 1914, refused to build a cheaper version of the car, and rather than give in to the New York bankers holding the purse strings, he simply quit and the company was sold shortly thereafter to Westinghouse.

In 1919, Ray S. Deering, Thomas L. Cowles, and several former Stevens Duryea employees purchased the name and factory back from Westinghouse and put the cars into production once more, only this time without J. Frank Duryea. The following year Stevens Duryea, Inc. purchased Baker Electric Cars and Rauch & Lang,

and began assembling electric taxicabs and cars in a new plant next door to the Duryea assemblyline. Unfortunately their timing was a bit off, as were sales of electric cars and Duryeas. The entire concern went into receivership, was taken over by a syndicate headed by Roy M. Owen, (late of Owen Magnetic fame), in 1924, and a year later it was announced that cars would only be built to order. The orders stopped coming in 1927, and that was the end of the Stevens-Duryea. ✥

1915 Stevens-Duryea

Chapter *Two*

THE VINTAGE YEARS

Cars From 1916 to 1924

1916 Packard

ankind tends to measure its achievements in decades: The Gay '90s, The Roaring Twenties, the postwar boom of the Fifties, everything neatly categorized in ten year increments, with one exception...automobiles. The history of the motorcar, from the late 1880s to present day has always been gauged in eras, some as short as a few years, others in sweeping decades like the Classic Era, from 1925 to 1948. One of the most dramatic periods in the automobile's rambling saga did in fact encompass a ten year span, it occurred from 1915 to 1925, a period that saw American and European auto industries take a

quantum leap forward in technology and design.

In the years from 1915 to 1925 the automobile matured from a mechanical contrivance, a mere curiosity to most, into a practical means of personal transportation. And with it came the beginning of an infrastructure that would change the face of America.

Nineteen Fifteen was a tumultuous year, not only for the automotive industry but the world at large. In Europe, war had broken out during the summer of 1914 and the automotive industry was gearing up for the production of military vehicles: Rolls-Royce was building armored halftracks instead of open tourers, and Daimler plants were manufacturing aircraft

engines rather than Mercedes. In the United States, a brief but dramatic expansion began within the American automotive industry as car makers increased their model lines, four cylinder engines gave way to sixes, sixes to eights, and eights to V-12s. At the same time custom coachwork became vastly more important as a means of differentiating makes and models. It was to be an era of change, and no one would benefit more from it than the automotive consumer, everyone from the laborer toiling long hours to purchase a Model T, to the industrialist contemplating his next limousine or town car.

1916 Packard

1916 PACKARD TWIN SIX LIMOUSINE

If building on the strengths of its prestige image was the goal, then 1915 was truly a watershed year for Packard. This was the year that Packard stunned the automotive industry with the introduction of the first twelve-cylinder automobile put into series production anywhere in the world--the Twin Six.

Designed by Packard's chief engineer, Jesse Vincent, the Twin Six so improved production techniques that the cars actually sold for less than the previous six cylinder models! With a base price starting at only $2,750 for the short 125-inch wheelbase five-passenger phaeton, Packard had not only built a more refined and more powerful car, but had built it for less.

At the time of its introduction, on May 1st, 1915, the Twin Six marked the greatest single advancements in automotive design since the debut of the Mercedes in 1901. The stately twelve-cylinder Packards were the car of choice for film stars, industrialists, politicians and heads of state. In 1921, President Elect Warren G. Harding, the 29th occupant of the White House, rode down Pennsylvania Avenue in a Packard Twin Six. This was the first time in history that an automobile had been prominently featured in an inaugural parade.

With the Twin-Six as its flagship, Packard sailed into the 1920s with a stunning line of automobiles to rival any on either side of the Atlantic.

The Packard Twelve engine was actually comprised of two banks of L-head cylinders, vee'd at a narrow 60-degree angle, thus the name Twin Six. It had a massive swept volume of 424 cubic inches with a bore and stroke of 3 x 5 inches, and a near silent output of 85 horsepower at 3000 rpm.

The Twin Six remained in production until 1923, the longest of any model up to that time, and accounted for a staggering total of 35,000 sales, establishing Packard as one of the world's leading manufacturers of luxury automobiles.

This stately 1916 Twin Six Limousine features an

1918 Pierce-Arrow

open driver's compartment and ornate, painstakingly hand-painted wicker canework decorating the rear body panels. Bodied by Packard, this was truly one of the most elegant looking cars of the 1910s. It originally sold for $3,150.

1918 PIERCE-ARROW MODEL 66 PROTOTYPE TOURING

Few automakers enjoyed more favor for as long a period as Pierce-Arrow. By the late 1910s they were neck and neck with Peerless and Packard for the title of America's premier luxury car maker. In 1918, Pierce increased its stake in the marketplace by introducing a new 825-cubic inch dual-valve engine, thus increasing

output from the same displacement inline six as used the previous year. The dual-valve six was also a quieter engine, and it returned better fuel economy than its single-valve predecessor.

The Pierce-Arrow engineering department in Buffalo, New York, had spent more than five months developing the dual-valve 66. Only four prototype cars were built, which reportedly went to dealers as demonstrators, before America's involvement in World War I curtailed automobile production. The Pierce 66 was the first American automobile to incorporate four wheel brakes. This handsome seven-passenger Touring is the only remaining example of the Model 66 prototypes!

1919 Pierce-Arrow

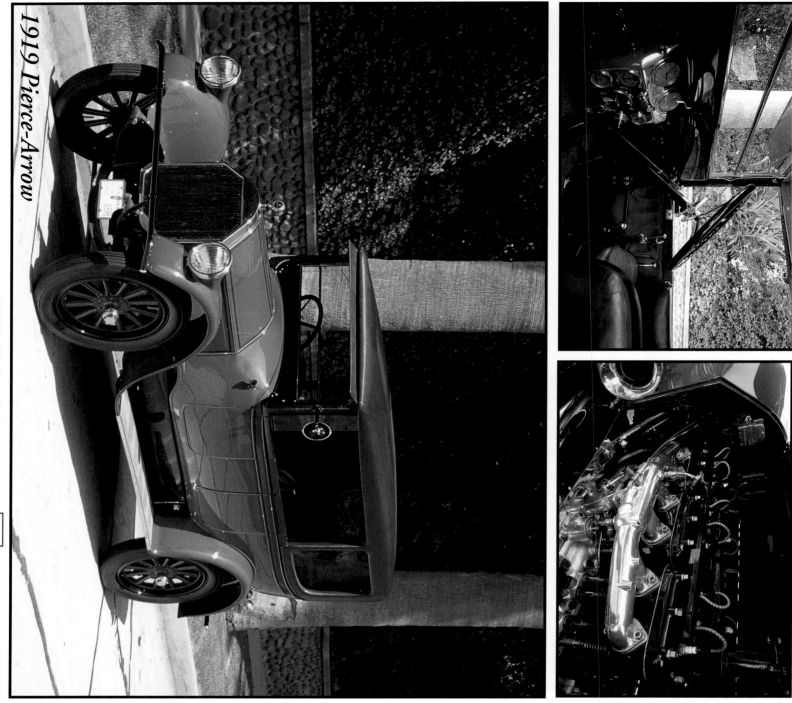

1919 PIERCE-ARROW MODEL 48 TOURING

Immediately following the Armistice, Pierce-Arrow resumed automobile production, and did so in a big way, introducing an even more advanced 524.8 cubic inch dual valve six with four valves per cylinder.

The new postwar model gave the earlier Model 66 a good run for its money in 1919, developing 48-horse-power, more swiftly and more efficiently than its pre-war predecessors.

In 1919, engineering and design began to share equal importance at Pierce-Arrow, and the company went to some lengths to stress that in their advertising, noting in one 1919 sales brochure titled "Rivalry Between Utility and Beauty," that "Always the engineer strives for mechanical advance, while the body design-er and finisher aim to enhance the appeal to the eye. In the current Pierce-Arrows the contest narrows down almost to a drawn battle. The power plant is as effi-cient as the car's appearance is distinguished. This beauty speaks for itself."

This striking 1919 Seven-Passenger Touring spoke louder than most, having been fitted with Pierce-Arrow's exclusive open coachwork combined with a custom top designed for the car by the Walter M. Murphy Company, in Pasadena, California. The Murphy top, added in the 1920s, featured sliding glass windows, thus permitting the same view from inside as an open touring, but with the wind-free ride of a closed sedan.

1923 McFARLAN MODEL 154 KNICKERBOCKER CABRIOLET

The Twenties marked a well-defined shift from the previous two decades, when nearly half of the coun-try's population had lived in rural areas and on farms, to one of a more mobile populace. Now, more people were moving to the cities, which in turn were spread-ing block by block further into what had once been the countryside. Taller and larger buildings were being erected, industry was growing, and from Main Street to the Lincoln Highway, roads were being built across the land, and the automobile was fast becom-ing the most popular means of personal transporta-tion in the country.

In 1909, in the quiet Indiana town of Connersville, where the McFarlan Carriage Company had been man-ufacturing wagons and carriages since 1856, it was

The Nethercutt Collection 59 The Cars of San Sylmar

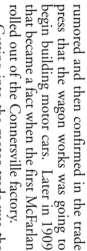

rumored and then confirmed in the trade press that the wagon works was going to begin building motor cars. Later in 1909 that became a fact when the first McFarlan rolled out of the Connersville factory.

Getting into the motor trade was the idea of Harry McFarlan, grandson of the company's founder John B. McFarlan. Harry chose to present his new cars to the public with some fanfare by testing them on the track at Indianapolis over the Labor Day weekend in 1910! The McFarlans finished third and fifth and fourth and fifth in two races held the year before the first Indianapolis 500. It was an impressive first outing and cars began to sell in small numbers, about 200 a year, which was all that Harry could build from the wagon works.

In 1913 the company was reorganized as the McFarlan Motor Car Company. As a manufacturer of exclusively hand-built luxury cars, McFarlans were very pricy from the start, beginning at around $2,000 and rising to a lofty $9,000 in 1923 when the company built this almost larger-than-life Knickerbocker Cabriolet for film star Roscoe "Fatty" Arbuckle.

Powered by the new Twin-Valve Six engine introduced in the 1921 Knickerbocker, it featured triple ignition, 18 spark plugs, and a menacing 120 horse-power!

Handsomely built atop 140-inch wheelbase chassis, the Knickerbocker was McFarlan's top-of-the-line model and as equipped for Arbuckle it came with a canopy that snapped onto the back of the roof and was supported some six feet hence by a pair of lance-like poles. It also came with a director's chair with Arbuckle's name embroidered across the back. It was said that the rotund actor would sit under the canopy between scenes and enjoy a libation or two from the amply stocked trunk.

With the exception of a 1923 Knickerbocker built for display in the Chicago Automobile Show and fitted with 24-carat gold trim and hardware (subsequently selling for a record $25,000 to the wife of an Oklahoma oil man), Arbuckle's Knickerbocker was the most lavishly appointed car the company ever built.

Fatty Arbuckle's career ended in scandal in the 1920s, and by 1928 McFarlan was gone, not because the cars were unpopular but simply, and ironically, because Harry McFarlan and his close associate Burton Burrows had always managed the company. Since 1924 McFarlan had been in very ill heath and there was no one else to direct operations but Burrows, who died in 1928, and with him the McFarlan Motor Car Company. The McFarlan assets were acquired that same year by automotive and aviation mogul Errett Lobban Cord. The McFarlan and the great Knickerbocker models sadly have become one of automotive history's more obscure and little remembered makes, except at the Nethercutt Collection, where Fatty Arbuckle's 1923 Knickerbocker Cabriolet is always on display.

Chapter Three

THE KINGS OF THE ROAD

American Cars From 1925 to 1941

t has always fallen upon those of us who live in the present to determine what of the past is worth remembering, what places, what people, and even what automobiles long gone deserve to be celebrated as high water marks in human history.

With more than a century of production to take into consideration, selecting a handful of cars upon which to hang the laurels is no easy task. There is, however, one period in the history of the American automobile that stands head and shoulders above the rest, the years from 1925 to 1948, better known today as the Classic Era.

From 1925 until America's entry into World War II in 1941, automakers had advanced the design and engineering of the motor car further than any other period since the turn of the century. Almost everything we consider modern today, such as overhead camshafts, four and five valves per cylinder, shatterproof safety glass, and even automatic transmissions, were developed before the 1940s. Traveling the road of progress, however, many automakers ran out of gas long before the Classic Era ended. They would never witness the sweeping changes that would ring down the curtain on many of the industry's most venerable traditions, the greatest of which was custom coachwork.

Here then, are the great cars from the greatest era in the history of the American automobile, names many will have heard, but few can recall having seen on the road.

The centerpiece of The Nethercutt Collection is this magnificent 1933 Model SJ Duesenberg Arlington Torpedo Sedan. Built for display at the 1933 Chicago "Century of Progress Exposition", it was named the "Twenty Grand" for its record setting price in 1933.

1925 DOBLE STEAM CAR

Steam power had been the driving force for a variety of American cars in the early 1900s, the most famous of which was the Stanley. White had made inroads into steam propulsion in the early years of the new century as well, but no one was more daunless than Abner Doble and his brothers.

Scion of a wealthy industrial family, the Doble brothers had been fascinated with steam power since their early childhood. While attending MIT in 1910, Abner visited the Stanley Brothers in Newton, Massachusetts, where he became further intrigued by the idea, taking the Stanley's design and improving upon it through the use of a condenser which recycled exhaust steam back into the engine.

Doble's design became the most advanced in the world, a concept that in theory proved superior to any other, but in practice a mechanical nightmare surpassed only by the Doble's lack of marketing sagacity and willingness to compromise in the interest of profitability. Their first venture failed in 1914. The design, however, succeeded in attracting the interest of C.L. Lewis, head of the Consolidated Car Company of Detroit, which launched the Doble steam car in 1916.

The new models were so advanced in design that they required no more preparation to start than a conventional gasoline engine automobile. In just 90-seconds a Doble had a full head of steam and was ready to roll. Once underway the cars were almost silent until the boiler kicked in to produce additional steam, unleashing a thundering roar similar to a small jet engine. The operation of the Doble required deft attention to pressure and

The Cars of San Sylmar

1925 Duesenberg

a keen eye on the road as the application of brakes had to be timed with cutting back the flow of steam via a regulator lever on the steering wheel hub. There was no floor throttle, no transmission, only the foot brake, a lever to change from forward to reverse, and another regulating output from the four-cylinder engine -- a staggering 150 horsepower and 1000 lbs-ft of torque delivered at 1 rpm!

One could challenge the logic of the Doble, or any steam car for that matter, since they required gasoline, kerosine, or heating oil to fire the boiler. The Doble averaged 10 miles per gallon of fuel, so while the range of the car on 17 gallons of water was touted to be up to 1500 miles, the driver had to refill the 24 gallon gas tank every 240 miles!

The average Doble measured 150 inches between the axles and weighed nearly three tons, yet from behind the wheel there was a seamless flow of power, and were it not for the complexity of the design and the sheer cost of the car, from $8,800 to $11,200 in 1925, the mighty steam car might well have succeeded long into the 1930s. Unfortunately, Doble ran out of steam, figuratively speaking, in 1931. Fewer than 30 cars in the E and later F Series were produced by the Doble

Brothers in their new Emeryville, California, facility. The Dobles never made a profit. Factory records show that each car cost them $55,000 to make!

The example in The Nethercutt Collection was bodied by the Walter M. Murphy Company of Pasadena, California, for Howard Hughes. The handsome roadster body has a completely disappearing convertible top, and a specially modified engine ordered by Hughes with higher steam pressure, (2000 psi), and a 1:1 ring and pinion. As equipped for Hughes, the Doble E-20 could attain a top speed of 133 mph!

The car was completely restored at The Nethercutt Collection in 1996-97 and is the only known example operating with a square top firebox. Most E Models were retrofitted with the later F type boilers, which added an additional 125 feet of tubing.

The Doble engine is a compounded design with a double bore of 2.625 and 4.500 inches and stroke 5.000 inches, for a cubic inch displacement of 214.14 x 2 cubic inches. The Doble steam engine and boiler is one of the most facinating automotive designs of this century. To further explore this unique achievment in automotive history, the Collection is currently building a cut-a-way display chassis and engine for exhibit in the new museum.

1925 DUESENBERG MODEL A PHAETON

Few automakers built their reputation on racing with more success than Fred Duesenberg, who began his career building and racing hill climb cars in the early 1900s for Maytag and Mason motorcars in Waterloo, Iowa. With more than a dozen years of racing experience behind them, Fred and his younger brother Augie, longed to produce a passenger car that would incorporate the advanced engineering they had developed for racing. After several failed ventures and a stint at manufacturing marine engines during World War 1, in 1920 they were able to organize the Duesenberg Automobile & Motors Company with financial backing from venture capitalists Newton E. Van Zant and Luther M. Rankin. The first passenger car to bear the Duesenberg name, the Model A, was shown at the 1920 New York Auto Salon. The car introduced two features appearing for the first time in an American automobile: a straight-eight engine and four-wheel hydraulic brakes. The Nethercutt Collection's 1925 Model A is one of the finest examples known from this early era in Duesenberg passenger

1925 Locomobile

car production.

Although the straight-eight chassis were fitted with bodies manufactured by several of America's leading coachbuilders, including the renowned Walter M. Murphy Company in Pasadena, California, the Model A Duesenbergs were not overly successful. This was not necessarily due to the cars, which had been superbly engineered, but rather a combination of the postwar recession and poor management by company executives, most of whom were replaced in 1923. For the most part, the company's sales and operating problems were out of Fred and Augie's hands, since the Duesenberg Automobile & Motors Company, as with previous ventures, was theirs only in name.

Somewhat disillusioned by their foundering automotive business, the Brother's again pursued their one true passion, racing, and in 1924 they entered four Duesenberg Specials in the 12th Indianapolis 500,

1925 LOCOMOBILE
MODEL 48 VICTORIA SEDAN

Unassailable quality, in an era when quality and reliability were the greatest problems plaguing the flowering automotive industry, was the hallmark of yet another

claiming the checkered flag with America's first supercharged race car. Of all his achievements, even the legendary Model J, Fred Duesenberg cherished the 1924 victory at Indianapolis as his greatest moment.

With sales of approximately 600 cars in five years, the Model A was not a failure, but it was hardly giving

Packard or Cadillac night sweats. The Model A did, however, set the stage for the intervention of E.L. Cord in 1928, and the subsequent creation of the greatest American automobile ever produced, the Model J Duesenberg.

er pioneering American automaker, Locomobile. The company was incorporated in 1899 by John Brisben Walker, editor and publisher of Cosmopolitan magazine. Walker's partner in the venture was Amzi Lorenzo Barber, who had made a fortune in the asphalt business, one could say, paving his way into the automotive industry.

The initial enterprise was for the production of Stanley Steamers, Walker having used Barber's 50% investment in their venture to purchase the entire Watertown, Massachusetts, operation. Thus the first Locomobiles, technically, were Stanley steam cars. The business lasted for less than a year with Walker and Barber splitting up Stanley. Walker moved his part of the operation to Tarrytown, New York, Barber kept the Stanley works in Watertown and renamed the cars Locomobile. The Stanley Brothers, incidentally, decided to get back into the steam car business themselves, and with their handsome profit from Walker and Barber (around $200,000), did just that in 1901.

Under the direction of Barber's son-in-law, S.T. Davis, Jr., Locomobile prospered into the early 1900s, by which time the company had abandoned steam for a new line of four-cylinder gasoline powered cars known for uncompromising quality. Locomobile became one of the best built luxury cars in the country, and following the introduction of a six-cylinder series in 1911, rose in prominence among America's most affluent families, including the Wrigleys, Carnegies, and Vanderbilts.

The finest examples of the Locomobile were produced in the early 1920s, with cars featuring luxurious custom coachwork and lavishly appointed interiors. The company's fortunes, however, began to decline around the same time, and Locomobile was forced into receivership, which landed the Bridgeport, Connecticut, firm in the hands of no one other than William C. Durant, who, having lost control of General Motors, was building his second automotive empire comprised of the Star, Flint, and Durant makes. Sadly, with a new line of six and eight-cylinder models in the wings, Durant was nearly wiped out by the stock market crash, and in the aftermath his new conglomerate collapsed and Locomobile ceased to exist after 1929.

By the 1930s the roadside was littered with fallen marques, great cars that had set the standard for excellence and performance in the first quarter of the 20th century. Long gone from the highways of America, these once proud kings of the road play a pivotal role in The Nethercutt Collection, preserving for future generations an era in automotive history that might otherwise be all but forgotten.

1925 Locomobile

1927 Star

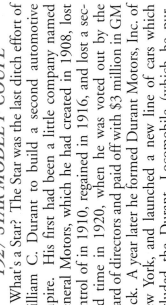

Henry Ford's Model T, and to the Chevrolet, which, ironically, Durant had created with Louis Chevrolet in 1912, and had used to leverage his way back into control of General Motors in 1916 by trading Chevrolet stock for GM shares.

For a brief period the low-priced Star, just $448 in 1922, did indeed give Ford and GM a run for their money. Less than a year after the first car rolled off the assembly line, Durant Motors built the 100,000th Star!

By 1927 when the Model F was introduced, still competitively priced at $675, the Star had become one of the most popular lower-priced cars in the country. Unfortunately, it was just a year later that Durant would make the first of several poor decisions, one of which was to phase out the Star name at the end of 1927 and make the new 1928 models Durants.

The stock market crash in 1929 dealt Billy Durant a staggering blow, (he was heavily invested), and with his second automotive empire teetering on the edge of bankruptcy by 1932, the 70 year old founder of General Motors finally called it quits.

The crowning achievement of his second venture, oddly enough, was not the Durant or Flint automo-

1927 STAR MODEL F COUPE

What's a Star? The Star was the last ditch effort of William C. Durant to build a second automotive empire. His first had been a little company named General Motors, which he had created in 1908, lost control of in 1910, regained in 1916, and lost a second time in 1920, when he was voted out by the board of directors and paid off with $3 million in GM stock. A year later he formed Durant Motors, Inc. of New York, and launched a new line of cars which included the Durant, Locomobile (which he purchased in 1922), the Flint, and the Star.

The little Star was to be Durant's challenge to

1930 CADILLAC V-16 MODEL 452A TOWN CAR

In October of 1929, everything was being readied at Cadillac for the introduction of the most remarkable automobile America had ever seen. Then came Black Thursday, October 24th. In one afternoon a record number of shares changed hands on Wall Street and the New York Stock Exchange went into free fall. All in all, not a good day. By the following Tuesday, the even

bile, but the lowly Star, which had succeeded in becoming the equal of Chevrolet, Ford, and Dodge in the eyes of the workaday man.

This was true of J.B. Nethercutt, who as a young man working for his aunt, Merle Norman, drove an old 1927 Star Coupe, just like this one, to run errands for the first Merle Norman Studio in Ocean Park, California. Because of the fine memories J.B. had of the Star, he had this one equipped with an authentic battery radio (mounted on the rear package shelf) identical to the one

he had used in the company's delivery car more than 50 years ago.

The Star's 30-horsepower four-cylinder engine (which was actually built for Durant Motors Corporation by Continental), had a swept volume of just 152 cubic inches, but as the company advertising stated in 1927, the Star was "...the greatest dollar-measured car value in the field of low-cost Fours." Billy Durant should have read his own ads!

C.B. DeMille's 1930 Cadillac

blacker October 29th, the values of securities had plunged by more than $26 billion! The world was about to plummet into the worst economic catastrophe of the 20th century, just as Cadillac prepared to debut the most expensive automobile in its history, the V-16.

It is ironic that the greatest automobiles of the Classic Era were designed and built during the 1930s, just as the Depression hit its stride and America lost faith in the government's ability to reignite the economy. By the end of 1932, more than 11 percent of Americans, 13.7 million people, were out of work, including President Herbert Hoover.

Two years earlier, on January 4, 1930, the long-term effects of the stock market crash had yet to be realized. At the fashionable Waldorf Astoria Hotel the annual New York Automobile Show opened to the public and Cadillac formally introduced the all-new V-16 model.

One of the first people to order the luxurious new Cadillac was legendary film director Cecil B. DeMille. This beautiful Fleetwood Transformable Town Cabriolet was to become one of DeMille's favorite cars. A true automotive aesthete, he not only enjoyed being chauffeured around town in the stately Cadillac, he also liked to slip behind the wheel on occasion.

Beneath the long stretch of ebony black hood was the largest number of cylinders any American automaker had ever offered up to that time, a 452 cubic inch, overhead valve V-16, producing a near silent 185 horsepower. The Cadillac engine was so quiet, in fact, that at idle it was almost impossible to tell if the car was running.

In the first full year of production Cadillac was barely able to keep up with the demand, delivering an impressive 2,887 cars in 1930, each with an average price of $7,500--as little as $5,350 for a 2-door Roadster, and $8,750 for DeMille's Transformable Town Cabriolet, which was the second most expensive model offered. The V-16 Town Brougham sold for a stratospheric $9,700 at a time when the average Ford or Chevrolet was priced at under $500!

Cadillac offered 54 different body styles for the V-16, three different dashboard layouts, and a seemingly endless variety of interior fabrics and trim. Counting all the variations on basic body styles there were more than 100 different ways to order a Cadillac V-16! Few, however, were as impressive as C.B. DeMille's Transformable Town Cabriolet. Design number 4220, only nine of these stately cars were built.

1930 Cord L-29

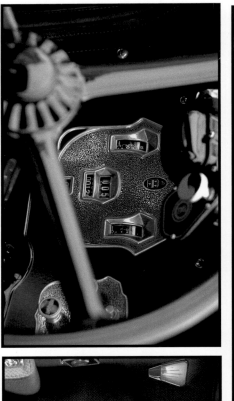

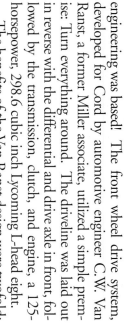

1930 CORD L-29 TOWN CAR

In 1999 we celebrated the 70th anniversary of a monument to innovation, the most successful engineering idea in automotive history, front wheel drive. The car which brought this imaginative concept to market was the L-29 Cord.

The L-29 was a ground breaking design that virtually stunned the automotive world when it appeared in the Summer of 1929 as a 1930 model. With international debuts in both Paris and London, the Cord was regarded by the foreign motor press as the first American automobile to capture the spirit of European design. The crowning achievement of the car's debut year was its selection as Official Pace Setter for the 1930 Indianapolis 500, which, as luck would have it, was won by a front-wheel-drive Miller, the very car upon which the Cord's

1930 Cord L-29

engineering was based! The front wheel drive system, developed for Cord by automotive engineer C.W. Van Ranst, a former Miller associate, utilized a simple premise: Turn everything around. The driveline was laid out in reverse with the differential and drive axle in front, followed by the transmission, clutch, and engine, a 125-horsepower, 298.6 cubic inch Lycoming L-head eight.

The benefits of the Van Ranst design were twofold: better traction, since the drive and steering wheels were one and the same, and a lower body height, with the traditional front-to-rear driveshaft and transmission tunnel having been eliminated. In an era when every change in automotive styling or engineering was newsworthy, the Cord L-29 was the stuff headlines are made of.

This handsome L-29 Town Car is one of only three produced by Cord. Simply defined, a Town Car is a long wheelbase limousine with divider window and an open driver's compartment for the chauffeur.

One early variation on the traditional Town Car design was penned in 1925 by a young stylist working as a consultant to the Duesenberg Brothers. John Tjaarda proposed lowering the beltline of the Model A Duesenberg, increasing the length of the front fenders and placing the spare wheels into fender recesses alongside the hood in order to give the car a longer, lower overall profile. There is no known evidence that such a car was ever built, at least in 1925, but by the late '20s, the fender design was almost de

igueur on everything from Model A Fords to Model J Duesenbergs.

When the stock market made its meteoric slide into disparity in October 1929, Town Cars had become the most popular of all designs among New York's café society, the nouveau riche, and the Hollywood Film Colony. Of the latter, were film stars John Barrymore, Dolores Del Rio, and Lola Montez, who ordered Cord Town Cars custom bodied by the Walter M. Murphy Company of Pasadena, California.

While many of the Murphy company's best designs came from the talented hand of Franklin Q. Hershey, the Cord Town Car was the work of stylist Phil Wright, a former member (like Hershey) of Harley Earl's original Art & Colour Section at General Motors. Wright's first Town Car design for Murphy was on the standard 137-1/2 inch wheelbase L-29 chassis. The close-coupled Town Car appeared very sleek with sweeping fenderlines, dual-stack rear-mounted spares, but given the short wheelbase was very tight on legroom for both driver and rear compartment passengers. Fortunately, this was of little consequence to the car's original owner, the petite and popular actress Dolores Del Rio.

The second version, built by Murphy for John Barrymore, was atop the long wheelbase 152-1/2 inch chassis. Perhaps more elegant in its execution, the Barrymore car differed from the Del Rio Town Car in ending the cowl at the front windshield, and also offered substantially more legroom. The car in

The Nethercutt Collection was the second long wheelbase model built. It differed from the Barrymore car having traditional side-mounted spares, a look quite similar to Tjaarda's 1925 Model A Duesenberg proposal. The custom-built Murphy Town Cars are believed to have cost $7,000 each.

Built by a new division of Errett Lobban Cord's flowering Indiana-based automotive and aviation empire, which included Auburn and Duesenberg, the L-29 was E.L. Cord's zenith. Now, like Henry Ford, the Dodge Brothers, Fred and August Duesenberg, and Walter P. Chrysler, Cord had a car bearing his name, and for the moment, it was the most advanced and most publicized automobile in

the world. In the first three days of public showings more than 1.5 million people visited Auburn showrooms. By September 5, 1929 there were some 3,000 standing orders for the car, said to be a record for any newly introduced model priced above $3,000.

Despite its technological advances and voguish good looks, the L-29 arrived at an abysmal period in American history. The economic tidal wave that had swept prosperity from Wall Street and most of the nation late in 1929 had greatly weakened automotive sales, and even with an affordable price, compared to any other car in its class, the seemingly long list of buyers soon dwindled. This was compounded by servicing problems on the front wheel drive system, and a general shift away from glitzy cars as the Depression-torn economy stumbled along. By 1932 the L-29 was out of production.

1931 CUNNINGHAM ENCLOSED DRIVE LIMOUSINE

In 1931, the price of the average American automobile, a Ford, Chevrolet, or Dodge, had dropped to less than $900, and a top-of-the line Cadillac V-12 commanded no more than $4,895. One can imagine then, that with a retail price of more than $9,000, the market for Cunninghams was extremely limited.

Although cars built by James Cunningham, Son & Co., in Rochester, New York, were usually of very large proportions, they were always clean and simple of line, elegant, but patently conservative. The company, founded in 1882, had been one of the nation's leading luxury carriage makers before entering the automotive field in 1907.

Every Cunningham motor car produced between 1907 and 1931 was hand-built to order, and after 1911 the company even began assembling their own engines, which multiplied from an inline four-cylinder motor into a massive 442 cubic inch V-8 by 1916.

Throughout the 1920s the Cunningham was one of the most expensive cars sold in America, with an average price of $5,000. One of the most desirable luxury and sporting makes on the road, with coachwork ranging from a swanky 2-seat Boattail Speedster to an extravagant 6-passenger Town Car, Cunningham's roster of customers included among others the wealthiest and most powerful actress in Hollywood, Mary Pickford, comedian Harold Lloyd,

legendary film director Cecil B. DeMille, and department store tycoon Marshall Field.

Like Rolls-Royce in England, Cunningham had an equally unparalleled reputation for service in the U.S. No matter where an owner lived, if a Cunningham became disabled, a company mechanic would be immediately dispatched to the scene.

Cunningham built the majority of bodies for their cars and this stately 142-inch wheelbase Series V-9 model was delivered on April 7, 1931 to the New York City residence of Miss Ruth Twombly, the daughter of Florence Vanderbilt and Hamilton Twombly. An Enclosed Drive Limousine body style, it was ordered with custom headlights and taillights, and in the traditional Vanderbilt color scheme of dark maroon. Restored by The Nethercutt Collection to its original condition, the car even bears the Twombly family crests on the rear doors.

James Cunningham, Son & Co., remained a leader in its field until the Great Depression. The market for fine cars all but disappeared and Cunningham had no interest in going into mass production. As a result, 1931 was the final year for the true Cunningham, and it is believed that this particular car was the very last one ever built.

1931 Cunningham

The Cars of San Sylmar

The Nethercutt Collection 75

1932 Packard Twin Six

the urging of Indianapolis 500 winner and Packard consultant Tommy Milton, the company hired Van Ranst in 1930. Although the front-wheel-drive model never materialized, the V-12 engine was just what Packard needed to keep pace with Cadillac.

With the new Twin Six the men of East Grand Boulevard had set their sights high, suggesting that the car would be a competitor, not to the Lincoln or Cadillac twelves, but rather to the Marmon and Cadillac V-16s! In many respects it was.

When the first Twin Six was delivered in April 1932, it boasted an output of 160 horsepower from a 445.5 cubic inch displacement, and was certified to reach 100 mph, a speed few twelve and sixteen cylinder Cadillacs could obtain unless fitted with lightweight open coachwork. The Twin Six models, and later Packard Twelves, were accompanied by a "Certificate of Approval" signed by two-time Indy 500 winner (1921 and 1923) Tommy Milton, and Charlie Vincent, director of the Packard Proving Grounds, attesting that the car had been driven 250 miles and conformed, quoting Packard, "to the best Packard standards in acceleration and maximum speed, in control including steering, speed changes and brakes, in roadability and riding qualities, and in all adjustments necessary for...all riding and driving conditions."

The Twin Six was vested with a sumptuous variety of body styles, designed for Packard by Ray Dietrich. On two wheelbase lengths, Model 905 (142-1/8 inches) 10 body styles were offered, and for the Model 906 (147-1/8 inches) 11 styles, nine of which were Individual Custom series.

Originally selling for $7,000, the 1932 Model 906 Twin Six Convertible Roadster in The Nethercutt Collection is a Dietrich custom featuring the designer's trademark vee-type windshield, and side glass that completely disappears into the tops of the doors, giving the car the appearance of a true Roadster.

Technically, the Twin Six was a single year production model, succeeded in 1933 by the new Packard Twelve, which also featured an improved chassis. The '32 Twin Six was just the first salvo in a war of cylinders and coachwork targeted at what remained of America's upper class in the years of the Great Depression. Packard scored a direct hit.

1932 Marmon Sixteen

Having solidly ensconced itself in the hierarchy of American luxury auto makers for more than three decades, by the 1930s Packard had become the most prestigious American car on the road.

True, Duesenbergs may have been faster and more exciting cars to own, but they were too limited in production to be considered competition by Packard, and the same was true of Pierce-Arrow, one of the original great Three P's of the American automotive industry, now a troubled company barely surviving. Peerless,

the third "P" was already gone, having folded its tents in 1931. The real battle Packard faced was with Cadillac, which now had both a V-12 and a V-16 engine. Thus in 1932 the men of East Grand Boulevard were about to throw down the gauntlet once more.

While it may have appeared a bit ill-timed given the state of the auto industry, not to mention that of the national economy, in 1932 Packard dusted off the Twin Six name once again, and introduced a brand new twelve-cylinder engine as an option on the Deluxe Eight chassis.

The Twin Six of 1932 was a byproduct of Packard's plans in 1930 to develop a twelve-cylinder, front wheel drive automobile to compete with the new L-29 Cord. The engine, as well as the entire Packard front wheel drive concept, had been the work of Cornelius Van Ranst, who had worked with Leon Duray, Harry Miller and Leo Goossen on the prototype L-29. At

1932 PACKARD MODEL 906 TWIN SIX CONVERTIBLE ROADSTER

introduced. Priced at $995, it was the first straight eight ever offered for under $1,000, although hardly any were sold at that price. The Roosevelt was continued as a separate model line beginning in 1930, in essence, Marmon's LaSalle. The changes in models, designs and marketing made from 1924 to 1930, only brought about the decline of the prestigious image Howard Marmon had created, and all for naught; after five years under Williams, the company was still foundering.

In the end, Marmon went out like it came in, with an advanced motorcar of stunning proportions, and like the first, it was the work of Howard Marmon. While Williams had been building his bread-and-butter cars, Howard had spent the same five years developing what would become the marque's greatest model, the Marmon V-16.

Introduced in 1931, it displaced 490.8 cubic inches, developed a full 200 hp and could effortlessly reach 100 mph. Eight different LeBaron-built body styles were penned by Walter Darwin Teague, Jr., with prices ranging from $5,200 to $5,500. The cars were about $150 lower in price than comparable Cadillac V-16 models, added to which the Marmon was 10 mph faster and of equal if not greater quality and design, with some of the era's most beautifully-styled coachwork.

After delivering 223 cars the first year, sales began a slow decline (as did the American economy) and Marmon reduced the Sixteen's base price to $4,825 in 1932, when this elegant dark green LeBaron Sedan

was built. A full custom, it was sold to W.K. Haverstick of St. Louis, Missouri for $5,800, making it one of the most expensive Marmon Sixteens ever built. Wrote pioneering American car collector D. Cameron Peck of the luxurious Marmon Sixteen Sedan, "As a whole, the car is a thing of quiet, honest beauty, with brilliant performance...a joy to drive."

Had Marmon only received such lilting praise in the 1930s. The market for sixteen-cylinder luxury cars was limited and Cadillac had the advantage of being the first. With only the V-16 to sell after the 1932 model year, the long established house of Marmon fell in January 1934 after building 390 Marmon Sixteens.

1932 Marmon Sixteen

Duesenberg. And just like those famous-faced siblings who brought us the Model J, Marmon's legacy also begins with two brothers, Howard and Walter.

By the 1920s, they had built a thriving business in America's original automotive manufacturing hub, Indianapolis, Indiana. The Marmon motorcar had proven itself early on in the greatest test of man and machine, by winning the inaugural Indianapolis 500 in 1911. Five years later a Marmon Model 34 made automotive history when Samuel B. Stevens headed a contingent which drove the car cross-country in less than six days, beating the record set by Cannon Ball Baker in a Cadillac V-8 by some forty-one hours! The crowning glory for Howard Marmon, however, came at Indianapolis in 1920, when a Model 34B Speedster was chosen as the Official Pacesetter for the eighth running of the Memorial Day classic, and Barney Oldfield as the driver.

To everyone's amazement, Oldfield led the starting grid around Indy at a sensational 80 mph clip before pulling off at the end of the pace lap. Even Oldfield's legendary rival Ralph DePalma--who was on the pole that year--remarked that the Marmon may have been the fastest car on the track. Oldfield was so impressed with the Speedster's performance that he purchased the car after the race and then drove the Marmon Pacesetter coast-to-coast eight times to promote a line of tires bearing his name.

Trying to remain competitive in the Post World War I recession, Marmon lowered its prices for the first time, gradually improving sales but not enough to stave off an upheaval within the company. In May 1924, George M. Williams, a former General Motors executive and a major stockholder in Nordyke & Marmon, was hired as president, succeeding Walter Marmon who became Chairman of the Board of Directors--a more ceremonial than purposeful title. Howard Marmon, while still holding the rank of Vice President of Engineering, became progressively less involved with the company as Williams ushered in the era of "The New Marmon."

In 1927 a new Little Marmon 3-liter straight eight was introduced, with the entire Marmon model line switching from sixes to eights the following year. Much to William's chagrin, the new 3-liter was a monumental failure, and a harbinger of his tenure.

In 1929, a light car, the L-head Roosevelt was

1932 Lincoln

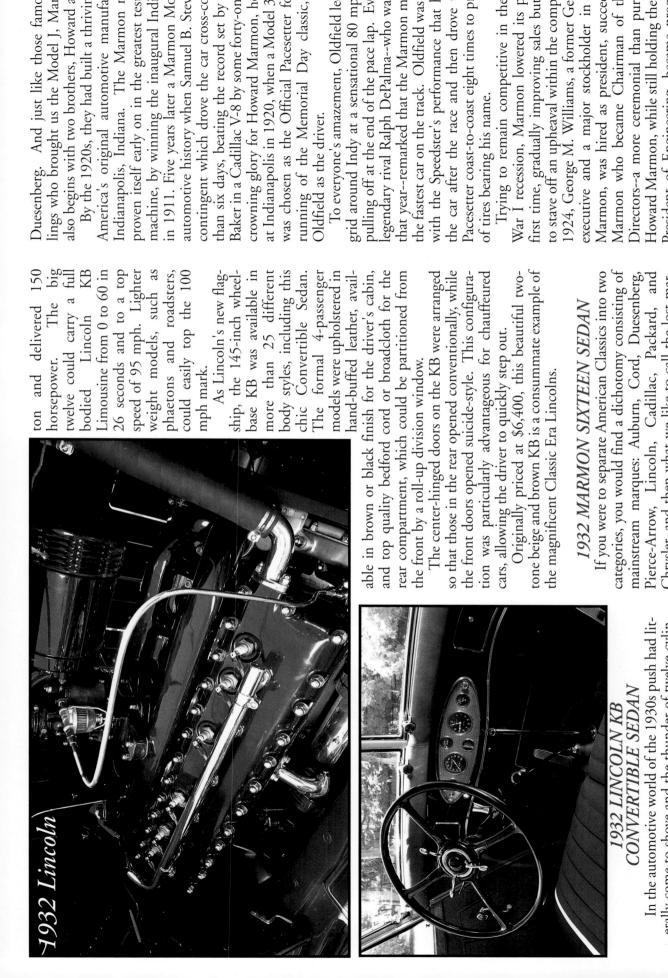

ton and delivered 150 horsepower. The big twelve could carry a full bodied Lincoln KB Limousine from 0 to 60 in 26 seconds and to a top speed of 95 mph. Lighter weight models, such as phaetons and roadsters, could easily top the 100 mph mark.

As Lincoln's new flagship, the 145-inch wheelbase KB was available in more than 25 different body styles, including this chic Convertible Sedan. The formal 4-passenger models were upholstered in hand-buffed leather, avail- able in brown or black finish for the driver's cabin, and top quality bedford cord or broadcloth for the rear compartment, which could be partitioned from the front by a roll-up division window.

The center-hinged doors on the KB were arranged so that those in the rear opened conventionally, while the front doors opened suicide-style. This configuration was particularly advantageous for chauffeured cars, allowing the driver to quickly step out.

Originally priced at $6,400, this beautiful two-tone beige and brown KB is a consummate example of the magnificent Classic Era Lincolns.

1932 LINCOLN KB CONVERTIBLE SEDAN

In the automotive world of the 1930s push had literally come to shove and the thunder of twelve-cylinder engines could be heard from Indianapolis and Detroit all the way to Buffalo and Syracuse, New York. Auburn, Cadillac, Packard, Lincoln, Franklin, and Pierce-Arrow were all offering V-12s in an effort to attract buyers with the most powerful cars the country had ever seen up to that time. Lincoln weighed in with one of the most potent, a 447.9 cubic inch V-12 that tipped the scales at more than half a

1932 MARMON SIXTEEN SEDAN

If you were to separate American Classics into two categories, you would find a dichotomy consisting of mainstream marques: Auburn, Cord, Duesenberg, Pierce-Arrow, Lincoln, Cadillac, Packard, and Chrysler, and then what we like to call the lost marques: Franklin, DuPont, Wills-Sainte Claire, Peerless, Stearns Knight, Ruxton, Reo, and Marmon; automobiles that seldom get the literary attention or collective notoriety of the others.

All are equally important, but Marmon, perhaps more than any of the aforementioned, boasts the richest and most colorful history, one not too distant from that of another famous Indianapolis automaker,

1932 Lincoln

1932 Chrysler Custom Imperial

1932 CHRYSLER CUSTOM IMPERIAL CONVERTIBLE SEDAN

In 1925, the newly formed Chrysler Corporation headed by retired General Motors vice president Walter P. Chrysler, sold more than 100,000 cars, and in a single year transformed itself from an unheard of automaker into a company competing with Ford, General Motors, and Packard, for a share of the mid-priced luxury car market flourishing in the latter half of the 1920s. By 1926 Chrysler had established more than 3,800 dealerships from coast to coast, and topped the previous year's sales by 62,242 cars.

Spearheading the drive to west luxury car sales from Cadillac-LaSalle, Packard, and Lincoln, was the luxurious Chrysler Imperial, with custom coach-work designed by the country's top stylists including Ray Dietrich, and Ralph Roberts of LeBaron.

During the early 1930s when most automakers were feeling the pinch of the Depression, more Chrysler Imperials were finding their way into the hands of affluent owners than competitive makes. Despite having to cut production in 1932, Chrysler sold more cars than Oldsmobile, Cadillac-LaSalle, or Packard.

The Imperial line was divided into two distinct categories in 1932, semi-customs, designated as the CH Series and built on a new 135-inch wheelbase; and the senior CL Series, also known as the Imperial Custom, assembled on a new chassis with a 146-inch stretch between the axles. The Imperial models were powered by two new straight eight engines introduced the previous year, the largest with a swept volume of 384 cubic inches developing 125 horsepower at 3200 rpm—sufficient to launch the Imperial CL models from 0 to 60 mph in 20 seconds, and to a top speed of over 90 mph.

The most distinctive Imperials were the long hood CL models, designed by Ralph Roberts and built to order by LeBaron in eight different body styles. The full length hood, which extended to the base of the windshield, gave the eight-cylinder cars the same long, lean look as twelve-cylinder Lincolns, Packards, and Cadillacs, and in the opinion of many modern-day collectors, were the best-styled automobiles Chrysler ever built.

Within the Imperial line the most popular open car was the Convertible Sedan offered in both CH and CL

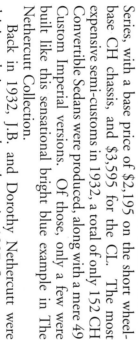

Series, with a base price of $2,195 on the short wheel-base CH chassis, and $3,595 for the CL. The most expensive semi-customs in 1932, a total of only 152 CH Convertible Sedans were produced, along with a mere 49 Custom Imperial versions. Of those, only a few were built like this sensational bright blue example in The Nethercutt Collection.

Back in 1932, J.B. and Dorothy Nethercutt were driving their somewhat decrepit 1927 Star coupe through Los Angeles when a stunning blue Imperial CL Convertible Sedan swept past them. The young Nethercutt's eyed it enviously, hoping that someday they

1932 Chrysler Custom Imperial

too, could have such a car. Thirty-five years later, in March 1967, J.B. Nethercutt purchased a rather worse for wear Imperial CL convertible sedan in a faded shade of maroon, and began a complete restoration. When the paint was stripped away, the cars original shade of blue was discovered. Research of the LeBaron's history revealed that only one such example had been sold in Los Angeles, and it had been blue. This was the very car that J.B. and Dorothy had seen back in 1932! Today, in its beautifully restored condition and original color scheme, is a much-loved part of their renowned collection.

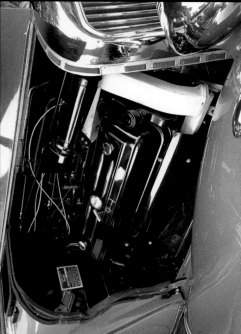

1933 Franklin

the corporate drafting table a custom department was established in Syracuse, New York, and the years which followed saw an expanding line of custom bodies featuring coachwork by Brunn, Holbrook, Derham, Willoughby, Locke, and Merrimac.

Following the death of de Causse in 1928, Franklin turned to the inimitable Ray Dietrich for designs, and it was Dietrich who added the Franklin's stylish Ryan headlamps and matching parking lights.

For Franklin, 1928 was to be a landmark year. The Airman Series, named in honor of Charles Lindbergh, was introduced as an all-new model line. Although having been besieged with offers and gifts following his epic transatlantic flight in 1927, Lindbergh accepted only a new Franklin. Lucky Lindy was also hired by the company as an engineering consultant. With Lindbergh on staff and Amelia Earhart as a their spokeswoman, Franklin boasted itself as "The most comfortable mile-a-minute car ever built...the automobile's nearest approach to flying."

Franklin's biggest year ever was 1929, with production reaching 14,432 cars, but by 1932 the Depression was weighing heavily in Syracuse. Franklin sales had more than halved each year through 1933, and in 1934 Franklin would be forced to close its doors after selling only 360 cars.

The company did, however, go out with a bang. In the Fall of 1932 Franklin brought out what was perhaps the best multi-cylinder automobile of the era, powered by a supercharged, air-cooled 6.8 liter 150-horsepower V-12. Fitted with sleek, LeBaron-designed coachwork, the Franklin V-12s were absolutely awe-inspiring.

By the time Franklin sold its patents to the Air-Cooled Engine Company–later called the Franklin Engine Company, which supplied Preston Tucker with the motors for his innovative rear-engined Tucker Torpedoes in 1948–a total of 200 V-12 Franklins had been delivered.

This handsome 1933 LeBaron-bodied Club Brougham was among the last of the great Franklins produced. One of four body styles offered in 1933, the LeBaron line also included a 5-Passenger Sedan, 7-Passenger Sedan, and a 7-Passenger Limousine. Ironically, the best cars in the company's 32 year history, were its last.

1933 Duesenberg "Twenty Grand"

THE DUESENBERGS

After more than 60 years, whenever automotive authorities are called upon to list the greatest cars of the 20th Century, the name Duesenberg consistently comes up as number one, and for good reason. In 1928 the Model J offered a straight eight engine with dual-overhead cams, four valves per cylinder, and an output of 265 horsepower. Even by today's standards these are impressive figures. The Model J was simply the most powerful American car on the road--faster than anything that wasn't turning laps at Indianapolis in the 1930s. When the Duesenberg brothers added the supercharged SJ version in 1932, they boosted the mighty straight eight's output to a heart pounding 320 horsepower, making it the most powerful non-racing automobile of the 1930s. While it has been argued that the performance figures for the cars might have been slightly inflated by the factory, by any standard of comparison, the SJ still surpassed every other American automobile, even the Cadillac V-16, by at least 100 horsepower, and could effortlessly exceed 100 mph.

To create such a car Fred Duesenberg needed two things: first, a reason to design it, and secondly, the money to finance the research and development. The Duesenberg brothers had neither. Fortunately for automotive history, Errett Lobban Cord did.

For several years industrialist E.L. Cord had been watching Duesenberg from afar. An admirer of Fred and Augie's creative genius, Cord deplored the sloppy management that had driven the company to the brink of failure in 1924. Two years later he stepped in, purchasing a controlling interest and reorganizing the Indianapolis, Indiana, firm as Duesenberg Inc.

Every one of the approximately 485 Duesenbergs built between December 1, 1928 and the last to leave the factory in 1937, when E.L. Cord's Auburn, Cord, Duesenberg empire collapsed, were fitted with hand-made, coachbuilt bodies of extraordinary quality and equally extraordinary cost. A coachbuilt Model J averaged $15,000, making it the most expensive American automobile on the market.

1933 DUESENBERG "TWENTY GRAND"

In 1933, Duesenberg raised the standard for automotive design with a car so spectacular that it commanded a price of $20,000! The Arlington Torpedo Sedan was designed by Duesenberg's legendary chief stylist Gordon Miller Buehrig and built atop a supercharged SJ chassis by Rollston, Inc., in New York for display at the Century of Progress Exposition, better known as the Chicago World's Fair of 1933-34.

This car received more attention to detail and chassis finish than any other Duesenberg ever built. When the car was acquired by Mr. Nethercutt in 1978, Gordon Buehrig was called upon to consult on the restoration, as was former Duesenberg president Harold T. Ames. After a year in San Sylmar's restoration shop, the "Twenty Grand" emerged looking exactly as it had the day it left the Duesenberg factory for the World's Fair.

The car's distinctive low profile, built-in trunk (most unusual for 1933), and elegant silver-gray art deco interior, set this Model SJ apart from any other Duesenberg built. Winner of the Auburn-Cord-Duesenberg Club's Best SJ, and Best of Show award, and Best of Show at the 1980 Pebble Beach Concours d'Elegance, the stunning silver Duesenberg Arlington Torpedo Sedan is now the centerpiece of The Nethercutt Collection's Grand Salon.

1934 DUESENBERG MODEL J MURPHY DUAL COWL PHAETON

Although there were many one-of-a-kind designs like the "Twenty Grand", most of the coachwork designed for the Duesenberg chassis was produced in series, the numbers ranging from as few as four, to the Walter M. Murphy Company's record of 53 convertible coupes. The celebrated Pasadena, California, coachbuilder also bodied this distinctive two-tone green J Dual Cowl Phaeton, which was one of the very first cars J.B. Nethercutt purchased. He bought the sporty Duesenberg back in 1966.

Although it is a Dual Cowl Phaeton, the Murphy design differed from the traditional definition in that it had roll-up glass windows for the front seat passengers, and only the requisite drop-in isinglass side curtains for the rear compartment. The Murphy design also has a severely angled vee windscreen over the rear cowl, rather than an upright windshield, which was the more common style. Like many of the Murphy Company's best designs, this Dual Cowl Phaeton was created by chief stylist Franklin Q. Hershey, who is perhaps better remembered by automotive enthusiasts as the man who designed the 1955 Ford Thunderbird.

1934 Duesenberg Model J

1936 DUESENBERG SJN CONVERTIBLE COUPE

The third Duesenberg on display at San Sylmar is a sporty, supercharged 1936 SJN Rollston Convertible Coupe. One of the most powerful open cars of the 1930s, this sleek black roadster could race from zero to 100 mph in a mere 17 seconds, and remember this was in 1936!

The beautifully sculptured apple green SJ engine had a whopping 420 cubic inch displacement, and with the Duesenberg-designed supercharger engaged, unleashed 320 horsepower posthaste. A sensational maximum speed of 129 mph was attributed to the SJ, which had an equally intoxicating price in 1936 of $18,000.

Offered in two gigantic wheelbase lengths, 142-1/2 inches and 153-1/2 inches, the Model J, SJ, and JN Duesenbergs would one day become the quintessential American automotive icon. Not bad for a company that was recapitalized in 1926, introduced its first new model in 1928 and was out of business by 1937!

1933 FRANKLIN CLUB BROUGHAM

The Franklin had an almost charmed existence. We say almost because the company went out of business in 1934, but up until that time, Franklin had been the most successful air-cooled automobile ever built. The H.H. Franklin Company had been blessed in the late 1920s with the patronage of America's top two aviators, Charles Lindbergh and Amelia Earhart, who chose Franklins over every other car because of its innovative air-cooled, aircraft-type engine design.

Following what could only be called a dealer rebellion in 1923, Franklin was forced to redesign its cars, which up until that time had never sported a conventional grille. When H.H. Franklin agreed to change the design in order to please his dealers, John Wilkinson, Franklin's chief engineer, and the car's original designer, tendered his resignation. Franklin had to turn to an independent design firm to create an entirely new car for 1925. He went to the Walter M. Murphy Company in Pasadena, California, and to New York automotive stylist J. Frank de Causse, renowned as designer of the Locomobile Sportif. Franklin chose the de Causse design as the basis for the all-new model line.

Among the new cars was a long, low and racy boattail speedster, one of the first such designs to grace an American-made chassis. With de Causse at

1933 PIERCE-ARROW MODEL 1247 CONVERTIBLE SEDAN

Pierce-Arrow's fortunes had risen and fallen, and were in the hands of Studebaker, which had purchased the New York automaker in 1928 in the hopes of cre-

ating a luxury division to compete with Cadillac and long-time rival Packard had a V-12, and virtually every other luxury automaker in the country offered Lincoln. It had been a marriage of necessity for Pierce-Arrow, which had fallen well behind the competition in the late 1920s, still building conservatively-styled cars powered by massive six-cylinder engines. Pierce's either a straight eight or a V-8. With Studebaker's money Pierce was able to introduce an eight in 1929 and in 1932 a powerful V-12 of 462 cubic inches developing up to 150 horsepower. The following year output was increased to 175 horsepower, and Pierce-Arrow was once more a force to be reckoned with, but only for a brief time.

This Dark Brewster Green LeBaron Convertible Sedan was one of the most expensive, at $5,250, and beautiful Pierce-Arrows built in 1933, a year which was to be a turning point for the New York automaker. At the Chicago Century of Progress Exposition, Pierce-Arrow introduced the revolutionary Silver Arrow, one of the most influential automotive designs of the era. It brought attention to the company as had no other car since the early 1900s. The following year a production version of the Silver Arrow was introduced and Pierce-Arrow sales rebounded briefly, but at year's end fell short of the company's projected break even point by nearly 1000 cars. From there it was a downhill ride. Studebaker was now in deep financial trouble and had to sell Pierce-Arrow to a group of Buffalo, New York, bankers and businessmen. They bankrolled the company for another four years, but as sales continued to dwindle, only 875 cars in 1935; 787 in 1936; and a dismal 167 cars in 1937, they finally pulled the plug, auctioning off the company's assets the following year.

Of the original great "Three P's", Packard was now all that remained by the end of the 1938.

1934 PACKARD MODEL 1108 DIETRICH CONVERTIBLE SEDAN

After Packard introduced the Twin Six in 1932, the 1933 models came to be known as Packard Twelves. It was the right car, at the right price, at the wrong time.

The 1933 model year was the shortest in the company's history. Packard president Alvan Macauley had delayed the debut of the new Tenth Series until January, and then halted production eight months later to introduce the 1934 models. As it turned out, the delay had no adverse effect on Packard sales, which still came up short of expectations as the Depression deepened and even those with the money

1933 Pierce-Arrow

1934 Packard Dietrich

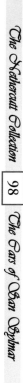

America's troubled economy.

The 1106, 1107 and 1108 models were Packard's top-of-the-line in 1934. The 1108 body designs, which included this sporty Convertible Sedan, were built on the long 147-inch wheelbase chassis, and with the exception of three custom LeBaron designs, were the work of Ray Dietrich, whose name seems to come up more often than almost any other as the designer of the best looking cars built in the 1930s.

Dietrich had been a stylist for Packard since 1925, and although he had moved on to Chrysler by 1933, he had left behind a wealth of designs for Packard to use. In 1934 there were six Dietrich models offered on the expansive 147-inch wheelbase 1108 Packard Twelve chassis: Convertible, Sport Phaeton, Victoria, Coupe, Sport Sedan, and Convertible Sedan.

The Convertible Sedan was one of the most attractive of all Dietrich designs, with an elegant elongated hood, vee-frame windshield, gracefully skirted fenders, and both front and rear doors hung at the center pillar from enormous chrome-plated hinges.

Priced at $6,555, the 1108 Convertible Sedan was powered by Packard's 160-horsepower, 445.5-cubic-inch V-12. On the average, a Packard Twelve could accelerate from 0 to 60 mph in just 20.4 seconds and claim the 100 mph mark with all but the heaviest of coachwork. Respectable for a car that weighed more than 5,000 pounds.

Although the dazzling color of The Nethercutt Collection's Dietrich Convertible Sedan was never available in 1934, it was the actual color used to illustrate a body style in a 1934 Packard advertisement. After J.B. Nethercutt purchased the car in 1965, he decided to have it restored to the color in the Packard ad, which, after a lot of blending and experimenting turned out to be a combination of orange and yellow, thus the car's nickname, Orello.

The Eleventh Series Packards, which were produced from August 1933 through August 1934, have come to be regarded as the finest models ever produced by the men of East Grand Boulevard.

to purchase a new Packard did not, some just being conservative, others waiting to see if the administration of President Franklin Delano Roosevelt, a Packard owner himself, could mend tom 1933 Boattail Speedster, and the Alexis de Sakhnoffsky false hood, a clever deception created by taking the hood all the way back from the grille shell to the base of the windshield, thus concealing the front cowl and giving the car the illusion of being longer than it actually is. Packard also used the false hood on a number of Dietrich customs to give the cars the appearance of additional length, not that any was needed on a body stretched between axles set 147-inches apart.

Since 1934, the Sport Phaeton has been described as the most beautiful open car ever built, and the sportiest four-door convertible of the 20th century. It's hard to argue with either appraisal. The LeBaron design epitomizes the very essence of a classic car. Not surprisingly, all four of the original 1934 Sport Phaetons still exist.

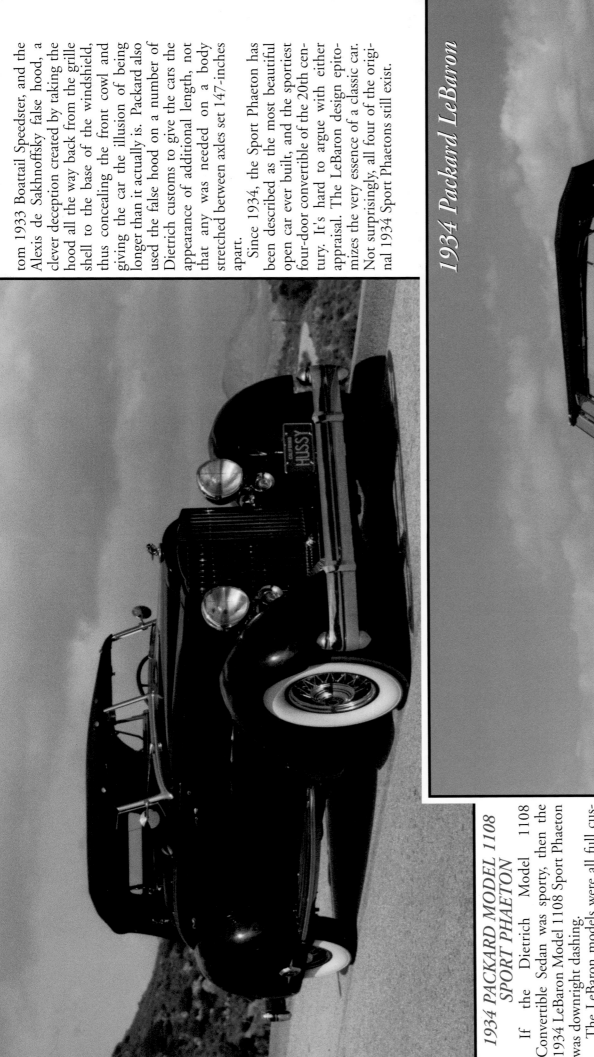

1934 Packard LeBaron

1934 PACKARD MODEL 1108 SPORT PHAETON

If the Dietrich Model 1108 Convertible Sedan was sporty, then the 1934 LeBaron Model 1108 Sport Phaeton was downright dashing.

The LeBaron models were all full customs, and very expensive, even by Packard's standards. Only four Sport Phaetons were built by LeBaron, each selling for $7,065, almost double that of a standard 1934 model, and nearly $1,000 more than any of the other seven Dietrich and LeBaron custom body styles.

The LeBaron design for the 1108 Sport Phaeton combined a number of unique styling elements, including the teardrop pontoon fenders that had been created for Packard design chief Ed MaCauley's cus-

1935 CADILLAC V-16
FIVE-PASSENGER CONVERTIBLE

With the financial resources of America's largest corporation behind it Cadillac waded into the 1930s with what some might have called reckless abandon, others called it the most exciting series of luxury cars ever built by General Motors, the V-16 Cadillacs.

By 1935, the Cadillac sixteens were the undisputed winner of the multi cylinder wars. It was something of a hollow victory though, as V-16 sales dropped in 1935 to a dismal 50 cars. In the overall scheme of things at GM this was insignificant, but such declines had killed Marmon in 1933. Among the V-12's, Franklin had folded in 1934, Packard and Lincoln were holding their own, and there was little competition from either Auburn or Pierce-Arrow. With both twelve and sixteen cylinder cars, Cadillac pretty much in the driver's seat.

The 1935 model year was generally a carry over except for a change in the V-16's classification, which became the Series 60, and the introduction of a new bumper design. Gone were the wispy two-piece biplane bumpers of 1934–in their place a sturdy one-piece bumper of impressive dimensions. Not nearly as attractive but a good deal more protection for the costly Cadillac grille. The 1935 V-16 line was noted for having some of the largest sedans in Cadillac history, huge five and seven-passenger cars that weighed over three tons and commanded prices upwards of $7,500. A bit more dashing in appearance and a little lighter on tonnage to make better use of the 185-horsepower V-16 engine, was the sporty Five-Passenger Convertible Victoria.

Fleetwood design number 5885, the convertible's low windshield, lengthy fabric top with blind rear quarters, and bold pontoon front fenders contributed to the car's racier stance.

Though still built on the lengthy 154-inch wheelbase chassis used for the four-door models, the Victoria managed to appear smaller, almost as small as the number produced, just two examples in 1935, priced at $8,150 apiece.

The car in The Nethercutt Collection was originally sold to Grover Whalen, a former New York City Police Commissioner and well-known political figure who became The Big Apple's official host and president of the 1939 New York World's Fair.

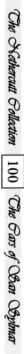

1935 Cadillac V-16

1935 Cadillac V-16

shower, kitchen, two separate bedrooms, a built-in radio, refrigerator, and propane gas heater.

The Travelodge was built like a car, using weather-resistant sheet aluminum, and the finest mountain birch woods and fabrics for the interior furnishings. It was the Pierce-Arrow of travel trailers. There were three versions, the thirteen-foot Model C, priced at $785; the sixteen-foot Model B for $972, and the top-of-the-line Model A.

More people had been taking to the open road since Wally Byam invented the Airstream travel trailer in 1931. The Pierce-Arrow Travelodge was introduced in 1936, just as President Roosevelt's New Deal work projects were bearing the fruit of newly paved roads and better highways.

To pull this lovely house on wheels to a sunny vacation spot required a car with a substantial engine, and there were few better equipped for the task than the 144-inch wheelbase, 185-horsepower V-12 powered Pierce-Arrow Limousine. An estate-sized car without the trail-

1937 PIERCE-ARROW LIMOUSINE & TRAVELODGE

In an era when camping out meant driving to some remote location (say about 35 miles outside of the Los Angeles city limits to a veritable wasteland known as the San Fernando Valley), and pitching a tent, the revolutionary Pierce-Arrow Travelodge was like a home away from home. In fact it was. Travel trailers were still relatively new, and expensive, the Pierce-Arrow commanding $1,282, a lot of money for something that didn't even have an engine. It did have a bath, a

er in tow, the big Pierce Limousine could comfortably seat five, and with the jump seats lowered, an additional two could squeeze into the back.

Pierce-Arrow was devoted solely to the manufacture of luxury cars and that was to be their undoing in the late 1930s. In 1933 total production was a mere 167 cars, including a handful of Limousines, such as this beautiful dark blue model in The Nethercutt Collection. During the same period Pierce-Arrow delivered a total of 440 Travelodges. Better than one for every other car sold. At the end of 1937 Pierce-Arrow suspended all production, and on the 13th of May 1938, a Friday, Pierce-Arrow ceased to exist.

1937 Pierce-Arrow
Limousine & Travelodge

The Nethercutt Collection   103   The Cars of San Sylmar

1937 Pierce-Arrow Limousine & Travelodge

1937 CADILLAC SERIES 90 V-16 AERO-DYNAMIC COUPE

In 1933 Cadillac took a bold step forward in automobile design with another Fleetwood-bodied model, the Aero-Dynamic Coupe. First shown as a concept car by General Motors at the Chicago Century of Progress Exposition, the prototype Aero-Dynamic Coupe was built on a 149-inch wheelbase Series

452-C chassis. The Chicago World's Fair car featured Fleetwood's advanced streamlined body styling, pontoon-type fenders and a fastback roofline that would not only influence American automotive designs well into the 1940s, but automotive styling the world over. In 1934 a Mercedes-Benz 500K competition model featured similar lines and a year later went into production as the Autobahn Kourier. Packard also produced three fastback models in 1934, and Cadillac began offering production versions of the Aero-Dynamic Coupe to fit V-8, V-12 and V-16 chassis.

The V-16 models were built on a massive 154 inch wheelbase, the longest ever used on a Cadillac production car, and sold for $8,100. Fleetwood produced 20 of the ultra streamlined five-passenger bodies through 1937, eight of which were mounted on the V-16 chassis--three in 1934, four in 1936 and one in 1937, the car pictured, which was the very last

1937 Cadillac V-16
Aero-Dynamic Coupe

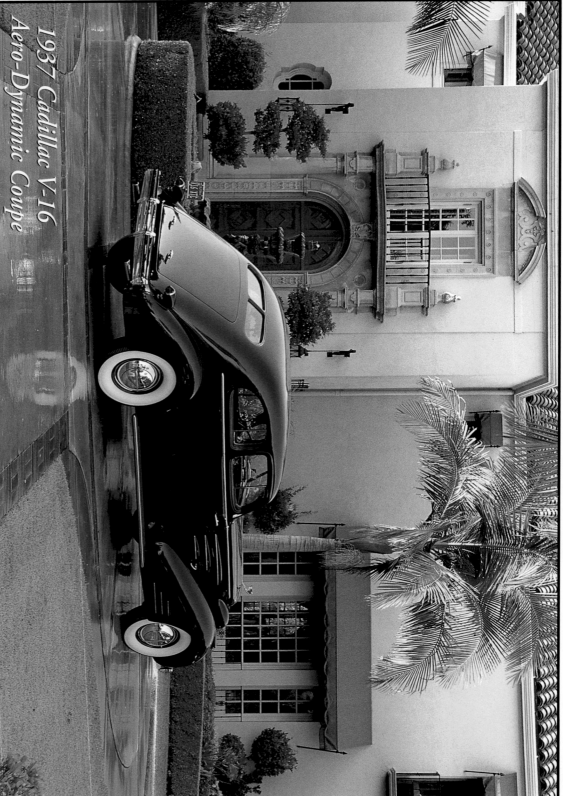

1937 Cadillac V-16 Aero-Dynamic Coupe

V-16 Aero-Dynamic Coupe built.

After a few minutes behind the wheel of this car you really forget that it is more than 60 years old. V-16 Cadillacs from the late 1930s were very modern, they had a kind of sensational styling that was in many ways transitional between the Classic Era and those that would appear just before World War II. General Motors stylists managed to carry that off fairly well on many of their cars, but no better than on the Fleetwood Aero-Dynamic Coupe.

1937 LINCOLN V-12 JUDKINS BERLINE

Formality was a matter of style at Lincoln, and Edsel Ford, who was a stylist at heart and President of Ford Motor Company by birth, chose the best designers in America to create the coachwork for the twelve-cylinder Lincolns.

The 1937 Lincolns were dramatically different in appearance, having adopted styling cues from the benchmark 1936 Lincoln-Zephyr. The Zephyr was a completely new kind of car for Lincoln, a competitively-priced model targeted at Auburn 852, Chrysler Airflow, and LaSalle buyers.

The aerodynamic Zephyr body design had come from Briggs, the largest factory coachbuilder in Detroit, and specifically from the drafting board of John Tjaarda, the brilliant Dutch-born designer whose signature appeared on everything from the Lincoln Zephyr and Graham Hollywood, to the finishing touches on Dutch Darrin's design for the 1941 Packard Clipper.

On the Zephyr, Tjaarda integrated teardrop-shaped headlamps into the fender design, a first for Lincoln, raised the rear roofline to emulate the fender contours, and then curved it into a sheer dropping from just below the backlight to a built-in trunk. Like the Chrysler Airflow, the Zephyr was very streamlined, but

far better in appearance. The new model established a styling trend that would dictate both Ford and Lincoln designs well into the postwar '40s.

In 1937, the Merrimac, Massachusetts, firm of Judkins, one of the country's most renowned coach-builders, designed three exclusive body styles at Edsel Ford's request, including this luxurious 5-passenger Berline.

Judkins followed the same design discipline dictated for the entire 1937 Lincoln line, but added a bustle back trunk to increase luggage capacity on the long 145-inch wheelbase chassis, and tailored a sublime interior for the car as only Judkins could. Priced at $7,500, a total of 66 Model K Berlines were built during the 1937 model year.

1937 PACKARD TWELVE TOURING SEDAN

Among all of the great models produced during the 1930s, the 1937 Fifteenth Series Packard Twelve is considered to be one of the first really fine driving American cars, a car of both uncommon comfort and performance.

These were the first senior models to benefit from the technology developed by Packard for the lower-priced One-Twenty line.

The Fifteenth Series Twelves, introduced in September 1936, featured new 16-inch wheels, Packard's Safety Plus bodies, made of hardwood and steel, and new Double Trussed frames, which factory literature claimed were over 400% more rigid than before. The new models also boasted Packard's exclusive Safe-T-FleX independent front wheel suspension, and Servo Sealed four wheel hydraulic brake system, all of which had been developed for the lower-price six-cylinder One-Twenty (the cars that saved Packard from going broke in the late 1930s by becoming one of the best-selling models in the company's history.)

Powered by a 67 degree V-block twelve cylinder engine, the average 1507 model could accelerate from a stand to 60 mph in under 15 seconds and attain a top speed of 85 mph to 90 mph. To best utilize the Twelve's output of 175 horsepower, (180 horsepower with the high compression heads), Packard's three speed selective synchromesh transmission was geared considerably low, providing quick throttle response and low end torque. The Twelves reached their maximum power at around 3500 rpm, with a standard final drive of 4.41:1. Packard offered both higher and lower over-all ratios, ranging from 4.06:1 to 4.69:1 and 5.07:1. While the top end may have suffered some for the capability of reaching highway speeds in short order, the ride and handling in a Fifteenth Series Packard Twelve more than compensated for failing to reach that all desired 100 mph mark.

The new independent front suspension instilled a feeling of comfort and stability previously unknown to Packard drivers. Additionally, the rear suspension now employed a Panhard rod, complimenting the front suspension's anti-sway bar, and contributing significantly to reduced body lean. As such, the 1937 Packards were uncommonly agile for long wheelbase cars, and at highway speeds handled far better than either the

Lincoln or Cadillac Twelves.

The 1507 models, such as this curvaceous Touring Sedan, were built on a 139-1/4-inch wheelbase. The shorter length 1506 was built on a 132-1/4-inch platform, while the long wheelbase 1508 models measured 144-1/4-inches. The longest stretch available for the Super Eight model line was 139 inches, so if one wanted a really long wheelbase car, they had to opt for a Packard Twelve in 1937. This contributed to the Fifteenth Series being the best year ever for twelve cylinder Packard, posting a record 1300 sales.

Packard offered a total of 13 catalogued body styles, one for the 1506, eight for 1507 and four for the 1508 chassis. The 1507 chassis could be bodied with factory coachwork ranging from the Touring Sedan, Formal Sedan, Club Sedan, Coupe, Convertible Victoria, 2-4 Passenger Coupe, and Coupe-Roadster to the custom bodied LeBaron All-Weather Cabriolet.

As the decade of the Thirties neared its turbulent finale, the era of full custom coachwork had nearly come to an end and almost all Packard bodies were being built in-house. Even the Dietrich-built customs had been discontinued. All that remained was the styling and the Dietrich name, which would be dropped after 1937.

The Touring Sedan in The Nethercutt Collection was delivered to Howard R. Bendixon in October 1937, purchased from Mr. Bendixon by J.B. Nethercutt in the late 1950s, sold to Bill Harrah in 1962, and purchased back by Mr. Nethercutt at the Harrah auction in 1984. Except for new paint and re-chromed bumpers, this handsome touring car is in original condition. The Syracuse name, incidentally, was not Packard's, but was given to the car by Mr. Nethercutt in honor of the Touring Sedan's first owner, who lived in Syracuse, New York.

1938 CADILLAC V-16 SERIES 90 CONVERTIBLE SEDAN

After selling approximately 4,000 V-16 Cadillacs over a period of eight years, GM's luxury car division discontinued the model line in 1937. This, however, was not the end of the V-16! To everyone's surprise, Cadillac stunned the automotive world a second time with the introduction of an entirely new line of cars in 1938, powered by an even better flathead V-16.

The new 431 cubic inch engine, using a smaller and lighter monoblock design based on Cadillac's 1936 V-8, developed the same 185 horsepower as its predecessor, but calling it a V-16 was almost an abstraction of the term. With the twin banks of eight splayed at 135 degrees, the side valve, L-head sixteen was virtually flat, and so recessed within the engine bay that one had to peer over the fenders to even see the top of the heads.

The new 1938 models, such as this opulent Midnight Green Convertible Sedan, were scaled down from the earlier 154-inch wheelbase V-16 chassis and built on the same 141-inch wheelbase platform used for the lower-priced Series 75 V-8.

While some 13-inches had been lost between the axles, Fleetwood continued to build the same overall length bodies, resulting in an exceptional rear overhang, which in most instances was consumed by a trunk large enough to hold luggage for a family of five.

Although essentially a V-8 chassis with a V-16 engine, the senior Cadillacs were distinguished from the eights by a bolder eggcrate grille, fender lamps, and streamlined louvers on the hood side panels and on all four fender skirts.

V-16 interiors were accented with a handsome array of art deco style instruments, most notably a square speedometer, a wide variety of upholstery options from hand-buffed leather to broadcloth, and a steering column-mounted selective synchro 3-speed shifter. Overall, the cars were a little less flashy than those of the early 1930s, but still the most impressive luxury automobiles sold in America for the money. This Convertible Sedan, pictured with a 1935 Waco Cabin bi-plane, originally sold for just $6,000. Back in 1933 a Fleetwood V-16 Convertible Sedan would have listed for $8,000. So, in many respects Cadillac was offering more car for the money in 1938.

1938 Lincoln V-12 Judkins

sive one-off and limited semi-custom designs. Mass production at Judkins customarily meant building more than one. In the case of this unique looking Lincoln V-12 Touring Coupe, only a single example was produced, and it was Mr. Judkins' personal car.

The novel window treatment was inspired by the Delage D8 120 Aerodynamic Coupe built in 1938 by Letourneur et Marchand in Paris, France. The Delage, which was displayed in the French Pavilion at the New York World's Fair, had the same design and fastback roofline. Since the Lincoln's 136-inch wheelbase chassis was half-a-foot longer than the Delage's, Mr. Judkins was able increase legroom, give the passenger compartment a bit more length, and mount massive rear-hinged doors that permitted access to both the front and rear seats.

With the Touring's swept back pillarless windows, the view from the back seat was spectacular. As with all Judkins designs, the rear compartment was lavishly appointed and upholstered in a combination of bedford cord and broadcloth.

J.B. and Dorothy Nethercutt knew Mr. and Mrs. Judkins, and had admired the handsome two-tone tarragon green & black Lincoln for many years. When Mr. Judkins passed away in 1969, his wife advised J.B. that if he wanted the Lincoln, she very much wanted him to have it. The car soon joined the collection, and has since become one of the main attractions.

1938 LINCOLN V-12 JUDKINS TOURING COUPE

Coachbuilders like Murray, Fleetwood (which had been a subsidiary of General Motors since 1927), and Briggs, (which also owned LeBaron), catered mostly to the Detroit establishment designing and building bodies in series. Judkins, on the other hand, was one of the true custom coachbuilders, creating exclu-

1940 Cadillac V-16

1940 CADILLAC V-16
SERIES 90 SPORT COUPE

It was 1940 and Cadillac was about to put the V-16 out to pasture for the second and last time. The luxury car market was totally dominated by V-8s, including Cadillac's own. There was simply no place for a car

with sixteen cylinders in the coming decade. The proof was the sales tally. Just 61 Series 90 "Sixteen Fleetwoods" were delivered compared to the thousands of V-8 Cadillacs sold in 1940.

Nearly all of the V-16s built in 1940 were semi-customs, with the exception of a few coachbuilt models

like this sleek Five-Passenger Sport Coupe bodied by the distinguished firm of Derham & Co., in Rosemont, Pennsylvania. This was the only full custom offered on the V-16 platform.

Derham was known to have an occasional flair for the dramatic, and that was evident in the upholstery total redesign Packard had seen in more than a decade. The sporty new Clippers made everything else obsolete overnight, with the possible exception of a few coachbuilt models that managed quite well to bridge the distance between 1930s styling and the coming look of the 1940s.

One such example was this Model 1907 Custom Super Eight One-Eighty bodied in 1941 by LeBaron Detroit, a division of the Briggs body company since 1927, and descendent of the legendary LeBaron coachworks founded by Ray Dietrich, Tom Hibbard, and Ralph Roberts. (In 1953, Briggs was purchased by Chrysler, and that is how the LeBaron name came to be used on so many Chrysler models.)

The 1941, Packards were very modern cars, engineered to make the best use of body styling, which Detroit had finally realized was more important to buyers than V-12 engines and technical innovations, unless, of course, they were convenience features like power windows, a push-button radio, or air conditioning, all of which Packard loaded into the Custom Super Eight One-Eighty.

The cars were powered by a straight eight of 356 cubic inches delivering a substantial 160 horsepower through a new semi-automatic transmission that eliminated having to depress the clutch. It would automatically disengage by manifold vacuum when the accelerator was released, at which point the driver shifted gears and stepped on the gas pedal to re-engage the clutch. It was all very simple. The age of convenience was on the way.

LeBaron packaged all of this new technology in a handsome four-door body sporting a lower roofline and trim profile that by no small coincidence looked very similar to the dazzling 1940 Darrin-bodied Packard Sport Sedan.

All One-Eighty Super Eight models were special orders in 1941 and a total of 11 different body styles were cataloged, three by LeBaron, two by Darrin, one by Rollston, and the rest by way of Briggs which now handled all of the Packard's factory coachwork. The Sport Sedan sold for $3,545, which wasn't much to pay for the privilege of driving around in a car that bore the LeBaron signature.

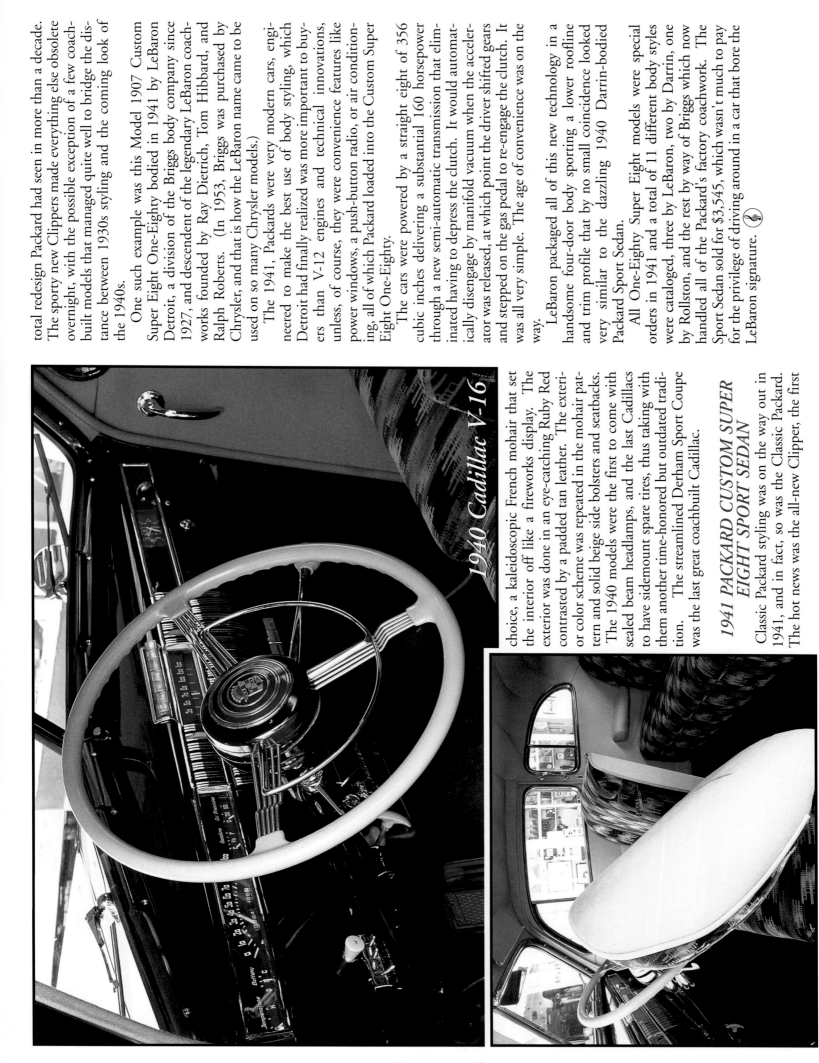

1940 Cadillac V-16

choice, a kaleidoscopic French mohair that set the interior off like a fireworks display. The exterior was done in an eye-catching Ruby Red contrasted by a padded tan leather. The exterior or color scheme was repeated in the mohair pattern and solid beige side bolsters and seatbacks.

The 1940 models were the first to come with sealed beam headlamps, and the last Cadillacs to have sidemount spare tires, thus taking with them another time-honored but outdated tradition. The streamlined Derham Sport Coupe was the last great coachbuilt Cadillac.

1941 PACKARD CUSTOM SUPER EIGHT SPORT SEDAN

Classic Packard styling was on the way out in 1941, and in fact, so was the Classic Packard. The hot news was the all-new Clipper, the first

Chapter Four

EUROPEAN CLASSICS

The Greatest German, Italian, And French Cars

Chapter Four

lmost every automobile built from the turn of the century up until the late 1930s was comprised of two essential and separate elements: the chassis, and then the coachwork. Each without the other was incomplete, but a great chassis and powerful engine clothed in an unattractive body was far worse than a mediocre chassis surrounded with exquisite coachwork. In the motor car's golden age it was the coachbuilders more often who held the key to success; all the manufacturers held was the key to the ignition.

The styling and construction techniques used by French coachbuilders in particular were considered among the most advanced in the world, and for the better part of the 1920s and throughout the whole of the 1930s, Paris was the place to go for exotic coachwork and expensive cars.

The work of French designers was largely confined to

the national marques (those produced in France and Belgium) such as Bugatti, Hispano-Suiza, and Minerva.

The Nethercutt Collection has acquired some of the finest examples of these superb European marques, along with a few that are less known in this country including a very rare French Avions Voisin, which was built for film star Rudolph Valentino, a pair of immense Renault touring cars, from an era when Renault was one of Europe's foremost luxury automakers, and two of Germany's most legendary cars, a Maybach Zeppelin and a Mercedes-Benz 540K Cabriolet.

Here then, are the great European Classics of San Sylmar.

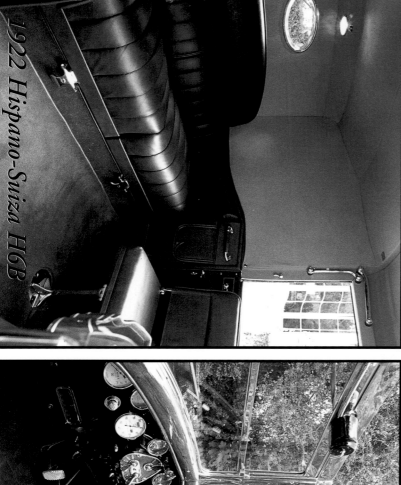

1922 HISPANO-SUIZA H6B
CABRIOLET DEVILLE
&
1928 HISPANO-SUIZA H6C BINDER
CONVERTIBLE COUPE

As popular and as expensive as a Rolls-Royce, Hispano-Suiza had one of the most colorful histories of any European automaker. Although the history of Hispano-Suiza dates back to 1898, it was during the late 1920s and up until 1937, when the company ended automobile production in France, that the Sociedad Hispano-Suiza Fabrica de Automoviles rose to international prominence.

Although considered to be French cars, the company was of Spanish origin and under the direction of Swiss engineer Marc Birkigt, who joined the firm in 1898, thus the name Hispano-Suiza--Spanish-Swiss. The confusion over the marque's heritage stems from the opening of a new Paris factory in the early 1900s. All of the great designs to bear the Hispano-Suiza name and flying stork mascot would come from France after 1919.

For those whose interests include the history of aircraft, many will recognize the Hispano-Suiza name more readily than will automotive enthusiasts. The development and manufacturing of aircraft engines, among the best ever built, was the company's principal business, and the ultimate cause of the French division's demise. Having converted the automotive factory to manufacture V-12 aero engines at the beginning of World War II, the Paris works was confiscated by the Germans when they invaded France. The remaining factories in Barcelona and Madrid continued to produce cars up until 1944, but by the end of the War Hispano-Suiza was out of the automobile business.

One of the company's greatest designs was the 1919 H6 and its subsequent development into the H6B and H6C, both of which are featured in The Nethercutt Collection. The cars in the H6 series were powered by an overhead cam, light-alloy six-cylinder engine so well engineered that it would remain in production from the end of World War I up until the mid-1930s. Considered the best built automobile in Europe and priced several thousand dollars more than a Rolls-Royce, the Hispano-Suiza was regarded with the highest esteem by everyone from General Motors' chief stylist Harley Earl, (who copied Hispano-Suiza styling for the 1927 LaSalle, right down to a version of the flying stork hood ornament), to the Rothschilds, who owned several examples, artist Pablo Picasso, and a list of owners that

1928 Hispano-Suiza H6C

read like a who's who of the wealthiest families on two continents.

The majestic H6B Cabriolet DeVille in the collection was bodied in 1922 by Paris carrossier Jacques Saoutchik. Known for his superb sense of style, tempered with just a hint of extravagance, Saoutchik designs were always a little ahead of their time, and in 1922 this spicy brown Hispano-Suiza was nouvelle vague compared to the starched collar coachwork still befitting formal livery. Originally selling for $15,000, the car was equipped with a removable leather cover over the chauf-

feur's compartment, and luxurious leather-upholstered seating in both the front and rear.

The collection's second H6 model, a 1928 Type C (known as a Boulogne, in honor of André Dubonet's success with a prototype in the 1924 Coupe Boillot race at Boulogne), is also fitted with a cabriolet body but in a more genteel 2-door style by Henry Binder.

Binder's designs were less exciting to the eye than Saoutchik's, but sporty nonetheless, particularly on the H6C chassis which was equipped with the 135-horsepower, 8-liter engine introduced in 1924.

The H6C had a rather ribald reputation for speed, having been the platform for Dubonet's 1924 Tulipwood race car, and it had been an H6C that trounced a Stutz Blackhawk in the famous 24-hour endurance race at Indianapolis Speedway in 1928.

Henry Binder had to build a body that lived up to that kind of reputation. It takes little more than a glance to know that he did.

1923 AVIONS VOISIN

1923 AVIONS VOISIN C5 SPORTING VICTORIA

Rudolph Valentino lived a fast life, and a relatively short one, he died at age 31 from a ruptured ulcer. At his funeral in New York City, there were so many mourners the lines outside the church stretched for 11 blocks. His career in silent movies was epic, the part of Julio in the 1921 film The Four Horsemen of the Apocalypse was Valentino's first major role, after which he quickly became Hollywood's silver screen heartthrob in films like The Sheik (1921), Blood and Sand (1922), The Eagle (1925), and The Son of the Sheik (1926).

By the early '20s he was one of the wealthiest actors in Hollywood, and his passion for beautiful cars was almost as legendary as his love of beautiful women.

In 1923, he was in Paris, where he drove virtually every exotic make of car then available. He decided to purchase a Voisin and ordered a Victoria Touring body from Carrossier J. Rothchild et Fils. The cost for the custom-bodied Avions Voisin was $14,000. It took several months for the car to be completed and Valentino didn't take delivery until his next European trip in 1924. He proudly drove the handsome Sporting Victoria through the streets of Los Angeles, Hollywood, and Beverly Hills for the next two years, and kept the car at

his Hollywood Hills retreat, known as Falcon Lair, until his death on August 23, 1926.

Although the Voisin had a rather stylish aluminum bird sculpture for a hood ornament, Valentino's close friends Douglas Fairbanks and Mary Pickford had presented him with a silver-plated coiled hooded cobra to place atop the hood of the car when he completed the film Cobra. Some say it was a gesture of friendship, others a publicity stunt to promote the movie. Either way, it became one of the most famous hood ornaments of the era.

The C5 Voisin was famous, too, an uncommon car, even in France, it was the product of Gabriel Voisin, who

had built airplanes from the turn of the century through World War I. When the aircraft business dried up after the war he decided to build automobiles.

With a huge factory and 2000 employees at his disposal, Voisin not only designed and built his own chassis, he produced the engines as well, an almost unbreakable sleeve valve four that delivered a robust 90 horsepower. By 1920 more than 1000 cars had been delivered, and the Voisin quickly become one of the more fashionable automobiles in which to be seen. Much of the credit for that also went to Gabriel Voisin who had a hand in body designs, which were quite often just short of bizarre, but always interesting.

After Valentino's death an estate auction was held at Falcon Lair and the C5 Voisin was purchased by Robert M. Lawson of Los Angeles. "I kept the car for many years," wrote Lawson in a letter to the car's third owner. "While it was seldom driven, it was an interesting possession." An apt term. In 1973 the Voisin was purchased from car collector Richard Alexander, and it has been a "star" in the Nethercutt Collection ever since.

The photographs for this book, incidentally, were taken at Falcon Lair in the exact same place Valentino parked his Avions Voisin 73 years ago.

1923 RENAULT ALL-WEATHER CABRIOLET AND 1925 TOURER

France was not only home to many of the world's finest coachbuilders, but also one of the oldest automakers in Europe, Renault, which opened its doors in 1899.

While Daimler is often credited with producing the first front-engined automobile in 1900, Renault actually introduced its 1 3/4 hp buggy with front-mounted engine, shaft drive and a three-speed gearbox a year ear-

lier. With a capital investment of 40,000 francs put up by his elder brothers, Fernand and Marcel, Louis Renault established a factory on the grounds of the family home in Ballancourt, and with a staff of 60 workers produced 71 cars. The following year production rose to 179 cars and Renault was on the road to success as one of France's premiere automakers.

Throughout the early years, Renault continued to advance the design of the automobile, albeit in the French idiom, disposed to his own styling ideas, partic-

ularly the unique shape of the Renault hood, which became an early trademark. By 1913 Renault was France's largest motor vehicle manufacturer with an output of more than 10,000 cars a year and a workforce of nearly 4,000.

During World War I, Renault produced V-8 aero engines for the Farman biplane, manufactured light tanks, and developed a powerful V-12 aero engine which was used in the celebrated Bregurt 14 biplane fighter. Following the Armistice, Renault resumed automobile

1923 Renault All-Weather Cabriolet

production, but continued to expand into the aviation field becoming the largest aero engine manufacturer in the world by 1930.

As an automaker, Renault produced cars that were affordable and practical, leaving the luxury car field to contemporaries like Bugatti, Delage, and Delahaye. On occasion, however, a customer of means and national pride would come to Monsieur Renault's door and request a custom-built car. Two such examples are the Model 45 Tourer and Model 45 All-Weather Cabriolet in The Nethercutt Collection.

Two of the most luxurious models built in the 1920s, the open Tourer and semi-enclosed All-Weather Cabriolet were powered by Renault's L-head six-cylinder engine with a massive swept volume of 548 cubic inches, or 9.1 liters! Noted Renault literature, "The Renault Big Six is a car of unusual power and flexibility, easy to manipulate in traffic. The four wheel Servo-braking device permits quick stopping with a minimum of effort and avoids skidding. The length of the chassis permits the various types of closed and open bodies."

For the period, it was an ideal car. Fitted with factory coachwork the Model 45 was affordable, practical, very much the kind of car Louis Renault liked to build, and for those who desired a coachbuilt body, the same chassis was equally suitable, just so long as you didn't want to change the hood!

1926 Bugatti

1926 BUGATTI TYPE 23 BRESCIA CONVERTIBLE COUPE

Of all the French marques, Bugatti was perhaps the greatest automaker to provide chassis for custom coachwork. Ettore Bugatti was to his small region of Alsace, France, what Henry Ford was to Dearborn, Michigan.

From around 1910 to 1951, nearly 8,000 cars bearing the Bugatti signature were produced at the factory works in Molsheim.

The Type 23 Brescia was

Bugatti's little car, affordable, not in the same class as the more costly sports models, but still a Bugatti. This example is a bit unusual as it has a fabric body built by Carrossier Gaston Grummer in Clichy, (Siene) France. It is powered by a small 90.6 cubic inch Bugatti four-cylinder engine developing 40-horsepower.

The fabric body, which was patented in France by Charles Weymann in 1921 and licensed to more than 30 different French coachbuilders, was comprised of a color-impregnated Zapon cloth resembling leather in both appearance and texture. The bodies were padded with either curled horse hair or cotton waste, tacked and stitched to the car's ash framework, and backed by muslin or oil cloth for waterproofing. The bodies were light, only a few hundred pounds, surprisingly durable, and if properly maintained, long lasting, as evidenced by this 73-year-old example which is all original.

1928 Isotta-Fraschini

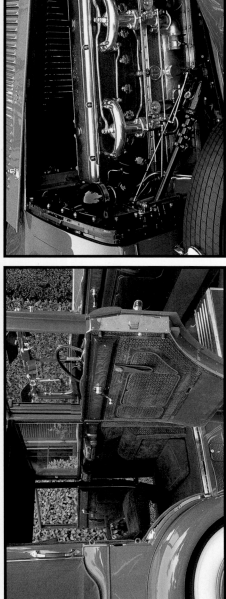

1928 ISOTTA-FRASCHINI 8A
ALL-WEATHER LANDAULETTE

Were beauty alone the only reason for the Isotta-Fraschini's existence, it would have been reason enough. One would have to search long and hard to uncover an ungainly example of this proud marque, the true thoroughbred of Italian motorcars in its day.

The company was founded before the turn of the century, by Cesare Isotta and the brothers Fraschini—Oreste, Vincenzo and Antonio. Societa Anomina Fabbrica di Automobili Isotta Fraschini, referred to simply as IF, started producing its own engines in 1903. Their first all-Italian-built model, the Tipo 12 hp, launched three decades of Isotta-Fraschini automobiles.

In the early 1900s, Isotta's marketing and sales priorities were directed not wholly toward Europe, as one might expect, but far across the Atlantic to the eastern seaboard of the United States where race-prepared Isottas won the 1908 Briarcliff in New York, the Lowell Trophy in Massachusetts, and the Savannah Challenge Trophy race in Georgia. The strong showing by the Milanese firm resulted in their rapid climb in popularity among America's automotive elite.

A company driven by innovation, at the 1909 Paris salon, Isotta-Fraschini introduced one of the automotive world's first successful applications of four-wheel-brakes.

Following World War I, IF embarked upon its greatest era with Oreste Fraschini directing the company's new postwar marketing and design strategies. The prewar years had seen a flurry of Isotta models and the firm's continued support and involvement in motorsports competition. The new Isotta policy would be to offer a single model with the emphasis on luxury and elegance. It would be called the Tipo 8.

1928 Minerva

Powered by a new in-line eight-cylinder engine introduced in August 1919, it was the first of its type put into series production anywhere in the world and, of course, the car also offered four-wheel-brakes.

By the 1920s Isotta-Fraschini was one of the world's most desirable automobiles. Names on the firm's prestigious list of clients included the kings of Italy (Victor Emmanuel) and Iraq (Faisal), Queen Marie of Romania, the Empress of Abyssinia, Prince Louis of Monaco, the Maharajahs of Alwar and Patiala, and the Aga Kahn. In America, Clara Bow, Jack Dempsey, Newspaper publisher William Randolph Hearst, and film star Rudolph Valentino had all become Isotta-Fraschini owners.

With the improved Tipo 8A, introduced in 1924, horsepower was increased to 120 at 2400 rpm, making it one of the most powerful touring car chassis of the early 1920s.

The regal 8A All-Weather Landaulet Cabriolet in the collection was bodied by Italy's leading coach-builder, Carrozzeria Castagna, in Milano. It was delivered to the New York City dealership Isotta-Fraschini Motors on Park Avenue, and sold to a Mrs. Lynch, who also happened to have a Park Avenue address.

Built on a 145-inch wheelbase chassis, the elegant Castagna body came with right hand drive so the chauffeur could quickly alight from behind the wheel to open the curbside door for his employer. This masterpiece of coachwork design has a most interesting feature, a series of buttons on the right rear armrest with a corresponding lighted dial on the dash panel, just to the right of the steering wheel. The dial gives instructions to the driver either to SPEED UP, SLOW DOWN, STOP, TURN RIGHT or LEFT, TURN AROUND, or GO HOME.

The Crash of '29 hit IF very hard, considering its largest market was the United States. With virtually no automobile sales and only aircraft engines being built, the company was sold in 1933 to aircraft manufacturer, Count Caproni di Taliedo. Isotta-Fraschini attempted a return to automobile manufacturing after World War II, but the road which these great cars had once traveled no longer existed.

1930 Minerva

1928 MINERVA CONVERTIBLE TOWN CAR & 1930 LIMOUSINE DEVILLE

The first Minerva was a bicycle. Not the most auspicious beginning, but that is how Minerva founder Sylvain de Jong started his business in Antwerp, Belgium, back in 1895. Not entirely satisfied with the quality of his bicycles, he traveled to the United States in 1896 and spent the better part of the year studying American machine tools and machining techniques, skills that he used to produce his improved two-wheelers, the Minerva and Romania.

With an obvious fondness for mythology, de Jong settled on Minerva, the ancient Roman goddess of wisdom and the arts, as the name for his first motorized cycles added to the company's product line in 1899. By the turn of the century Minerva had over 200 employees turning out 800 bicycles and motorcycles a month. Most men would have been content to leave well enough alone, but de Jong was an inventor, and the allure of the motor carriage finally got the best of him.

In 1904 he introduced a 636cc single-cylinder "Minervette" motor car. At around the same time he changed the company name from Sylvain de Jong et Cie. to Minerva Motors SA. Larger cars, including a 6250cc 40-horsepower six, were on the market by 1907, and the Antwerp factory, now with 1200 employees, was turning out 600 cars and 1500 motorcycles a year. Minerva automobiles finally exceeded the number of motorcycles produced in 1909 becoming the company's principal product. This was also the year de Jong adopted Charles Yale Knight's sleeve-valve engine design making Minerva only the second European firm, after Daimler of Coventry, to use the Knight sleeve-valve engine.

The Knight was one of the most reliable engines in the world, almost indestructible and good, it was said, for 120,000 miles before requiring any major overhaul. It was also a very expensive engine to manufacture, but considering the well-to-do clients that patronized Minerva, price was never a question.

King Albert of the Belgians bought a Minerva in 1910 and drove it himself on a tour of the Tyrol. By 1914, other royal owners included the Kings of Norway and Sweden. Another famous Minerva customer in 1912 was none other than pioneer automaker Henry Ford.

With American luminaries like Ford endorsing Minerva, de Jong was well on the road to establishing an export market in the U.S. when Archduke Franz Ferdinand, heir to the Austrian throne, was assassinated

in Sarajevo. This initiated a chain of events that led to Germany invading Belgium and declaring war on Russia and France. From there it was like dominos falling. Britain declared war on Germany, Austria declared war on Russia, France and Britain went to war with Austria and Turkey, and by August of 1914 all of Europe was embroiled in the war to end all wars.

After the war De Jong visited the United States once again, this time to study the latest production methods and to restock with modern machine tools. By 1920 Minerva 20-horsepower cars with four-cylinder monobloc engines were leaving the Antwerp factory in respectable numbers. A six appeared in 1920, followed by a small 2-liter four in 1922.

Practically the whole car was made in-house, with the exception of chassis frames, magnetos, carburetors and tires. Bodywork was made at a newly-acquired factory at Mortsel, an Antwerp suburb, although many of the larger Minervas carried custom coachwork by the leading carrosserie, D'leteren in Belgium, Vanden Plas, Hibbard & Darrin, and Labourdette, in France.

By the mid-1920s Minerva was one of perhaps half a dozen European cars considered among the best in the world, and once more very popular in the United States where they were imported by Paul Ostruk in New York City. One of the highest priced automobiles for sale, a bare Minerva chassis was approximately $10,000, with additional thousands required for custom coachwork. In New York, Minervas were frequently seen delivering their highborn owners to the theater, club, or social gatherings. And more than a few were known to be parked in the garages of America's most distinguished families. The Vanderbilts and duPonts were both Minerva customers, in fact, at one time the duPont family owned no fewer than fourteen Minervas!

By 1925 annual production was up to 2,500 and nearly 3,000 in 1926, more than half of which were being exported. For Minerva there appeared to be no end in sight as sales continued to climb, but in January 1928, the founder of Belgium's most renowned motorcar died, and with him, the driving force behind the company. A year later a decline in sales brought on by

1930 Minerva

the Depression marked the beginning of Minerva's slow demise. On the way out, though, the company produced a handful of spectacular cars, including the 1928 Convertible Town Car in The Nethercutt Collection, which was originally built for General Billy Mitchell and fitted with a body by the Floyd-Derham Company of Philadelphia.

The 1928 models were powered by a 362.5 cubic inch Sleeve-Valve six-cylinder engine. While this was a strong motor, it was no match for Packard's Twin Six, or the Cadillac V-8. It was the company's reputation and a selection of handsome coachwork that kept customers knocking on Minerva's door.

By the 1930s, when the second Minerva in the collection was built, the company had introduced a straight eight and regained a foothold in the foreign as well as home market. It was to be short-lived, however, due to the economic malaise that was spreading from Wall Street to London, Paris, Rome, and Berlin.

The body for this stately Limousine deVille was made in Belgium by the country's leading coachmaker, D'Ieteren Frères, S.A. in Brussels. The car was used by French lecturer Pierre Doriaan, who had vowed to drive it to Cape Horn in South America, and then make the famous trek up the primitive Alcan Highway to Alaska. Unlike most people who only dream of such deeds, he did it and for nearly eight years this Minerva carried the Frenchman and his wife Marie over all manner of terrain on two continents, from Terra del Fuego, across the United States, and up to British Columbia, where the car came to rest after completing 300,000 miles of travel. The Doriaans never

made it to Alaska because the long-traveled couple had a falling out, (can't imagine why), sold the car to a dealer in Canada, and returned to France.

Needless to say, this is not a low-mileage original car, but it is one of the most beautifully restored in The Nethercutt Collection, lavishly appointed in the rear compartment with ornate upholstery, wood trim, and accessories. There is even an intercom, vanity set, and clock. If you had to travel around the world by car, this was probably the car in which to do it.

1932 AUSTRO DAIMLER ALPINE SEDAN

Austro Daimler, as the name implies, was the Austrian division of Daimler Motoren Gesellschaft in Germany. The company was originally established in 1899 through the Austrian company of Bierenz-Fischer in Vienna. In 1902, after developing the Mercedes, Paul Daimler went to Austro Daimler as chief engineer, and in 1905 he returned to Germany and Ferdinand Porsche took his place in Vienna. Needless to say, Austro Daimler has been tied to some rather historic figures. The company became independent of the German branch in 1906, and went its own way, merging with Puch in 1928 and in 1934 tieing the knot with Styer-Werke A.G. to form Styer-Daimler-Puch A.G., still one of the most successful industrial concerns in Austria.

1932 Austro Daimler

Thanks to a diversity of business relationships and a host of talented engineers, (Dr. Porsche, for example, being replaced in the late 1920s by Karl Rabe, who would later work on the design of the Porsche 356), Austro Daimler was able to produce a substantial number of well-built and innovative motorcars throughout the 1920s and 1930s.

In 1932, when this sporty red Alpine Sedan was produced by the Austro Daimler-Puchwerke in Osterreich, the company was building straight eight engines of 279.5 cubic inches that delivered a robust 115-horsepower. The new Austro Daimlers were both comparable and competitive to Mercedes-Benz models of the same period. (Over the years Daimler had unknowingly helped establish all of its major competitors: Austro Daimler, Maybach, and BMW!) The Model ADR8 chassis used for the Alpine Sedan was a unique single spine tubular design (tuning fork-shaped), with a swing axle independent rear suspension, Alfin drum 4-wheel hydraulic brakes, and race-tested dry sump lubrication. It was essentially a very large sports car.

The Alpine Sedan was built to order for a Mr. Moser in Switzerland, where the car remained until 1947 when it was shipped to South Africa. It changed hands several times and was finally purchased in the mid-1970s by well known California auto importer and racing historian Otto Zipper. The ADR8 Alpine Sedan joined The Nethercutt Collection in 1982. Only around 300 ADR8's were produced. The very last cars to bear the Austro Daimler name were built in 1934.

1932 MAYBACH ZEPPELIN DS 8
SPOHN SPORT CABRIOLET

The automobile has become one of modern man's preeminent obsessions, one of the few objects that we assume to be extensions of our own personality. Like a bespoke suit or a lavish home, an automobile makes a statement about its owner. In the early years of the automotive trade, it also made a statement about its builder, and the cars of Wilhelm and Karl Maybach spoke volumes about their creators.

While history credits Gottlieb Daimler and Carl Benz as the two independent automotive geniuses who put the world on wheels in the late 1880s, it has always been the work of three men, the third being Wilhelm Maybach, Daimler's friend and protege throughout the founding years of Daimler Motoren Gessellschaft. Today, when one visits the Daimler-Benz Museum in Stuttgart, there are three bronze busts displayed near the entrance, Carl Benz, Gottlieb Daimler, and Wilhelm Maybach. It is mute testimony to the role Maybach played in Mercedes-Benz history. It was Maybach who helped create the first modern car, the 1901 Mercedes, the benchmark against which all other automobiles would be judged for the first decade of the 20th century. For his effort, Maybach was hailed as "King of the Carmakers."

By 1901, the company he had helped establish with Gottlieb Daimler had patented the first vee-twin engine, a 4-speed gearbox with gated linkage, a jet-type carburetor (still the basis for modern carburetors), and the first production motor car with a front-mounted engine.

Following Daimler's death in March 1900, Maybach suddenly found himself in disfavor with the DMG board which had consigned him, along with his son Karl, a brilliant engineer in his own right, to heading research and development, a far less important role than Maybach's earlier position as technical director under Gottlieb Daimler. It was in the end a political strategy to strengthen the position of Daimler's two sons, Paul and Adolf, but at the cost of Maybach's prestige within

the company. In October 1906 Maybach decided to resign. He was 61 years old.

Rather than go into retirement, Maybach joined Ferdinand Graf (Count) von Zeppelin in the development of a new aero engine for his giant lighter than air ships. He was given responsibility for overseeing the construction of the engines and his son Karl was appointed technical director. A separate company, Luftfahrzeug-Motorenbau GmbH, (changed in 1912 to Maybach Motorenbau Gessellschaft) was established to produce the Zeppelin engines, and it would be from the M.M.G. factory in Friedrichshafen, Germany, that the first Maybach automobiles would emerge following World War I.

While Mercedes were regarded as very stylish automobiles, the majority of Maybach body designs were conservative in nature, primarily limousines, pullman-cabriolets, four-door cabriolets, and a few sports cabriolets, most of which were built by Karosserie Hermann Spohn in Ravensburg.

In 1929, the same year that the air ship Graf Zeppelin, powered by five 550-horsepower Maybach V-12 engines, circled the world, Karl Maybach introduced the company's first V-12 automobile. He followed the 1929 "12" with the 150-horsepower, 7-liter, DS 7 Zeppelin model, and in 1931 introduced an even more powerful DS 8 version, with an 8-liter, 200-horsepower

engine. Despite the size and weight of the cars, better than three tons, a Maybach Zeppelin DS 8 could reach 100 mph.

The DS 8 model in The Nethercutt Collection was built in 1932 and bodied by Karosserie Spohn in Ravensburg, as a sporty four-door cabriolet. Although the majority of Maybach's were black, befitting the dignified styling of the cars, a few coachbuilt models were done in colorful two-tone paint schemes, such as this distinctive combination of green and gold.

The DS 8 interior was luxuriously appointed, upholstered throughout in supple leather and trimmed in hand-polished burled walnut. The original selling price for the Spohn Cabriolet was $12,000.

The DS 8 line, which was produced up until 1940, conferred upon Maybach a stature regarded by the proletariat as closer to that of Rolls-Royce than Mercedes-Benz.

1933 BUGATTI TYPE 51 GRAND PRIX

The chassis design for all Bugattis retained traditional Bugatti architecture, this most notably being a solid rear axle suspended by quarter elliptic springs, and at the front an artistically striking solid beam axle confoundingly pierced at its outer corners by semi-elliptic springs passing through the axle housing!

Engines, too, were awe-inspiring in their layout, unique in appearance, having squared housings with finely damascened finishes. The logic of this seemingly complicated design was debated for decades. Was it, as some have speculated, Ettore Bugatti's sensitivity to the Cubist movement of the 1920s that inspired the damascene-finished rectangular shapes, or was there a more practical reason for their unique appearance? It was the latter, according to Roland Bugatti, who told noted historian Griff Borgeson, "The Boss (as Ettore was referred to) did not tolerate the waste of time, labor, or materials. The factory workers were mostly the sons of farmers with few mechanical skills. Slab-sided construction and engine-turned finishes were the most simple." So much for the romance of the Cubist Movement.

The T51 Bugattis were swift cars suited to virtually any type of road competition. Beneath the removable hood was one of the most powerful inline eight-cylinder engines of the 1930s, a 2.3 liter (136.5 cubic inch) dual overhead cam motor capable of developing 180-horsepower. The Bugatti-built gearbox was almost unbreakable, and the massive mechanical brakes adequate to the task of scrubbing off speed until they overheated, which was the one weakness of most early Bugatti cars.

The body on the example in The Nethercutt Collection is an authentic reproduction of a T51 Grand Prix. The car was originally owned by the famous Bugatti team driver Louis Chiron, and fitted with a competition coupé body. That was the prototype for the Type 57S Atlantic. When the car was purchased by J.B. Nethercutt in 1959, all that remained was the bare Type 51 chassis. He turned to internationally renowned Bugatti authority and restorer O.A. "Bunny" Phillips, who built the current racing body, which is identical to those campaigned in the early 1930s. The car is "road equipped" with fenders, skirts and a windshield, which were removed in competition.

Capable of speeds reaching 140 mph, the Type 51 Grand Prix is still a formidable sports car, even by today's standards.

1933 HISPANO-SUIZA J 12 COUPE DEVILLE

By 1930 Hispano-Suiza found itself falling behind the competition. While still one of the most powerful cars in Europe, in the United States, which was the

1933 Hispano-Suiza J 12

1933 Hispano-Suiza J 12

largest export market for Hispano-Suiza, both Packard and Cadillac had V-12 engines. Not to be outdone for long, in 1931 Hispano-Suiza created the most expensive car in the company's history, the J 12, powered by a massive 9424 cc V-12 engine producing 200-horsepower at 3000 rpm. Later models equipped with a high-performance crankshaft increased output to a staggering 250-horsepower, which put the J 12 in direct competition not only with Packard and Cadillac, but the fastest car built in America, the mighty Model J Duesenberg.

A J 12 was capable of reaching a top speed in excess of 100 mph and could clip the distance from 0 to 60 mph in just 12 seconds, faster than

almost any other car in the world.

With the international economy in turmoil, the number of buyers for the J 12 was limited, and production of the car was commensurate, only 100 were produced through 1937, each with coachwork by the leading design houses on both sides of the Atlantic.

The J 12 was available in four wheelbase lengths which included the 134-1/2-inch "short," the 146-inch "light" chassis, 150-inch "normal," and 157-3/4-inch "long" chassis.

The 1933 J 12 in The Nethercutt Collection was bodied as a Coupe deVille by Paris coachbuilder Henry Binder. The car is unique in that it is a two-door hardtop Coupe deVille, with a removable front roof section. One could consider it a precursor of today's targa-style and removable T-top roofs.

The elegant, rounded contours of the roofline complement the sweeping fenders and semi-built-in rear trunk. Designed for MM. Deutsch de la Meurthe, France, this is one of the most beautiful Hispano-Suiza bodies ever built. The car has been a part of The Nethercutt Collection since 1965.

1938 MERCEDES-BENZ 540K CABRIOLET A

With an appearance that one journalist in the 1930s described as having "aggressive styling and Teutonic arrogance," the Mercedes-Benz 540K was indeed an awe-inspiring automobile.

The 5.4 liter (540K) overhead valve straight-eight with Roots blower was the final evolution of the 380/500K/540K series delivering a breathtaking 180-horsepower with the supercharger engaged. It was advertised as the fastest standard production automobile in the world with well over 100 mph maximum speed and the ability to cruise the new German Autobahn effortlessly at 85 mph. In 1937 any automobile that could achieve triple digits was immediately legendary.

For Daimler and Benz, the 1930s had marked the first full decade of their amalgamation as a single company, an era highlighted by far-reaching advancements in engine, chassis and suspension design that would put the Mercedes-Benz 540K at the forefront of the European automotive industry. At a time when most automakers were still using solid axles, the Mercedes-Benz chassis featured four-wheel, coil spring, fully independent suspension.

The Nethercutt Collection's 1938 540K Cabriolet A is a seldom seen right-hand drive version built for sale in Great Britain. While this is worthy of note for a German car built in the late 1930s, up until the 1920s right-hand-drive was more the rule than the exception throughout the world. Both Daimler and Benz kept the steering to the right for more than 20 years, when they were Germany's two leading independent automakers, and following their 1926 merger, right-minded thinking continued to prevail until left-hand-drive models began appearing on the sporty S, SSK and SSKL series in 1927. By the 1930s, either left or right-hand-drive versions could be ordered on any Mercedes-

Benz chassis, including the 500K and 540K.

The total number of 540K chassis produced, 406 from 1936 through early 1940 (in addition there were 354 500K chassis built from 1934 to 1936), suggests that fewer than 200 right-hand drive cars were built and of those only a handful would have been fitted with the luxurious Cabriolet A body. Bearing serial and chassis number 835305 and engine number 169316, this striking light blue 540K is equipped with the later 5-speed gearbox usually considered first available on 1939 models, so it is very likely that this car was built late in the 1938 model year.

Chapter Five
5

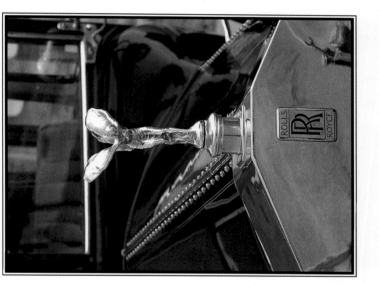

THE ROLLS-ROYCE COLLECTION

Ghosts & Phantoms & Wraiths To Spirit You Away

n Great Britain there was only one word for luxury, well, actually two words, Rolls-Royce, created by the amalgamation of C.S. Rolls & Co. and Royce & Co. Ltd., in March 1906. The following year Messrs. Frederick Henry Rolls and Charles Stewart Royce introduced the Silver Ghost, so named for the 13th car produced, which featured a distinctive gray color scheme and silver-plated fitments. All 40/50 hp six-cylinder Rolls-Royce models were known thereafter as Silver Ghosts.

From the onset, Rolls-Royce automobiles set an international standard for quality, luxury, and engineering, and by 1910 the Silver Ghost was the most desirable luxury automobile in the world, a car for monarchs, potentates, and captains of industry. It remained in production until 1924.

1913 ROLLS-ROYCE SILVER GHOST TOWN CARRIAGE

Bodied by the House of Mulliner in Longacre, London, in 1913, this dashing closed car has a sporting character emphasized by a rakishly veed windscreen and plunging hoodline which drops almost 20 degrees from the cowl to the radiator shell. The car is pictured with a

DeHavilland Moth of the same year. Like the legendary DeHavilland, one of England's greatest aircraft, the Rolls-Royce Silver Ghost was an engineering masterpiece, powered by an inline six-cylinder engine with a swept volume of 453.2 cubic inches and an output estimated at 50-horsepower. We say estimated because Rolls-Royce never published horsepower figures in its sales brochures, stating only that horsepower was adequate.

Elegant and sporty livery such as the 1913 Town Carriage commanded a significant price in 1913, converted from Pounds Sterling to Dollars, about $6,425. Painted a traditional dark green, the car is handsomely contrasted by an interior upholstered in fawn cloth. The body and hood are aluminum, for lighter weight and better performance, and protected by steel fenders.

Measuring 187-1/4 inches and tipping the scales at a modest 4,380 pounds (thanks to the aluminum body), the Silver Ghost could deliver its passengers to a top speed well in excess of 65 mph with the power of the engine being dispensed via a Rolls-Royce 3-speed transmission. Handsome, as reliable as Big Ben, and built to last, this Silver Ghost is the embodiment of the great British motor cars built during the 1910s.

1930 Rolls-Royce Phantom I

THE ROLLS-ROYCE PHANTOM COLLECTION

The Phantom I arrived in 1925 to replace the Rolls-Royce Silver Ghost which had been in production since 1907. The only significant change, however, was the introduction of a new 7.4 liter (453.2 cubic inch) overhead valve six-cylinder engine. The Phantom I was otherwise a transitional model displaying coachwork similar to that of the later Ghosts, the same chassis and suspension, and four-wheel brakes, which were first introduced on the 1924 Ghosts. All new body designs did not begin to appear until 1928 and 1929, by which time the Phantom I was scheduled to be succeeded by the Phantom II.

The new Rolls-Royce Phantom made its debut in September 1929, just two months before Wall Street went into free fall. The stock market crash would severely hamper Rolls-Royce sales in the U.S. market, and ultimately lead to the failure in 1934 of the American branch, Rolls-Royce of America, in Springfield, Massachusetts, which had built Ghosts and Phantoms known as Springfield Rolls, since 1919.

The Phantom II was equipped with a revised six-cylinder engine increasing output to around 120 horse-power at 3000 rpm. As the cylinder wars of the 1930s heated up in America between Cadillac, Lincoln, Packard, Pierce-Arrow, Auburn, and the rest, Rolls-Royce stepped up Phantom II performance to 158 horsepower by using a higher 5.25:1 compression ratio and a new carburetor. Produced through 1935, the body styles offered on the Phantom II marked the high point in prewar Rolls-Royce coachwork.

1930 ROLLS-ROYCE PHANTOM I MARLBOROUGH TOWN CAR

The Nethercutt Collection is one of the very few in the world that has all six versions of the Rolls-Royce Phantom, dating from 1930 to 1972. This extraordinary ornate Marlborough Town Car is a Springfield Rolls bodied in New York by Brewster & Co. The breathtaking coachwork features Brewster's meticulously hand-painted wicker canework on over two-thirds of the body, which is contrasted by a black paint scheme, leather-upholstered roof, and cream wire spoke wheels.

Originally selling for a staggering $22,000 in 1930, the car was built for Alma Spreckles, of the Spreckles Sugar Family in Salinas, California.

There were a total of 1240 Phantom I chassis built and delivered by Rolls-Royce of America from 1927 through 1931.

1930 Rolls-Royce Phantom I

1930 ROLLS-ROYCE PHANTOM II BREWSTER TOWN CAR

One of the best engineered and most reliable cars of its time, the Rolls-Royce Phantom II is best remembered for the striking array of hand-crafted coachwork which graced the 144-inch short wheelbase and 150-inch long wheelbase chassis. A total of 1,767 Phantom IIs were produced through 1935, one of the most spectacular of which was this regal long wheelbase town car bodied in the United States by New York City coachbuilder Brewster & Co.

This was the second body on the 1930 Phantom II chassis which was purchased by film star Constance Bennett in 1936. The original sales card from J.S. Inskip, the New York sales office for Rolls-Royce, shows the car having been originally sold with a Trouville body in 1931 and traded back in 1935, after which it was rebodied by Brewster for the 1936 New York Auto Show.

1930 Rolls-Royce Phantom II

The Brewster is one of the most striking town cars of the 1930s with a rakish v-windshield, luxurious interior appointments, and highly detailed, hand-painted canework along the body.

Bennett saw the car at the auto show, purchased it from Inskip for $17,000, and had the three-ton Rolls-Royce shipped to her Holmby Hills estate in Los Angeles, California. A pretty hefty sum for a second-hand car, the intrepid actress earned back all of the money she paid by renting the Town Car to the movie studios for $250 a day!

Because of its elegant one-of-a-kind Art Deco styling, Bennett's car appeared in a number of MGM films including the 1937 classic "The King and the Chorus Girl" starring Fernand Gravet, Jane Weymann, Edward Everett Horton, and Joan Blondell. "For its acting services," wrote Bennett to later owner William Young in 1961, "it was a standing joke in Hollywood that the car received more salary than many players. It was in a picture once with Carol Lombard for three weeks."

Bennett kept the car for more than a decade, until her husband lost it in a poker game in 1948. Young sold the Phantom to J.B. Nethercutt in January 1985. Restored to its original glamour, it is one of the signature cars on exhibit at The Nethercutt Collection, and is regarded by many classic car aficionados as the most beautiful town car ever built.

1932 ROLLS-ROYCE PHANTOM II CROYDON VICTORIA

In the 1930s, the economic climate in America and the rest of the world had substantially reduced the number of clients available to the leading manufacturers of coachbuilt luxury cars, and Rolls-Royce had concluded that declining sales in the U.S. no longer warranted the production of cars in Springfield, Massachusetts. Rather, the Phantom II chassis would be assembled in Derby, England, with left-hand drive, and sent to America where Brewster would manufacture coachbuilt bodies to order.

A Brewster body was considered one of the finest in America. In fact, by 1934, (the year Rolls-Royce of America went bankrupt), Brewster coachwork had become so popular, Cole Porter used it as one of the many praiseworthy objects in the hit song "You're the Top" from the Broadway musical "Anything Goes."
"You're the top, you're a Brewster body..."

Some 125 Phantom II chassis were built in Derby with left-hand drive for export; 116 came stateside, while the remainder were sent to Canada and Europe.

The Rolls-Royce of America/Brewster & Co. pamphlet produced for the new car carefully informed prospective customers that the Phantom II was "built in Derby, England, with left drive steering and for American road conditions." The Springfield cars were all given quaint English names, such as Piccadilly Roadster, Newport, Huntington, Henley and Croydon.

The Croydon was a sporty victoria body style, that being a convertible coupe with a blind rear quarter, a design that was more popular in Europe than the United States, although Ray Dietrich designed several spectacular victoria body styles for Packard around the same time, and Murphy built a few for Duesenberg. The victoria had the appearance of a sporty two seater, but there was actually a full width bench seat in the rear, which left passengers pretty much in the dark, since there were no rear windows and the backlight was usually a narrow rectangle of beveled glass.

The stylish Brewster-bodied Croyden from The Nethercutt Collection was originally sold to Mrs. Jessie Woolworth-Donahue, the daughter of 5¢ & 10¢ Store magnate Frank Woolworth, for a staggering price in 1932 of $18,600.

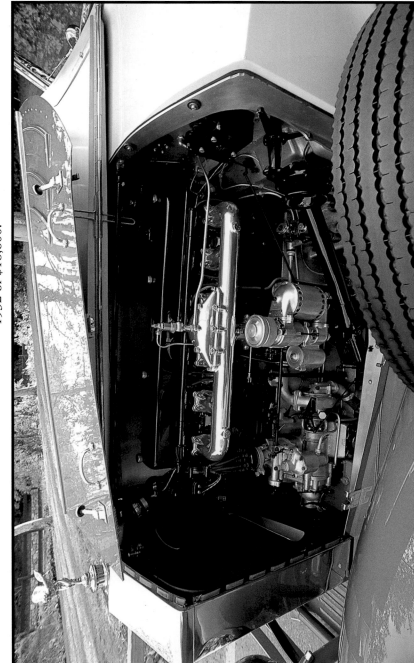

1932 ROLLS-ROYCE PHANTOM II KELLNER SALAMANCA TOWN CAR

When it came to a Rolls-Royce there was no such thing as national pride. Whether the owner was a London haberdasher, a Wall Street stock broker, or an Indian Maharajah, they all wanted the same thing, to own a Rolls-Royce Phantom II. There was, however, one defining characteristic: coachwork, and you could easily spot a British-built body from one done in the United States, Germany, or France, particularly France, because Parisian carrosserie had their own distinctive savoir faire when it came to dressing a Rolls-Royce chassis.

By the 1930s, Kellner had managed to design coachwork on everything from imported Packard chassis to Ettore Bugatti's unparalleled Type 41 Royale. In 1932, Carrossier Kellner built this dashing Salamanca-style Town Car which is quite uncharacteristic for a Rolls-Royce. The sweeping bodylines bear a strong French influence seen on cars styled by Parisian coachbuilders Jacques Saoutchik, Joseph Figoni, and the Franay brothers.

The doors are center hinged, with concealed hinges, the front opening in reverse of the rear, or suicide-style. The roofline is noticeably lower than most Rolls-Royce models of the period, especially with the retractable front panel, designed to fold under the rear roof section, thus permitting an open chauffeur's compartment in fair weather, the traditional town car configuration.

The most distinguishing characteristics of the Kellner body, however, are the beautifully shaped two-piece front and rear bumpers with their sculptured vee center drop. Not exactly the best protection for the car, but certainly something to look at. Ah, the French!

1937 ROLLS-ROYCE 25/30 HP SEDANCA DEVILLE

Not every great Rolls-Royce in the 1930s was a Phantom, in fact, since 1922 there had been a second series, politely known as a "baby" Rolls-Royce, essentially a lower-priced model to bolster sales in the post World War I recession. It became the bread & butter car for Rolls-Royce, although it was still considered the high-priced spread.

The first model was the Twenty, which remained in production until 1929, replaced that year by the new Model 20/25. This version was built through 1936, and joined later in 1929 by a second model, the 25/30, which was as close as one could get to a Phantom without spending considerably more.

The 25/30 was built atop a 132-inch wheelbase chassis with semi-elliptic springs supporting solid axles front and rear. The more powerful overhead valve six-cylinder engine used in the 25/30 had a swept volume of 259.7 cubic inches, and developed approximately 85 horsepower, delivered via a 4-speed transmission with single plate clutch.

The stately 25/30 Rolls-Royce remained in production for nearly a decade, with the last of 1,201 cars being produced in 1938, a year after this sporty Sedanca deVille was built to order for Mrs. Arthur Sainsbury of London, (later Lady Sainsbury), by British Coachbuilder J. Gurney Nutting.

Of the many British coachbuilders, J. Gurney Nutting was the most flamboyant, closer to French stylists in the flow of fenders and roof lines than more traditional square-rigged British designs by H. J. Mulliner, Park Ward, and Barker.

The car is more appropriately dubbed a "Sports Sedanca DeVille" or close-coupled town car because of its sleek bodylines. It is hard to believe that this is technically considered a chauffeur driven car.

This example carries two coachbuilder's plates, "Coachwork by J. Gurney Nutting" and "Designed and supplied by H.R. Owen". Although Gurney Nutting built several similar bodies on 25/30 and Phantom III chassis, this is apparently the only version with the stylish one-piece rear side windows, which results in an especially graceful rear compartment line. With a combination of downward sweeping moldings, pontoon rear fenders, and a strikingly sporty decklid embracing a semi-enclosed spare tire, the total effect of Owen's design is quite unlike any other British-bodied Rolls-Royce of the era.

Lawerence Dalton, the noted automotive historian and author of several books on Rolls-Royce coachwork described the 25/30 Sports Sedanca DeVille as "Gurney Nutting at its best."

1937 Rolls-Royce Phantom III

1937 ROLLS-ROYCE PHANTOM III SEDANCA DEVILLE

By the 1930s the multi-cylinder wars were raging on in the U.S. Packard, Cadillac, Lincoln, Auburn, Pierce-Arrow, and Franklin all had twelve-cylinder engines, and Cadillac and Marmon even had sixteen-cylinder models! In Europe, Hispano-Suiza had introduced the J12, thus Rolls-Royce, with an inline six was simply no match on either continent. In the fall of 1935 the great British automaker cast its lot into the fray with the Phantom III.

This was an entirely new Phantom, from the 142-inch wheelbase chassis and General Motors-type independent front suspension, to the massive overhead valve V-12 engine displacing 447.9 cubic inches. The Rolls-Royce twelve delivered up to 180 horsepower at 3000 rpm and could easily take a full-bodied town car up to 85 mph. Later models with overdrive were capable of nearly 100 mph in top gear, making this the fastest, and thanks to the improved suspension, best handling Phantom ever built. It was also to be the least produced prewar model, with total deliveries ending at the 710th chassis in 1939.

The PIII's had the most avant garde styling in Rolls-Royce history, even the traditionally reserved British coachworks like H.J. Mulliner were stretching fenderlines, rounding the rooftops and elongating the decklids.

One of Mulliner's finest and most elegant creations was this 1937 Phantom III built for the Hon. W.G. Bethell of Westminster, London, who retained ownership until 1950. The stylishly formal Sedanca deVille featured a rear division window, embroidered upholstery in the rear compartment and beautifully hand-finished cabinetry for bar and vanity.

As one of the six principal Phantoms in The Nethercutt Collection, the Mulliner Sedanca deVille symbolizes the most significant of all pre-World War II Rolls-Royce models.

1956 ROLLS-ROYCE PHANTOM IV SALOON

The Second World War had taken its toll on the European automotive industry, with air raids and land battles literally extending to the front doors of the world's oldest automakers, many of who returned to find their factories in ruin when the war ended in 1945. Rolls-Royce had fared better than most considering

that the company had built military vehicles and aero engines throughout the entire war and had been one of the German military's primary targets. With peace at hand and the resumption of civilian automobile production, Rolls-Royce began development of a postwar Phantom. The last had been done in the classic era of the 1930s, but now the market for such lavish and costly cars was smaller and Rolls-Royce decided to make the first postwar model available only to royalty and heads of state, thus the Phantom IV was the most exclusive yet produced. Only 18 were made between 1950 and 1956, the very first of which was delivered to their Royal Highness the Duke of Edinburgh and the Princess Elizabeth on July 6, 1950.

The new Phantoms were built on a long 145-inch wheelbase chassis and powered by a B80 Series straight eight with a swept volume of 346.3 cubic inches 164-horsepower output.

The car in The Nethercutt Collection was the 16th built in the series, ordered in 1955 by the Emir of Kuwait, H.H. Shaikh Sia Abdulla al Salim al Subak. It was fitted to order with green Connolly leather upholstery, a center division wall of burled walnut with fruitwood inlay, a silk rear window shade, and special foot rests and courtesy lighting. The coachwork was done by H.J. Mulliner & Co., and delivered on November 21, 1955 to The Kuwait Oil Co. Ltd. The Emir actu-

ally ordered a pair of cars, so both the 16th and 17th Phantoms built went to Kuwait. Measuring 19-feet in length and a height of over six feet, the stately Phantom provided the Emir with drawing room comfort for his brief 20 mile jaunts along Kuwait's only paved road, at the end of which it is said, he kept the second Phantom IV.

They were both resold to New York dealer Ed Jurist in 1966 and Mr. Nethercutt purchased this car in 1977 from well-known Scottsdale, Arizona, collector and auctioneer Tom Barrett.

Because of its low mileage, around 700 miles when Jurist took delivery in 1966, this unrestored, all original P IV is one of the most valuable cars in the entire Rolls-Royce collection.

1956 Rolls-Royce Phantom IV

1958 Rolls-Royce Silver Wraith Limousine

1958 ROLLS-ROYCE SILVER WRAITH LIMOUSINE

The Wraith had been the somewhat less costly stablemate of the Phantom III since it was first introduced in 1938. With the beginning of the war in Europe, the Wraith was hastily discontinued along with the Phantom III in 1939. As the name implies, the Silver Wraith was a direct descendant of the prewar Wraith, now equipped with a revised six-cylinder engine of 298.2 cubic inches. Output varied from 125 to 178 horsepower during the Silver Wraith's thirteen-year production span which ended in 1959, a year after this car was bodied by James Young Ltd. for Mrs. Eli Lily.

The car was equipped with a GM-licensed Hydra-matic automatic transmission, which was offered as an option on the Silver Wraith beginning in 1953, and a standard feature after 1955. The wheelbase measured 133-inches, which put the massive limousine body at close to 18 feet from bumper to bumper. Most of the cars were equipped with the large Lucas R100 headlamps (such as this example) which gave them a very stately appearance from the front, although a bit archaic by late '50s standards of design. Nonetheless, few motor cars appeared as regal in the 1950s as a Rolls-Royce Silver Wraith, and 40 years later that statement is still true.

1966 ROLLS-ROYCE PHANTOM V TOURING LIMOUSINE

The Phantom V is perhaps the most luxurious modern car of the late 20th century. Even 40 years after it was introduced the Phantom V is at home on the highway, still capable of cruising along at 70 mph, or faster should the occasion arise, still stylish enough to fit in with contemporary luxury cars, and exotic enough to turn heads wherever it is driven. Few automobiles built in the 1960s can make so bold a claim.

The Phantom V was a completely new car with a much longer wheelbase, 144-inches, and a new 380 cubic inch engine, the heady 200-horsepower aluminum V-8 used in the Silver Cloud II, which was also introduced in 1959. With the average Phantom V weighing almost three tons (5600 pounds), perform-

ance was never brisk, but adequate for the open road were a top speed of 100 mph could be obtained. Intended to be chauffeur driven, the Phantoms were equipped with the 4-speed GM Hydra-matic transmission.

The chassis lent itself to some rather exquisite coachwork during the car's nine-year production run, which concluded with the 832nd car in 1968. The most beautiful body design on the Phantom V was produced by James Young. It was Design PV22, a mammoth four-door limousine with bold sweeping fenderlines and a swank turtle deck trunk lid that belied the immense size of the car, just under 20-feet in length! A total of

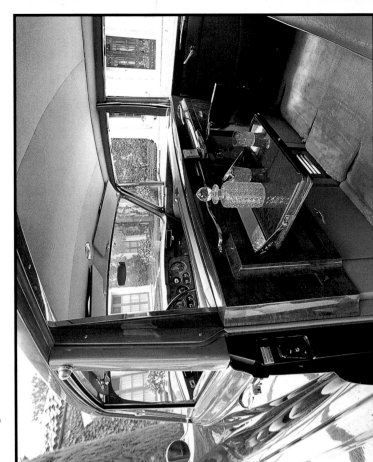

92 such examples were built, including this 1966 model in The Nethercutt Collection.

J.B. Nethercutt says that this is the most beautiful and most comfortable car in the entire collection.

1966 Rolls-Royce Phantom V

CALIFORNIA JBN

1967 ROLLS-ROYCE SILVER SHADOW

In 1965 Rolls-Royce introduced its first truly modern car, the Silver Shadow. Gone were the last vestiges of classically-inspired fenderlines, in their place, a contemporary design that drew mixed reviews when the car was introduced. History, of course, has proven the Shadow's critics wrong. The body design endured for over 20 years, the longest of any Rolls-Royce model in history.

The Silver Shadow was an innovative car for Rolls-Royce, the first to use monocoque construction, the chassis and body being all in one piece. The advantages were manyfold, not the least of which being improved handling and stability because of the design's lower center of gravity. Welded, rather than bolted together, the Shadow had a stronger and stiffer body that stood

up to the road far better than any of its predecessors, one reason why so many Silver Shadow's are still being driven today.

Powered by a 90 degree aluminum V-8 displacing 360 cubic inches and developing 200 horsepower, the Silver Shadow could race from zero to 60 mph in just 12 seconds and claim a top speed of 120 mph. At 17 feet in length and just a fraction under five feet in height, this was the sleekest car the men of Crewe, in Cheshire, England, had ever built.

The most beautiful of all Silver Shadows were

the two-door models first built in 1967 by the combined firm of H.J. Mulliner-Park Ward Ltd. of London. A total of 606 were produced between 1967 and 1971. After 1971 this body design became the very popular Rolls-Royce Cornish Coupe.

1972 ROLLS-ROYCE PHANTOM VI

This car completes the Phantom VI collection and is the only Phantom VI known to be registered in the United States. A total of 376 were delivered from 1968 to 1991, when Rolls-Royce announced that no further Phantoms would ever be produced.

A direct evolution of the Phantom V, the P VI was powered by a revised overhead valve V-8, now developing 220 horsepower from a 412 cubic inch displacement. With a wheelbase of 144-inches, the Phantom VI offered an unusually spacious rear compartment with

concealed hinge, center-opening doors measuring an impressive 49 x 36 inches, providing the easiest entry and exit of any limousine ever built.

Passengers rode in virtual silence within the cincture of the Phantom VI. Individual front and rear air conditioners, beautifully hand-crafted wood trim, leather seating and wool carpeting made the P VI the most luxurious limousine ever to bear the Rolls-Royce name. It was a fitting end to a lineage of Phantoms dating back more than 65 years.

Chapter Six

POSTWAR CARS

A New Generation Of Automobiles

I n the fall of 1945 every automotive design-er in the world was thumbing a pencil against a blank drafting table and wonder-ing out loud, "What do we do now?"

Somewhere in space those words are still floating around, echoing in the vast unknown along with radio waves carrying FDR's Fireside Chats and Milton Berle's first television broadcast on NBC. For Detroit, the war was over and assembly lines that had produced tanks and aircraft were coming to a halt. The time had come to get back to the business of designing automobiles, new automobiles for

a car-starved country with money in hand and plenty of empty garage space to fill.

How they filled it, changed the course of automotive history.

1946 VOLKSWAGEN

One of those changes began in Germany just as the dust was settling around what had become the British and American occupied sector. It was there that the Volkswagen was reborn from its own ashes in 1946.

Although Dr. Ferdinand Porsche is generally given credit for the Volkswagen, (literally People's Car), the lit-tle VW actually had many fathers, and not enough mothers to produce even one for sale to the Volk before the outbreak of hostilities in 1939.

Had it been sold in any number before the war, would the VW have been a decent car for the masses? By the standards of the day (deep, world-wide econom-ic depression, when the working class didn't have auto-mobiles), probably. It was supposed to have been afford-able, the equivalent of $250.00 U.S. At that, even a guy with a job flipping Weiner Schnitz ought to have been able buy one.

In 1938 the factory foundation was laid. The fol-lowing year the Stuttgart shop of Dr. Ferdinand Porsche built some prototypes used for publicity, and three VW race cars for the Berlin-Rome race, which was canceled because Germany invaded Poland on September 1. During the unpleasantries that followed, the VW works built the Kubelwagen and the 4-wheel-drive amphibious vehicles that went to Russia and never came back. When the madness ended and the smoke cleared, the four-power occupation of the once mighty Third Reich found Great Britain in charge of the real estate in Wolfsburg upon which the once hoped for People's Car Works remained, some parts still warm to the touch.

The British Military used the VW factory as a vehi-cle repair facility and shortly after ushered in a handful of former Porsche/VW workers to assess the damage and prospects of getting a few cars built from remaining parts so the occupying forces might have some VWs to drive. By 1946 around 1785 cars had been assembled, at which time the British began soliciting automobile manufacturers to come to Germany and get the VW fac-tory up and running. The English Motor Industry movers-and-shakers came and went, after giving the fac-

1947 Lincoln Continental Coupe

tory the once-over and leaving notes that mostly started with "You must be joking... Henry Ford II came, looked, and said something even less refined. The British finally caught on and it became obvious that if the German VW Works was to be revived, it would be the German workers who would revive it. And so it was.

The first production cars built in 1946, such as this handsomely restored example in The Nethercutt Collection, painted a typical early postwar shade of gray, weren't all that slick, (at least by U.S. standards), but they sure beat walking.

Tucked under the louvered rear hood was a small 68 cubic inch, air-cooled, horizontal-opposed four-cylinder engine designed by Dr. Porsche in the late 1930s. It turned out all of 25 horsepower, enough to push the little cars up to 60 mph given a good tailwind.

Models like this early sedan, which was among those originally built for the Allied Occupation Forces, (this particular car assigned to the U.S. Army Exchange Service for the Czech Military Mission), opened the door for an entire generation of VW cars.

J.B. Nethercutt calls the Volkswagen, "the message from Germany which Detroit ignored." In the fullness of time, the little rear-engine, air-cooled VW Beetle improved greatly, an American advertising agency put together a campaign that is still taught to marketing scholars, the Beetle began to be built far from Wolfsburg, (as far away as South America), to be driven by people who couldn't even point to Germany on a map, Henry Ford's 20-million car sales record for the Model T was eclipsed, and the VW came to be so loved, that a generation after the last was built, Volkswagen has introduced a new VW Beetle for the 21st century.

1947 LINCOLN CONTINENTAL COUPE

Inspired by Edsel Ford, who had become the head of Ford Motor Company's luxury car division following the acquisition of Lincoln from Henry M. and Wilfred C. Leland in 1922, the first Continental was designed for Edsel's personal use in 1939.

The body design by Edsel Ford and his chief stylist Bob Gregorie, characterized the long hoods, sweeping front fenders, high, narrow grilles, and trim bumpers seen on sporty European road cars of the late 1930s.

With Lincoln as his personal sanctuary, the one place where he operated, for the most part, free of his father's opinions and control, Edsel Ford produced some of the finest motorcars of the early 20th century. It was written that Edsel once said "Dad makes the most cars in the world, now I will make the best."

In 1939, Edsel drove his Continental around Boca Raton, Florida, where the Ford family had its winter estate. He was stopped so many times and received so many requests from wealthy friends for a car like his, that Edsel decided to put the Continental into limited production the following year.

The first 50 cars delivered in 1940 were virtually hand-built in one corner of the Lincoln assembly plant, using the V-12 Lincoln Zephyr as a foundation for the custom body. The very first Continental to be shipped to a dealer went to Long Beach, California, and was sold to film star Jackie Cooper.

Originally cataloged as a special version of the Zephyr, in 1941 the Continental became an individual model line with both Cabriolets and Club Coupes produced through February 1942, and again after World War II through 1948.

The first body design was revised in 1942 adopting most of the front end sheet metal used on the all 1942 Lincolns, thus giving the cars a noticeably different appearance from the original design. Under the hood, the powerful Lincoln V-12 engine got a performance boost in being bored out to 305 cubic inches. Unfortunately, the cylinder walls were too thin and after a considerable number of engine failures, when production resumed after World War II, the 1946 Lincolns were powered by the original 292 cubic inch V-12 used in 1940 and '41.

The Continental's return to production in 1946 was capped off with a Cabriolet model being chosen as the Official Pace Car for the first postwar running of the Indianapolis 500 Memorial Day Classic. Edsel's son, Henry Ford II, was the Pace Car driver that year.

In the postwar era, front end styling was revised from

1942 with a new larger double tier grille. The imposing 1948 Coupe in The Nethercutt Collection was among the last produced of the original Continental series. Discontinued in 1948, the Continental name would not return until 1956 with the introduction of the Continental Mk II.

Interestingly, the now legendary name has nothing to do with the stylish rear-mounted spare tire. The name was chosen by Edsel Ford to reflect the car's European or "Continental" flair. However, every automobile that has since copied the styling of the Lincoln, from the Cadillac Sixty Specials to Ford's own 1956 and 1957 Thunderbirds, refer to the rear-mounted tire as a Continental spare.

1951 BENTLEY COUPE DEVILLE

The Thirties were dead. They had died quietly in their sleep at 12:01 a.m. January 1, 1940. By 1951, when this rather classic-looking Bentley was designed few cars bore such storied Thirties' Era coachwork.

The car had been built for display at the 1951 Paris Salon by the esteemed French studio of Franay on the rue du Caporal Peugeot, the carrosserie to General Charles de Gaulle, England's Edward VIII, Prince Nicholas of Romania, the King of Sweden, several Maharajahs, French Noblemen and a Vanderbilt or two. In the postwar era, the Franay brothers produced several of the most avant-garde Bentley designs of the late 1940s and early 1950s. The cars had no resemblance whatsoever to anything even remotely British, with the exception of the grille and winged Bentley B hood ornament. In all other respects they could have been Delages, Bugattis, or Talbot-Lagos built in 1939.

It was, however, a 1951 Bentley Mk VI chassis, applauded as the best built, best handling car Rolls-Royce Bentley had ever produced up to that time. For coachwork, Franay Frères had the luxury of capitalizing on two decades of French styling, not only their own, but of Figoni and Saoutchik as well. The '51 Bentley show car was a stunning combination of styles that had been applied to the most exotic French marques in the 1930s by all three coachbuilders. Franay bodied seven Mk VI chassis between 1946 and 1952.

The early MK VI chassis were powered by a 4-1/4 liter F-head six-cylinder engine, and after 1951 by a new 4-1/2-liter producing a robust 150-horsepower delivered through a 4-speed gearbox. It was a very solid platform upon which to build virtually any type of coachwork, but most were fitted with factory-built stamped steel saloon bodies.

The one-off Franay, which was commissioned by Rolls-Royce, featured a Cabriolet style hard-top roof with a retractable front section, (similar to the Henry Binder designed Hispano-Suiza J 12 Coupe deVille bodied in 1933), which left the rear seat area covered with closed-quartered side panels.

To acknowledge the original horse-drawn Coupe deVilles of the 19th century, Franay mounted a pair of antique silver and blue carriage lamps on either side of the cowl. It was an elegant, understated touch, but very effective.

When Mr. & Mrs. Nethercutt saw the Franay a little over a decade later, they decided to add it to their collection. They consider it to be one of the most beautiful cars ever made. One look at this stunning automobile and it's easy to see why.

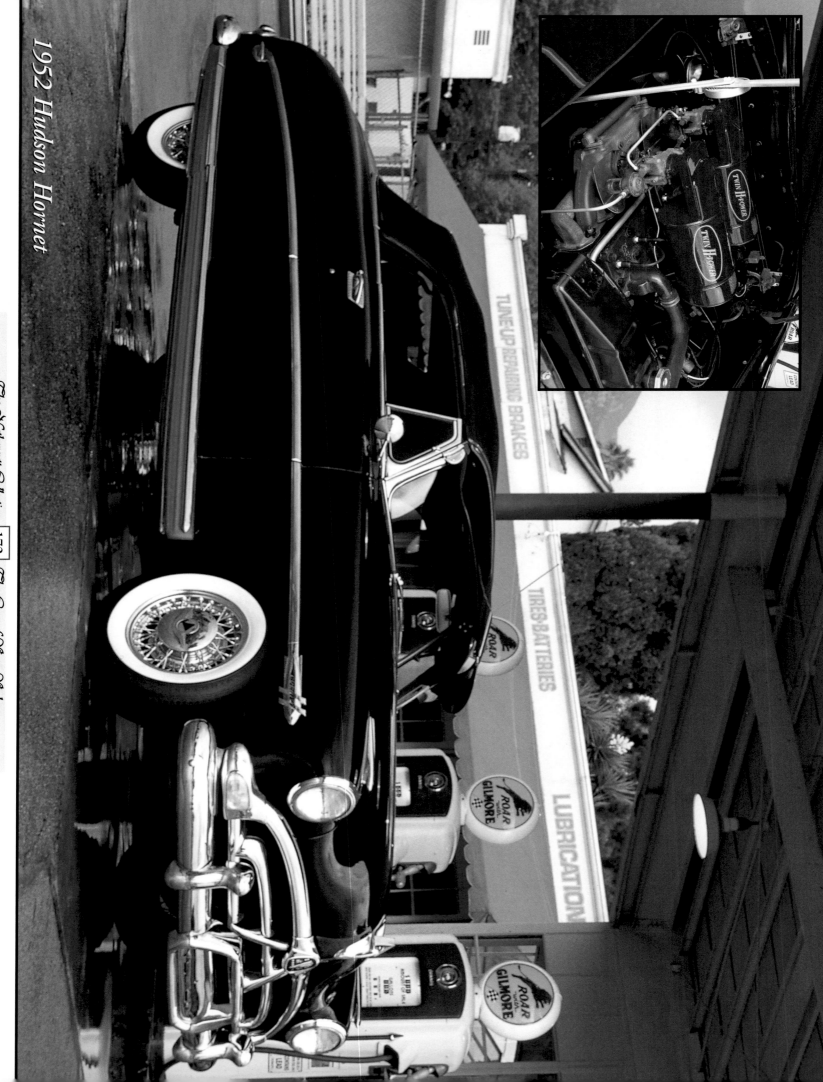

1952 HUDSON HORNET CONVERTIBLE BROUGHAM

There is nothing to compare with the sounds of a convertible, tires singing their song as they roll ribbons of pavement into fleeting images in the rear view mirror, the rush of wind surging over the windshield, the mechanical chant of the engine and the burbling of the exhaust pipes filling the air. In the postwar Fifties, this was driving at its absolute best, and few cars made it more enjoyable than a Hudson Hornet, America's leading high-performance champion. Hudson? Believe it or not, in the 1950s Hudson's cleaned just about everyone's clock in AAA and NASCAR competition!

From the very beginning Hudsons were known for their performance. At Daytona Beach in April of 1916, a Hudson set the one-mile straightaway stock car speed record at 102.5 mph. In May at Sheepshead Bay, the 24-hour stock car record was taken at 74.8 mph average, a mark that would go unbroken for 15 years. And it was a Hudson that set the world's first double transcontinental record, driving from San Francisco to New York and back in September 1916.

It was no surprise to those who knew Hudson's history that the Hornet burst upon the post World War II automotive scene and found almost immediate celebrity in AAA and NASCAR racing. From 1951 through 1954, Hudson Hornets won more stock car races and more season championships under AAA and NASCAR auspices than any other American make.

In the hands of skilled tuners, the Hornet's 308-cubic-inch L-head six could be urged to deliver up to 210 horsepower. Hudson also offered factory support through "severe-usage" options designed for racing applications. Hornets had responsive handling, quick steering and an almost unbreakable suspension.

The sporty Hudson models were offered in four different body styles: a sleek four-door Sedan, two-door Club Coupe (a favorite for racing), a two-door Convertible Brougham, such as this beautifully restored example from The Nethercutt Collection, and the swanky two-door Hollywood Hardtop, the glamour car of the Hornet line.

All new Hudsons featured an exclusive "step-down" chassis design that placed the passenger compartment within the frame members, allowing a lower overall height for the car, just 60-3/8 inches, and a lower roofline, without sacrificing headroom. For the early 1950s, Hudsons were considered among the safest cars on the American road, at least for passengers. Because of the "step-down" design, Hudsons had a lower center of gravity, thus were less likely to roll over, and the passenger compartment was surrounded on all sides by the base frame.

Proven in competition for three years, the entire Hornet line offered exceptional handling and cornering capability with an A-arm and coil spring independent front suspension and rugged solid axle rear with semi-elliptical leaf springs. Further contributing to the Hornet's road holding reputation were direct-acting shock absorbers at all four corners, a dual-acting front stabilizer, and a lateral stabilizer in the rear. The Hudson Hornet was very likely the best handling and best built American car in its price class.

The Hornets measured out at 208-inches from bumper to bumper (over 17 feet) on a 124-inch wheelbase and tipped the scales at 3,600 pounds. All four models were powered by a 308-cubic-inch, inline six cylinder side valve engine, drawing fuel from a Carter two-barrel carburetor. The Twin-H option, (twin carburetors) were added in 1952 and offered through 1954, as was a dual-range Hydra-matic transmission in place of the manual column shift.

From 1951 through 1953, output from the L-head six with the single Carter was a substantial 145 horsepower at 3,800 rpm, 160 horsepower with the Twin-H. Horsepower was raised to a vigorous 160 at 3,800 rpm and 170 horsepower with Twin-H in 1954, the last year for the Hudson line. It was a grand way to go out. On May 1, 1954, Hudson merged with Nash to form the American Motors Corporation. While the merger was the road to survival for the two automakers, it was a dead end street for Hudson. On May 27, Hudson employees were notified that production was being moved to the Nash automobile factory in Kenosha, Wisconsin. When the 1954 Model run ended on October 30, 1954 at Hudson's Jefferson Avenue plant in Detroit, so too, did an era in automotive history. The 1955 Hudsons were restyled Nash models, and all that remained of the great Hornets was a name, an unparalleled record in AAA and NASCAR competition, and a history which has made the Hudson Hornet one of the most collectible cars of the late 20th century.

1956 MERCEDES-BENZ 300SL GULLWING COUPE

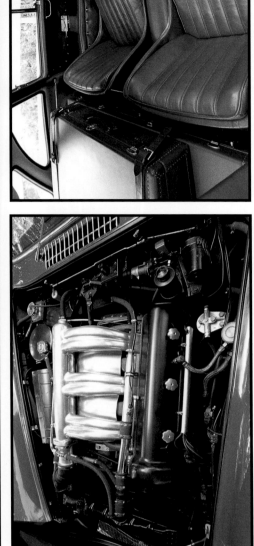

In the 1950s Americans learned about an entirely new kind of car, the sports car. True, America had built sporty cars for decades, Mercer, Stutz, the Marmon Wasp Speedster, even Duesenberg boattails were sporty, but they were nothing like the cars that crossed the Atlantic after World War II.

It began with square cut little MGs and the sexy new Jaguar XK-120 in the late 1940s, but by the early 1950s heads were turning whenever a 356 Porsche, an Alfa-Romeo, Ferrari, or Mercedes-Benz 300SL sped by.

At the time of its unveiling on February 6, 1954, at New York's International Motor Show, the Mercedes-Benz 300SL took everyone by surprise. The aggressive styling of Italian and British sports cars, however appealing, appeared almost passé alongside the dramatic Gullwing coupe, a luxurious street version of the Mercedes-Benz race cars which had dominated European racing in 1952.

What no one knew at the time, was that the men responsible for the 300SL race cars, and ultimately the production 300SL, Daimler-Benz Chief Engineer Rudolf Uhlenhaut, Technical Director Fritz Nallinger, stylist Karl Wilfert and Racing Director Alfred Neubauer, had literally created the Gullwing from off-the-shelf production car parts!

As a starting point in 1952, Daimler-Benz used the 300 and 300S series passenger car platform and 2996cc single overhead cam straight six engine. The SL's would also utilize other 300S components deemed suitable for racing, the rear axle, transmission, and front and rear suspensions. With minor modifications, Uhlenhaut extracted 170 horsepower from the standard engine without increasing its displacement.

The heart of the SL or Sehr Leicht, which roughly translates as "lightweight," was the car's new multi-tube spaceframe, comprised of 25x1mm, 25x2mm, and 18x1mm chrome molybdenum tubes. The entire structure weighed only 181 pounds with support for the engine, transmission and rear axle provided by three large oval crossmembers.

While ideal for a racing car, the spaceframe did present certain problems. Racing cars do not ordinarily have to be engineered for practical considerations, such as ease of entry and exit, but there was the possibility that the 300SL could become the basis for a road-going model--a design problem that led stylist Karl Wilfert to

conceive the car's most revered feature: its unique Gullwing doors.

In order to provide adequate beam strength, the spaceframe had to be elevated between the wheels, creating a high, wide sill that the occupants had to surmount when entering or leaving the car. This shape also eliminated the use of conventional door design. Uhlenhaut and stylist Karl Wilfert arrived at one in which entry was quite literally through the roof, a large panel hinged at the top which could be lifted straight up.

Although the engine and lightweight competition body had to be altered considerably to meet production car requirements, the fraternal relationship between the cars which had swept the 1952 racing season and those which would sweep sports car enthusiasts off their feet throughout the 1950s was unmistakable.

The 300SL engine (as with the 1952 race cars), was a direct adaptation of the single overhead cam six used in the 300 Series sedan, coupe, cabriolet, and roadster. The main differences was that the production 300SL received fuel through direct mechanical injection, the first such application of this system in a series production, gasoline-powered automobile.

The maximum 215 horsepower (240 horsepower with the sports camshaft) arrived at the rear wheels via a 4-speed synchromesh gearbox and a ZF limited slip differential. At peak performance the production 300SL could attain 150 mph and reach 60 mph from rest in eight seconds, making it the fastest production automobile available in 1954.

The Gullwings were built through early 1957 and total production came to just 1,400. Of that, 146 were manufactured in 1954 with approximately 125 cars being sold in the United States that year. Of the entire production run, roughly 1,000 coupes found their way to America.

The car pictured is of particular significance to Mr. & Mrs. Nethercutt, because it is an exact duplicate to one the couple owned in 1955.

This car was located in August 1979 but was in need of restoration. Since it was planned as a surprise for J.B. and Dorothy, the entire restoration had to be conducted in secret, with the shop staff actually taking parts of the car home to work on so Mr. Nethercutt wouldn't see it.

It took just over a month to complete the car, and on October 12, 1979, the entire restoration depart-

ment and executive staff, along with 380 invited guests introduced the Nethercutt's to the newest car in their collection. The couple was so surprised and happy, that for the first time ever, a car was started and briefly run in the marble floored Grand Salon!

Today it still remains among one of the most treasured cars in the entire collection.

1956 MERCEDES-BENZ 300Sc CABRIOLET

Virtually hand built to order, the Mercedes-Benz 300S and Sc were far more expensive than any other 300 models, the Sc demanding over $12,500, nearly twice that of the sporty Gullwing Coupe, and more than almost any automobile sold in America. Among the most rare of Stuttgart's early postwar offerings, the total sum of 300S and Sc models came to 760 cars built between 1952 and 1958. Of the scant 300Sc models produced from September 1955 to April 1958, 98 were Coupes, 53 were Roadsters and only 49 were Cabriolets, like this model in The Nethercutt Collection.

The 300Sc appeared late in 1955 as a '56 model, introducing sweeping changes to the 300 design, proof that Daimler-Benz was constantly improving its cars, even if they were only going to build 200 of them! The 3.0-liter, six-cylinder ohc engine was now fuel-injected (Einspritzmotor) and closely related to the 300SL's, utilizing a Bosch injection pump. With a compression ratio increased from 7.8:1 to 8.55:1, the Sc developed 175 horsepower, bettering the S by 25 horses from the same 182.7 cubic inch displacement. The drive was delivered through a fully synchronized four-speed manual transmission, with either a standard column or sportier floor-mounted shift available. Despite a curb weight of up to 4,450 pounds, the Sc could deliver its occupants from a stand to 60 mph in a respectable 14 seconds, and reach a top speed in excess of 110 mph.

1967 FERRARI 365 CALIFORNIA SPYDER

To a sports car enthusiast there is nothing to equal the sound of a Ferrari V-12, its intemperate exhaust booming through four shining tailpipes with the syncopated frenzy of distant drums. Enclose this mechanical furor with dazzling hand-built coachwork and you have created one of history's great combinations of passion and poetry, Ferrari's 365 California Spyder.

Ferrari got hooked on naming cars for the United States market when the company introduced the 340 America in 1951. It was followed in 1956 by the 410 Superamerica, and then the first Spyder California in December 1957.

The rarest cars to carry the California epithet were the 365 California Spyders, successor to the much vaunted 500 Superfast models introduced in 1964. For Ferrari, these were to be uncommon cars, hand-built, high-performance luxury models. Even more exclusive in number than the Superfast, the 365 California would be limited to just 10 month's production, from October 1966 to July 1967, allowing a mere 13 cars, plus the Geneva prototype built in July 1966.

By name, the car was related to the legendary two-seat 250GT Spyder California, but by design, closer to the Superfast with seating for four, albeit as a convertible rather than a coupe.

Since Ferrari first began selling cars in the late 1940s, tradition had dictated that body styling for both road and competition models feature a large oval grille, a pronounced, aggressive visage epitomized by such models as the 250 MM, 340 Mexico, 250 GTO, and 275 GTB/4. At the time the 365 California Spyder was penned, Ferrari designer Sergio Pininfarina was planning to break that tradition with the all-new 365 GTB/4 Daytona, a car that would abandon for the first time the historic oval grille that had become Ferrari's hallmark. The California Spyder fell somewhere in between, a byproduct of Pininfarina's archetypal school of design and the company's emerging aerodynamic vogue.

The 365 California Spyder in The Nethercutt Collection represents an amazing composite of Ferrari designs, a 2+2 convertible uniting elements from the ritzy 500 Superfast, the luxurious 330 GTC, itself a compilation of designs, and the sleek 206 Dino, all seamlessly tied to the formidable power of Ferrari's 4.4 liter, 320-horsepower V-12. Like its luxury counterparts the 365 offered power steering, power windows, and air conditioning.

While the California was nothing out of the ordinary under the skirts, basically a mirror image of the 330 GT 2+2, it was the only Ferrari convertible model at that time designed to seat four. Combined with Pininfarina's extraordinary body design featuring pop-up driving lights, Dino-like door-into-fender air scoops, and uncharacteristicly large, canted taillights,

the 365 California Spyder was a unique car, even among Ferraris.

The example in The Nethercutt Collection, serial Number 10077, was among the last four built in the series. It has been a part of the collection since 1981

and is one of the few contemporary automobiles deemed significant enough to share a place among the great American and European Classics that comprise the Collection.

Chapter Seven

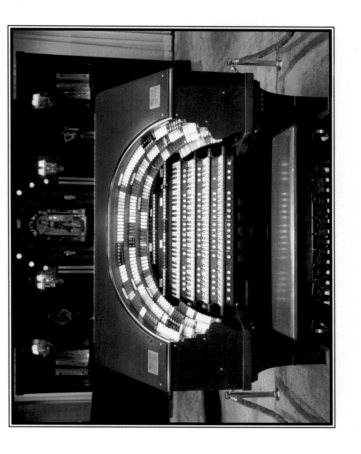

THE SOUNDS OF SAN SYLMAR
Cloud 99--The Nethercutt Collection's Music Room

any years ago, J.B. Nethercutt wanted something unusual and exquisite for his wife, Dorothy, on the occasion of their wedding anniversary. The thought of a music box led to an antique store and said purchase of a Swiss mechanical bird box of the 1830s.

At the time San Sylmar was being planned, J.B. Nethercutt was introduced to David Bowers and Terry Hathaway, who had begun a business in the acquisition, restoration, and sale of automatic mechanical musical instruments. J.B. Nethercutt wished to purchase yet another musical box for Dorothy, but was informed that while they did have some music boxes their specialty was a much larger type of musical instrument that would require an entire wall, and fill a room with music. It was called "Orchestrion". Here was something that the vast majority of Americans were unfamiliar with. The only similar instrument known by Americans were the so-called "Nickelodeons". Once J.B. Nethercutt saw and heard an Orchestrion, he was informed that those on display were for reference only. Should he wish to purchase one, their firm would seeks out one in Europe, arrange the purchase, shipment, then restoration. Mr. Nethercutt thought about this proposal. Within weeks he had purchased the entire Reference Collection along with many more that Hathaway and Bowers were able to find. This made the collection at San Sylmar one of the finest and most important collections of music boxes, disc and cylinder, nickelodeons, player and reproducing pianos, musical watches, and orchestrions.

These instruments have been restored much like the automobiles--to absolute perfection, both in their appearance and their ability to play music. "It's interesting to note that car collectors as a whole are generally quite interested in automatic musical instruments," says Mr. Nethercutt.

Tour guests are treated to the sights and sounds of the music room, known as "Cloud 99" as part of their San Sylmar Tour. After ascending the circular "Stairway To The Stars" which climbs upward from the Mezzanine level, guests encounter a splendid four-side vitrine--beautifully detailed and encrusted with ormolu mounts, produced by famous French cabinet maker Linke. On its shelves are rare musical watches, which have minute repeater movements. At the touch of a lever the time piece will ring the hour, the quarter of the hour, and how many minutes into that quarter! These date from the Late 18th to the Early 20th Century.

Among the most elaborate examples displayed are those which also have music box movements. Between 1700 and today, watchmakers created pocket watches that did much more than tell time. Some striker watches were created for a very practical purpose, to enable the unsighted to tell time by sound, and these actually have neither traditional watch faces or hands. Striker watches were also popular for people who worked at night, in dimly-lighted shops, or outdoors.

Ornate musical watches were pure enjoyment for the senses of sight and sound, with intricately-designed cases combining the skills of a jeweler, a goldsmith and an enameler. Many were of solid gold encrusted with precious stones. The vast majority of these exquisite little timepieces came from France and Switzerland. *Plates 1 through 8.*

Plate 1.

Plate 2.

Plate 3.

Plate 4.

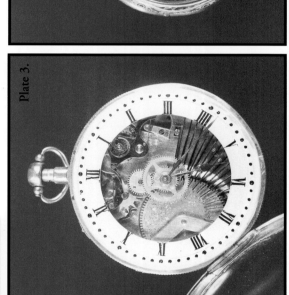

Plate 5.

Plate 6.

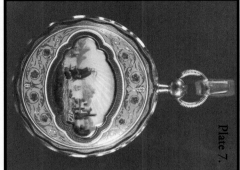

Plate 7.

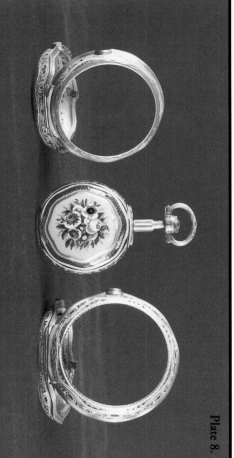

Plate 8.

Plate 9.

Plate 10.

MUSIC BOXES

Self-playing musical instruments have been around since ancient times. History records the existence of automatic flutes, mechanical birds, and other automated instruments in use as far back as 1500 to 1800 A.D. They were, however, the playthings of royalty and the very wealthy. The advent of the tuned steel comb music box made automated music makers available to the general public for the first time in the early 19th century.

The basic design required a rotating brass cylinder with raised prongs which were positioned along its length to strike a particular tooth in a metal comb placed opposite of the cylinder. Each strike produced a different sound, and examples could only manage one or two lines from a song, but as designs progressed, entire melodies could be played, and interchangeable cylinders allowed a variety of different tunes. The fundamentals of this design have not changed in more than century. This is still the basic formula for today's popular spring-wound Italian music boxes.

The exquisite Swiss cylinder music boxes on display in the Nethercutt Collection date back to the end of the

19th century. Some of these boxes include reed organs, silver bells and dancers, and would have been found in the homes of the well-to-do throughout Europe and America. Some of the top music box makers were Mermod, Paillard, Junod and Bremond.

Another type of music box that became very popular in the United States at the turn of the century was the Disc Music Box. Regina, from Ralway, New Jersey, was the biggest manufacturer in the U.S. Regina started in Germany under the Polyphon name and decided to open a Division in America. These were manufactured from 1889 to 1925. There range in size was a diminutive (5-inch disc) to huge (27-inch diameter). Some were coin operated for commercial use, while others with beautifully carved details were for residential use.

Polyphon Music Boxes, such as these ornate table top models, had interchangeable discs, much like phonographs. The pair in The Nethercutt Collection are among the finest examples known today. One is in the more elaborate curved or serpentine case and the other in a standard straight case. Both have beautiful sepia-toned chromolithographs mounted inside the underlid. There were manufactured in Germany in the late 1890s by Gustav Brachhausen and Paul Riessner who founded Polyphon shortly before 1890. They also established the Regina Music Box Company, in Rahway, New Jersey, which went on to become America's largest manufacturer of disc-style instruments. Plate 10.

"Stella" music boxes were made in Switzerland by Mermod Fréres (the French for Mermod Brothers), and were first marketed in America in the late 1890s. This example uses a 17-1/4-inch diameter interchangeable steel disc. The lower drawer was designed to hold additional discs. The perforated discs worked much the same as the paper rolls used on player pianos. By means of a special star wheel mechanism, these holes were "read" and the music arrangement transferred to a steel music comb, which then sounded the appropriate notes. Stella music boxes are quite rare today, almost as rare as the perforated metal discs that they play! Plate 11.

Capital "Cuff" Music Boxes were named for their cuff or conical-shaped note barrels. Neither a cylinder box nor a disc box, it was a cross between the two. The interchangeable metal sleeves or cuffs contained a series of raised projections representing the melody arrangements, these would strike the teeth of the steel comb and play the tune. The cuffs were available in different sizes, playing from forty-four to eighty-one notes. The Capital music boxes were manufactured in Jersey City, New Jersey by F.G. Otto & Sons in the late 1890s. Plate 12.

If you couldn't whistle while you worked, the combination writing desk music boxes of the late nineteenth century could play a tune for you instead. This desk in the Nethercutt Collection is beautifully crafted of burl Circassian elm, trimmed

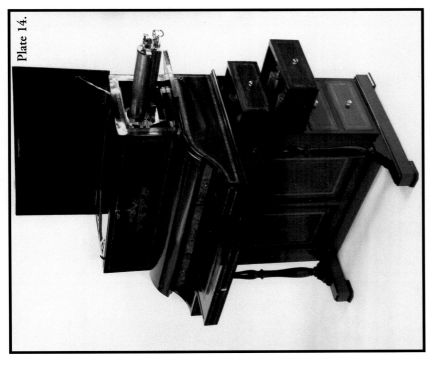

Plate 14.

Plate 13.

Plate 15.

Plate 11.

Plate 12.

with ebony. The bottom compartment and the side drawers offer storage space for extra cylinders, each of which plays six selections. Very elaborate compared to most music boxes, the large desk boxes played double musical combs, reed organ, six bells, drums and a wood block. Titles of the melodies available with the desk are hand-written on a paper which is fastened inside the lid of the box. *Plate 13.*

The second Swiss Music Box Desk pictured was built around 1875 and is an adaptation of a ship captain's desk that combines the art of automatic music with furniture making. The cabinet was manufactured in England, very possibly by the firm of Edwards & Roberts, famous for their work in parquetry. This music box had six interchangeable cylinders, each of which plays six melodies. *Plate 14.*

This Swiss music box with matching table was made between 1885 and 1890. The design in the wood is made by inlaying sections of pecan and pearwood into the burl walnut, and the black trim is ebony. The tiny pins on the cylinder pluck base and treble music combs, play ten bells, a reed organ, and cause a miniature ballerina to twirl and dance. The bells and ballerina can be seen through the glass window at the front of the case. This example is believed to be a one-of-a-kind design and was reported to have cost about $2,000 when it was new, more than 100 years ago. *Plate 9.*

The idea of a disc music box was patented in the United States in 1882 by Miguel Boom (making this the original boom box). The greatest name in music boxes, however, was Regina, of Rahway, New Jersey. It played tunes from movable pegs set in a revolving disc. In 1886, the first interchangeable disc instrument was made. This music box featured two combs, each mounted in a vertical position. Above the combs was placed a stationary perforated cardboard disc with projections on the underside which plucked the music combs. To many Americas of the post Civil War era, the name "Regina" was synonymous with the term "music box." With nearly 90-

percent of all music box sales, Regina dominated the market from the late 19th century up until World War I. This example is a deluxe table-mounted Regina in a richly gilded case with a matching disc cabinet. Produced around 1900, this instrument was probably made on special order. *Plate 15.*

The Regina Corona Automatic Disc-Changing Music Box was popularly known as the "parlor model" because it was the first to introduce a self-changing disc system. It became one of the leading products of the Regina Music Box Company. Standing nearly six feet in height, the instrument stores twelve 15-1/2-inch discs. By means of a dial on the right side, the desired disc can be selected for playing. Left unattended, the disc will play automatically in sequence. This rare example has a beautiful polished mahogany case with ornate brass trim. *Plate 16.*

The Gloria Double-Disc Music Box is undoubtedly one of the most impressive and unusual ever made. Melodies are played on two sets of tuned steel music combs, by two 26-1/2-inch discs. This "duet" by two discs produced a richer, more harmonious melody than is possible with a single disc mechanism. The case, of matched oak veneer, towers eight feet, seven inches in height and is ornately carved of handsomely-finished solid wood. The large metal discs are visible behind a gilded glass door. Of the Monopol "Glorias" produced in Leipzig, Germany, circa 1898, the one in The Nethercutt Collection is the world's only known surviving example. *Plate 17.*

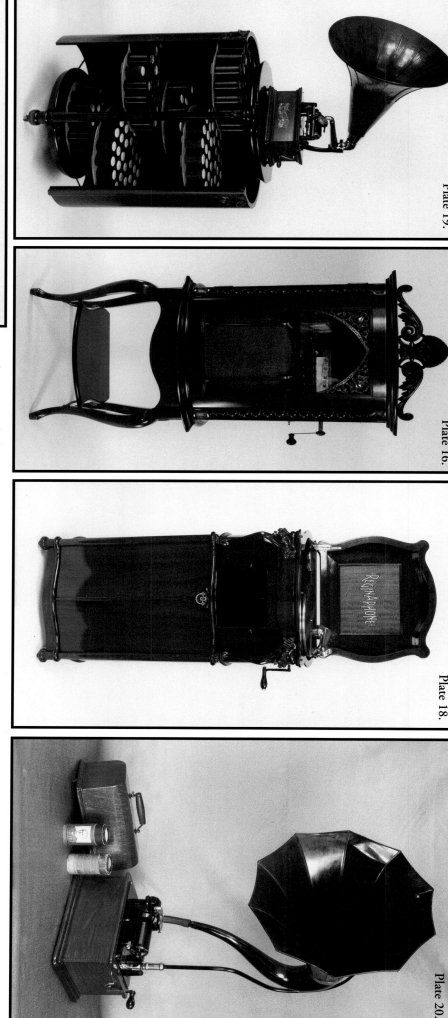

Plate 19.

Plate 16.

Plate 18.

Plate 20.

Plate 21.

PHONOGRAPHS

Incorporating the features of the disc music box with the disc phonograph, the Reginaphone, introduced shortly after the turn of the century, was a great attraction. The Nethercutt Collection has a Style 240, the most ornate instrument of the line. The exquisite serpentine mahogany case is ornamented with carvings of a lion's head at each of the front corners. The instrument is equipped to play the 15-1/2-inch metal music box discs and, by the addition of a removable turntable and tone arm, it can also play regular 78 rpm phonograph records. The phonograph components of the Regina were manufactured by the American Gramophone Company of Bridgeport, Connecticut, maker of the "Columbia" line of phonographs. According to the factory records of Q. David Bowers, just 365 examples of the Style 240 Reginaphone were manufactured, of which only a few exist today. *Plate 18.*

This Colombia Gramophone, circa 1900, features a large wooden horn which amplifies the sound recorded on the wax cylinder. The predecessor to the phonograph record, the wax cylinder phonograph was invented by Thomas A. Edison in 1877. His original intent for the device was a dictating machine and he scoffed at the idea of it becoming a means of entertainment. He was soon proven wrong, and by the late 1890s the demand for phonographs was tremendous. In its heyday, the cylinder phonograph, with its squeaky music, was a popular form of entertainment. The cylinders could play any-thing from an overture by a symphony orchestra to a political oratory by William Jennings Bryan or a speech by President William McKinley. The cabinet below the phonograph stored up to 120 cylinders. *Plate 19.*

A later version of the Columbia Gramophone featured a vertical metal cygnet horn and used both two-and four-minute cylinders. *Plate 20.*

The Victor Phonograph became the first successful "record player" in the world. The phonographic disc, first devised by Emile Berliner in the 1890s, provided an alternative to the wax cylinder disc and could play for a longer time. The model shown, dating from about 1900, portrays the famous Victor trademark of the dog "Nipper" listening to "his master's voice." The phonograph record, due to its ease of manufacture, completely replaced the wax cylinder by the late 1920s. The 78 rpm disc reigned supreme, and no one at the time could imagine a better way to bring music into one's home. How times change. *Plate 21.*

Plate 17.

Plate 22.

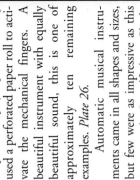

Plate 23.

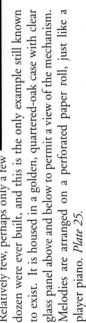

AUTOMATIC MUSICAL INSTRUMENTS

They say that necessity is the mother of invention. While that may be true, in some cases it was just curiosity. If one could make a mechanical piano, why then not a mechanical banjo, or a violin? Or an entire orchestra? Why not, indeed.

In the United States inventors were busy devising mechanical musical instruments both for private and public use. In 1896 in Massachusetts an automatic four-string banjo operating with an electric motor and continuous-feed paper roll was introduced. This was the first electric "nickelodeon". Unfortunately, the music arrangements were not very well-received and sales and rentals went from good to bad to worse. The company moved several times, but no investors were forthcoming. In 1904 the company was out of business. Since so few of these instruments were produced and few of these survived, the Encore Banjo is one of the most sought-after mechanical musical instruments of this era. *Plate 22.*

There is also a machine that can play one or more violins with piano accompaniment. Hand-played string instruments are considered the most difficult to master and therefore would not be possible to be made to play automatically. However, in 1902, Henry Sandell took out patents with the U.S. patent office, whereby he had designed an electrically played solo violin. It was manufactured by Mills Novelty Company of Chicago, Illinois, in 1909. The popularity was not impressive until Sandell added a 44 note piano to make a duet. In 1910, the Mills Violano Virtuoso was introduced as "The Mechanical Musical wonder of the World", which in fact it was. Although expensive for a nickelodeon, it sold quite well. In the teens a model with a second violin (making a trio) could be ordered. By 1930 when production ceased, it is believed that about 4,500 single and double Mills had been sold around the world. There is a single Mills of 1912 and Double Mills of 1921 in the Nethercutt Collection. *Plate 23.*

In 1915 the German firm of Hupfeld built a pneumatic action violin and piano combination called a Phonoliszt-Violina. Designed by Ludwig Hupfeld, it employed three vertical violins above an upright piano. The violins were fully strung but only one string on each was active—the equivalent of a three-string violin; "G" being omitted. When the piano rolls called for a violin to play, the violin would push forward into a bow wheel, resulting in some wonderful music to both see and hear.

An original advertisement for the Phonoliszt-Violina called it the "Eighth wonder of the world" and claimed that "great band leaders, after hearing the Phonoliszt-Violina have been astounded at the faultless technique and marvelous interpretation. The most admirable quality of the Phonoliszt-Violina is its soul, thus the most important factor in violin playing has been accomplished."

In a 1912 issue of Literary Digest, an author by the name of Toller was quoted as saying, "It is to be hoped that the mechanical violin may rid us forthwith of all our mediocre performers."

Listening to the music played by the Violina, it is obvious that no mediocre performer ever created any of the magnificent automatic music rolls that activate this fascinating instrument. *Plate 24.*

This is a self-playing xylophone. One might wonder why with automatic pianos and violins, there came a need for a xylophone. Well, the answer is one word: Glockenspiel. A very common and popular instrument in Germany. The manufacturer of this unique device, the Automatic Musical Company of Binghampton, New York, believed that such an instrument would be popular in the United States. Technically, a xylophone has wooden bars to sound the notes, and a glockenspiel has metal bars, but the New York company felt that the German pronunciation was too cumbersome for turn of the century Americans. Thus it became a self-playing xylophone. As it turned out it didn't matter which name they used, no body wanted one. Relatively few, perhaps only a few dozen were ever built, and this is the only example still known to exist. It is housed in a golden, quartered-oak case with clear glass panel above and below to permit a view of the mechanism. Melodies are arranged on a perforated paper roll, just like a player piano. *Plate 25.*

If you have a xylophone, a violin, a piano, and a banjo, obviously you need a harp. Wurlitzer believed so in 1905 when the Cincinnati, Ohio, firm began marketing the Automatic Harp, which was patented in 1899 by J.W. Whitlock of Rising Sun, Indiana. The first Wurlitzer harps, the Model A, were contained in a square case that had no resemblance whatsoever to a harp. Several years later, around 1908, Style B was introduced, and like this handsome example in The Nethercutt Collection,

it had the general appearance of a harp. Like a player piano, the harp used a perforated paper roll to activate the mechanical fingers. A beautiful instrument with equally beautiful sound, this is one of approximately ten remaining examples. *Plate 26.*

Automatic musical instruments came in all shapes and sizes, but few were as impressive as this Automated Grandfather Clock. Standing nearly eleven feet in height, this stunning piece, manu-

Plate 25.

Plate 24.

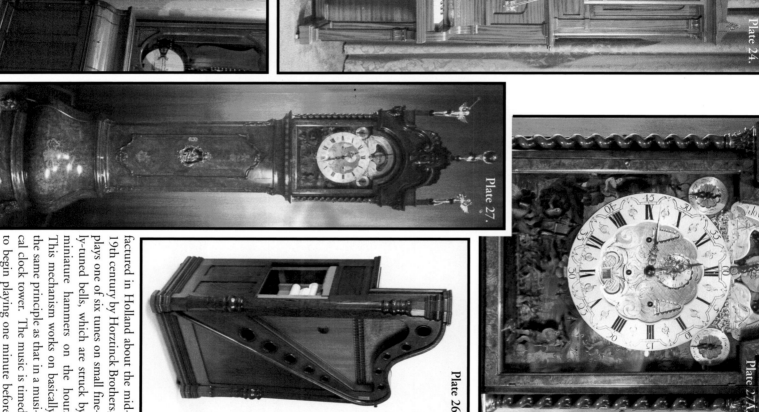

Plate 27.

Plate 27A.

Plate 26.

factured in Holland about the mid-19th century by Horztinck Brothers, plays one of six tunes on small fine-ly-tuned bells, which are struck by miniature hammers on the hour. This mechanism works on basically the same principle as that in a musical clock tower. The music is timed to begin playing one minute before the clock strikes the hour, and to finish in sixty seconds, so there is no possibility that the music will play and the clock strike simultaneously.

The case is an outstanding work of art, coupling beautiful-ly-carved burl walnut with marquetry of inlaid pecan. The Roman numerals on the face are hand-engraved, and hand-painted figures decorate the bottom portion of the clock face. At the top, the phases of the moon are depicted, and along the bottom a three-dimensional seascape moves back and forth with the swinging of the pendulum.

The clock is driven by weights, which are attached to strings. The strings run on drums, into which grooves have been cut. When the clock is wound, the strings run into the drums in proper sequence. There is a drum for the striking mechanism, one for the winding mechanism, and another for the music mechanism. All three are encased in solid brass plates.

By far one of the most beautiful Grandfather Clocks in the world, this large clock sits majestically in a corner of "Cloud 99." *Plate 27 & 27A.*

PLAYER PIANOS & REPRODUCING PIANOS

By the early 1900s, the player piano had begun to gain pop-ularity. Although a push-up piano player had been introduced in the 1890s, the "inside player" making piano and roll-player in one unit, captured the imagination of the American public. To date, over 3,000,000 have been made. There are several of these fine upright player pianos in the Collection. Some of these pianos were nickel-operated for commercial use.

The greatest innovation with a piano being made to play automatically was the introduction of the reproducing piano mechanism. The Europeans had begun the reproducing sys-tems, the most notable; Welte of Freiburg, Germany. They built a sophisticated system, which captured the expression of a live performance on a perforated paper roll and could replay that live performance with uncanny realism. The play-back unit was in a separate push-up cabinet called Vorsetzer (German - from the verb Vorzetsen: to sit before) - this device could be placed in front of any piano; spinet, upright, or grand and adjust to play the keys and push the expression pedals to re-cre-ate a live performance!

In this country, Charles Fuller Stoddard developed a like system. Stoddard placed his playback in a drawer that pulled out from under the keybed for roll playing and could be easily closed for hand playing. These were available on the many brands of pianos offered by the American Piano Company (AMPICO) of East Rochester, New York. Because of their high cost they never matched the high production of the player piano. But several thousand were sold by the several companies that produced them - notably Ampico, Aeolian Duo-Art, Welte Licensee and others.

Plate 29.

Plate 28.

Plate 32.

Plate 30.

The beautiful Steinway reproducing grand piano displayed in the Nethercutt Collection originally belonged to Henry Stetson, son of John B. Stetson, founder of the Stetson Hat Company. The Duo-Art reproducing mechanism in this piano was introduced in 1913 and immediately captured the fancy of music lovers everywhere. By means of complex recording devices, the performances of such great musicians as Paderewski, Joseph Hoffmann, Harold Bauer and others could for the first time be captured for posterity. The Duo-Art mechanism was installed in many brands of pianos, including Weber, Steck, Wheelock, Stroud, and, of course, the magnificent Steinway. *Plate 28.*

Another of the exquisite reproducing pianos in the collection, this 1917 Checkering Grand Piano utilizes the Ampico mechanism. The spool box and controls are housed in a drawer that slides out from beneath the keyboard. The case of the piano is made of African "fire grain" mahogany. *Plate 29.*

The most ornate reproducing piano in the collection is this regal Grand Piano manufactured by Mason & Hamlin. The Italian Renaissance art case and bench of solid hand-carved walnut were commissioned in Italy and took two years to produce. It is equipped with the deluxe Ampico Model B reproducing mechanism. From 1929 until the late 1930s, hundreds of Model B Ampico instruments were produced, but only 250 by top-of-the-line manufacturer Mason & Hamlin.

In an advertisement printed in 1926, American Piano Company (Ampico) stated that the greatest number of the world's ranking pianists were recording exclusively for Ampico, and that the Ampico offered the most imposing list of artists specializing in popular music and music for dancing.

As the most ornate and costly example of what may well be the world's most sophisticated reproducing piano, this instrument deserves its place of honor in San Sylmar. *Plate 30.*

The beautifully-carved Louis XVI cabinet of this Steinway Grand Piano is one of the most colorful in the San Sylmar collection. The bright red lacquer finish is ornamented with hand-painted scenes of a Chinese village, the underside of the piano lid is solid black lacquer, spangled with tiny stars to represent the heavens at night, and the lid top is done in the traditional style of a Chinese lacquer box with a garden scene hand-painted in gold.

Like the other Steinway in the collection, this stunning Grand Piano is equipped with the Duo-Art reproducing mechanism. *Plate 31.*

Even in the midst of the overwhelming elegance of "Cloud 99", this magnificent Ehrbar concert Grand Piano immediately draws rapt attention.

It was built by Ehrbar company of Vienna to commemorate the Golden Jubilee celebration of Franz Joseph I, Emperor of the Austro-Hungarian Empire, in September of 1898. The ten-thou-

sandth piano built by Ehrbar, it is one of the most elegant and ornate musical instruments ever produced.

This piano is not equipped with a built-in reproducing system. It is played automatically by a Hupfeld Dea "Vorsetzer" (not shown) which is positioned in front of the keyboard. *Plate 32.*

In 1929, the Steinway Piano Company sent a nine-foot Concert Grand action to the Aeolian Company in New York City and asked them to design a one-of-a-kind Louis XV art case to accommodate a special Aeolian Duo-Art reproducing mechanism.

This exquisite piano was the result, and was very possibly a prototype (or very specially modified model) as no machinery protrudes from the underside of the case. The reproducing mechanism has been restored, but the case, hand-painted in oils and decorated

Plate 34.

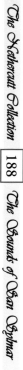

with gold leaf, is completely original. Because the piano was located in an estate called "Villa Leon," it is known by that name in the collection. This piano can be played manually, or with the Aeolian roll-playing system. *Plate 33.*

The firm of Bösendorfer was founded in Vienna, Austria, in 1828 by Ignatz Bösendorfer. He came from a family of cabinet makers but wanted to create something "exciting." So he decided to build the world's finest piano. Shortly after the company was in operation, the great pianist and composer, Franz Liszt,

Plate 33.

tried an early Bösendorfer and was so impressed that he gave the firm glowing endorsement. With that kind of help, the Bösendorfer Company was soon receiving orders from professional pianists, orchestras, wealthy families, and the courts of Europe.

The firm had its ups and downs with World War I, the Great Depression, and World War II, but managed to survive the worst of times, even the occupation of its factories during the Second World War when many of the company's gorgeous Grand Pianos were broken apart and used for fire wood!

In the postwar era Bösendorfer flourished once again and by the 1960s production was up to 100 pianos a year. In 1966 the Austrian firm was purchased by Kimball International Corporation in Jaspers, Indiana, one of America's leading piano manufacturers. A new factory was built for Bösendorfer and today production of these magnificent Grand Pianos averages around 600 per year.

The Imperial Concert Grand Model 290 in the Nethercutt Collection measures 9 feet 6 inches in length, is 5-1/2 feet wide and has 97 keys instead of the standard 88.

After purchasing the Bösendorfer in 1982, J.B. Nethercutt hired electronics and musical wizard, Wayne Stahnke, to develop an electronic reproducing system, so that live performances on the magnificent Grand Piano could be digitally captured and played back with much more accuracy than the pneumatic reproducing pianos in the collection. On September 29, 1984, a live audience heard the Bösendorfer for the first time. It is now electronically connected to the Collection's theater organ and can be played in duet with the mighty Wurlitzer. Part of the musical tour, the Bösendorfer is heard on a daily basis. *Plate 34.*

One of the Grand Pianos in the collection that is not seen on the tour is this gold-leafed Steinway Studio Grand in a Louis XIV

Plate 31.

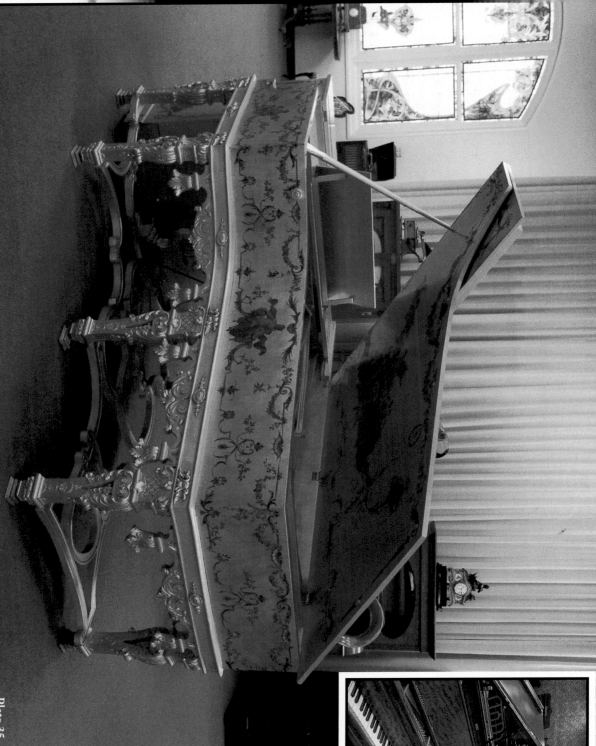

Plate 35.

Plate 36.

motif. The squared-off end of the piano gives the baroque appearance of a period harpsichord, and the gold leaf art case is hand-painted in oil. This elaborate Steinway is among the "Fifth Floor" collection, the fifth floor being the music department's executive offices, display room, and music library. *Plate 35.*

It is here that original paper music rolls, great treasures today in their own right, are carefully cataloged and stored. Some of these original rolls are autographed by the performing artist. While player piano rolls have been manufactured steadily

through the years, the reproducing rolls were not. Most of the equipment and master roll libraries were eventually destroyed. It was most fortunate for the reproducing piano owner that the Ampico perforators and much of the master library were found intact at East Rochester in the 1960s and have been restored so that re-cuts of the originals are available today.

Each company had it's own way of coding that would fit only the make of piano for which it was made. The San Sylmar Collection with so many pianos, nickelodeons, orchestrions,

etc., has developed a library of over 40,000 rolls! Theses rolls are kept in their boxes, in the roll library at an even temperature and humidity to ensure their life span. *Plate 36.*

ORCHESTRIONS

Another route for the player piano was to be adapted for commercial use with multi-tune rolls and a required five cents to be dropped into a coin slot. Hence, the famous name "nickelodeon" was born. While some were indeed just a piano, others were more elaborate--with organ pipes, percussion, and other tuned percussions to add an orchestral quality. Their cases were fancier and featured art glass and special lighting effects.

In Europe, the 1850s brought an automatic mechanical organ that was more sophisticated than anything that had preceded it. Welte of Germany added percussion and tuned percussions to the organ pipes which had been re-voiced to sound like orchestral instruments. These were huge instruments with heavy weights and cables that had to be hand-cranked to provide power for the bellows air pump and a large diameter pinned cylinder called a barrel had to inserted to program the playing mechanism. These amazing instruments found immediate popularity with the crowned heads of Europe, along with the emerging industrial rich who vied with each other to have the largest and finest sounding orchestrion-- as these came to be known.

When the electric motor and pneumatic paper roll playing system came to these instruments, the ease of operation made them more popular than ever. Every manufacturer offered their orchestrions in all sizes to fit any size room. The larger the size, the more complex the sound, and the more orchestra-like they became. One of the more interesting large pieces was produced by

the pioneer maker Welte, of Frieberg, Germany in 1910. Their largest model, Style 10, was called "Wotan". It stands nearly thirteen feet tall and is over nine feet wide.

The orchestrion's majestically painted art glass center "window" depicted the German mythological god "Wotan" in the final scene from Wagner's opera "Die Walkure". The castle Valhalla in the background and the sleeping form of his daughter Brunhelde at this feet as he summons the magic fire to surround her. The sound is just as majestic with its several hundred organ pipes and percussions playing the gamut of music from popular folk ballads, marches, overtures and potpourris from popular operettas and operas.

This example was originally installed in the ballroom of the Guest House of the Sun, a hotel in Batzenhausle, Germany. From the summer of 1910 until some time in the early 1930s, the Wotan provided music for thousands of delighted listeners and dancers. By the mid-thirties lifestyles in Germany had changed, the ballroom was no longer used, and the mighty Wotan fell silent, soon shrouded with dust. Some thirty years later the ballroom had become a bowling alley and the Wotan had been walled over. It was discovered by Q. David Bowers who purchased the massive orchestrion and had it disassembled and shipped to the United States for restoration. Today, it is one of the most popular musical instrument's in the Nethercutt Collection. Plate 37.

Flanking the Welte Wotan is a Wurlitzer Style 40 Mandolin PianOrchestra of 1910 vintage. While Wurlitzer of North Tonawanda, New York, made the case work and arranged and punched the music rolls, the playing chassis was contracted to J. D. Phillips & Sons of Frankfurt-am-Main, Germany. Over ten feet in height, it contains virtually an entire orchestra–piano, mandolin, forty-two "violin" pipes, twelve "viola" pipes, thirty "violoncello" pipes, a xylophone, drums, and various percussion effects.

It was set up in a large dance hall in Plant City, Florida in 1912. It survived the Prohibition years when these mechanical instruments were generally destroyed. They have a remarkable sound of the past–ragtime, early traditional jazz, and some like "If You Don't See Mama Every Night, You Can't See Mama At All". This is believed to be the only example of the Style 40 known to remain. Plate 38.

The Concert PianOrchestra (Style 32), was the largest orchestrion in the Wurlitzer line. This enormous instrument stands nearly twelve feet high and contains piano, bass drums, tenor and kettle drums, triangle, cymbals, xylophone, chimes, castanets, tambourine, first and second violin, viola and cello pipes, double bass pipes, flutes, clarinets, mandolins, saxophones, trombones, flageolets, French horns, oboes, piccolos, and bassoons! It is equipped with the famous Wurlitzer Automatic Roll Changer, permitting thirty different compositions to be played without repetition.

Wurlitzer advertisements enthusiastically described this orchestrion as being "without question the most wonderful self-playing musical instrument ever built. It is a combination of all the different instruments used in a full symphony orchestra, assembled in a single magnificent case, and arranged to play in solo and concert work, exactly the same as a human orchestra."

This style 32 Concert PianOrchestra is one of only three still known to exist, and the only example with this particular case style. Plate 39.

The Wurlitzer Style LX orchestrion was first manufactured in 1921. Many of these orchestra pianos, as they were also known, were installed in dance halls, hotel lobbies, restaurants and other commercial establishments. At the drop of a nickle, the music of the piano, mandolin, violin, flute, bass and snare drums, triangle, orchestra bells and xylophone would fill the room with impressive and delightful sound, while a rotating mirrored "wonder light" with a jeweled bulb produced the first glittering lighting effects.

Fewer than two dozen examples of this instrument are known to exist and this is the only one equipped with a xylophone. Plate 40.

In the first two decades of the twentieth century, orchestrions were in high demand to provide music for dancing. This beautiful, ornate Mortier orchestrion was made about 1920 in Antwerp, Belgium, and installed in a dance hall there.

Melodies for this instrument are recorded on a series of perforations punched into folding cardboard music "books," quite like cardboard sheets used to program the Jacquard device in knitting mills. This system provided extreme durability, a necessary feature for these hard-working instruments because they often operated around the clock.

The Mortier Company, founded at the turn of the century, was responsible for some of the most ornate examples of the organ-builders art ever produced. The cases were all made of rich, ornately-carved woods and were embellished with stained

Plate 37.

Plate 38.

Plate 39.

Plate 41.

glass panels, statues, and elegant lamps. There is only one other example of this Style 41 Mortier known to exist today. *Plate 41.*

Imagine being able to buy your own orchestra, beautifully housed in an ornate case made of the finest woods, for between five and ten thousand dollars!

During the period from 1890 to 1910, M. Welte & Sons of Freiberg, Germany, sold a number of these fabulous instruments to American businessmen; various dukes, barons, counts and other titled persons in Europe; and to many of the royal families of the day. Of course, the prices quoted above, in today's dollars, would have been anywhere from $50,000 to $100,000. A princely sum, but not too far from the cost of today's high-tech in-home theater systems.

Of the hundreds originally made, only a few dozen Welte orchestrions survive today. The Style 3 Cottage Orchestrion in the Nethercutt Collection is one of the largest and finest, standing nearly nine feet tall, and featuring over 200 pipes plus percussion effects. *Plate 42.*

The Weber "Maesto" Orchestrion was first produced in 1926, near the end of the "golden age of automatic music." It incorporated many refinements and new developments.

The "Maesto" was an electro-pneumatic orchestrion comprising a piano of the first order (by Feurich), organ pipes to make the sound of a violin, violoncello, flutes, clarinets, trumpets, saxophone, lotus flute, jazz trumpets, The "Maesto" also houses a complete xylophone, and assorted percussion instruments including bass drum, castanets, snare drum, tambourine, triangle, cymbal, and wood block.

A musical repertoire for the "Maesto" was arranged on perforated rolls by Gustav Bruder, one of the most talented musicians and roll arrangers in the world of automatic musical instruments. Selections included such favorites as the "Poet and Peasant Overture," "William Tell Overture," "Twelfth Street Rag," "My Blue Heaven," "Silver Threads Among The Gold," "Swanee," and "Indian Love Call." These songs prove, of course, that American popular tunes were also well-liked in Europe.

Only six examples are known to remain of the 60 to 70 instruments originally produced by Weber Brothers of Waldkirch, Germany. Harvey Roehl, a leading historian in the orchestrion field, has written that "there is little doubt that the Weber 'Maesto' orchestrion is the most life-like of anything in its class of instruments ever perfected by man." *Plate 43.*

Gladiator is an appropriate name for the massive Popper orchestrion in the Nethercutt Collection. This is one of the largest orchestrions in existence today, nearly twelve feet high and a stunning fourteen feet in width! Manufactured in the 1920s by Popper & Company in Leipzig, Germany, this immense instrument was originally installed in the plush New Batavia Restaurant in Brussels, Belgium.

With an air-pump system powered by an electric motor, the Popper contained a piano, mandolin, xylophone, bells, many different ranks of pipes, percussion effects, and other instruments.

It is estimated that about a dozen Gladiators were produced. The beautiful, ornately carved example in the Nethercutt Collection is the only one known to have survived, along with 100 original music rolls, of which 30 are still in good playing condition. *Plate 44.*

Considered by collectors of orchestrions as perhaps the finest ever built, and certainly to have survived, is The Nethercutt Collection's majestic Hupfeld Excelsior Pan Orchester (Orchester: the German word for orchestra). Built by the Ludwig Hupfeld Company of Leipzig, Germany in 1925, it's sophisticated orchestral sound and the staggering price of nearly $20,000, kept its production to only one! It was virtually custom-built for a hotel in The Netherlands where it was maintained playable for 40 years! While the mechanical portion needed a complete restoration, the case, unlike any of the others, only needed to be cleaned and polished to look as new. It came with 350 original music rolls in a variety of melodies to include the current popular dances: Charleston, tango, fox-trot, etc. Many American songs were popular in Europe as our pop music is well-known in Europe today.

The Pan Orchestra has 536 organ pipes, piano, drums, cymbals, orchestra bells, xylophone, glockenspiel, triangle, wood block, bird whistle, two functioning accordions, and a dinner chime (to call the hotel guests in to meals). The sound is phenomenal!

The orchestrion collection at San Sylmar represents the best of these wonderful creations, and are heard on a regular basis, playing their original paper music rolls. *Plate 45, 46, & 47.*

Plate 43.

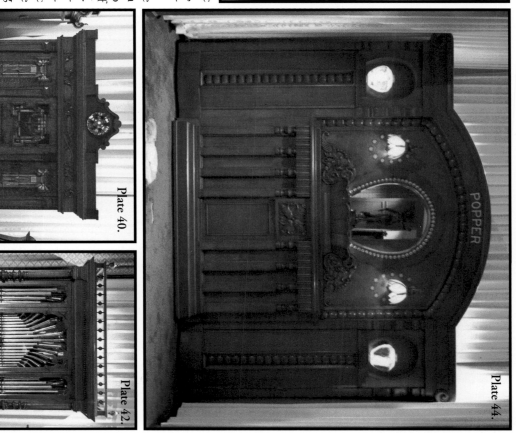

Plate 44.

Plate 40.

Plate 42.

THE MIGHTY WURLITZER THEATER ORGAN

The crowning glory and centerpiece of the musical instruments displayed at San Sylmar is a stupendous Wurlitzer concert pipe organ.

The first large pipe organs were largely built to play classical and religious music in Churches, concert halls, castles, palaces and mansions of the privileged and few.

In 1908, at Elmira, New York, a British emigree organ builder named Robert Hope-Jones, invented a new type of organ that synthesized the sound of an orchestra including percussions and tuned percussions. Wurlitzer took over management in 1910. Hope-Jones continued his experiments, variations of new sounds, and refinement of the Unit Orchestra organ. Hope-Jones died in 1914, but Wurlitzer went on to produce some of the largest and grandest sounding concert organs the world had ever experienced.

Other organ builders made their own version of the instrument, but the Mighty Wurlitzer is the best remembered in so many places. Civic and School auditoriums, fraternal lodges, skating rinks, restaurants and hotel ballrooms. But most of all, rising out of the orchestra pit of a motion picture theater, where the organist played a prologue concert, which was followed by a community sing. Then a live stage show was accompanied by the organ and other musicians. After an intermission, the console would recede into "pit position" where the organist would provide mood music and sound effects for the silent feature. In 1928 when movies found their own sound (soundtrack on film), the organs quickly became obsolete and the ensuing Depression ended their reign.

While many a grand organ was removed and dispersed from their original homes, they found new life in some residential and studio installations for recording purposes. In California in the 1960s organs were installed in pizza restaurants which led to a renaissance for the theater organ. Suddenly the public wanted to hear them again. Auditoriums, movie theaters, rinks, and other places began to restore their instruments to their former glory, and an international theater organ club came into being.

San Sylmar's magnificent theater concert organ began at the Keiths Theater in Atlanta, Georgia, where it was installed in 1926. It was removed in 1965, just before the building was demolished. The 3 manual, 17 rank organ was restored and enlarged to 25 ranks and then was installed in San Sylmar's 4th floor music room. Over the years many additional ranks were added to give this organ an even finer and larger orchestral sound. In fact it grew to 39 ranks (2800 pipes), which necessitated the purchase of a much larger, four manual console, which had been in the Denver City Auditorium organ from 1918 until the late 1950s, when it was removed and dispersed.

The 1994 earthquake virtually destroyed San Sylmar's

Plate 45.

Plate 46.

Plate 47.

It was specifically purchased from an antique dealer in Paris who specialized in former royal pieces from the 18th and 19th centuries. The cluster of royal white ostrich plumes produced in glass at the top indicates that it was a Royal Chandelier. As the centerpiece of the dining room, the magnificent crystal fixture is reflected in tall arched mirrors, creating a spectacular "Gallerie d' Glace" Hall of Mirrors effect.

The sixteen foot inlaid dining room table seats sixteen guests in unique one-arm chairs. While easily moved for seating like an armless side chair, when placed together at the table they form double arm chairs!

To bring the idea of music from the music room into the dining room, there is a montage of instruments beautifully arranged and fastened to the wall behind the table. Each has been carefully mounted so as not to be damaged.

The beautiful muraled ceiling in the dining room was hand-painted by the senior Mr. Heinsbergen, when he was nearly 77 years of age. The murals were sealed with an application of buttermilk, thickened with chalk, a technique used by mural artists for hundreds of years to enhance and protect ceiling paintings. *Plate 50, 51, & 52.*

THE CAMEO THEATER

Designed by Anthony Heinsbergen, Sr., who also designed some 780 other theaters during his career, the Nethercutt Collection's private "Cameo Theater" is decorated in the style of the great motion picture houses of the 1920s. The proscenium arch is of hand-cast plaster with hand-applied 24k gold leaf, while the satin, hand-painted curtain sets off the hand-glazed walls in traditional style. In keeping with the era of silent films, a theater organ rises out of the floor, and there is also piano accompaniment. The theater also has Seeberg motion picture player - a combination of pipe organ and piano which is played by hand or by music rolls.

The theater lobby features a huge stained glass window entitled "The Landing of Columbus." It was designed and produced in 1904 by Louis Comfort Tiffany.

The life-size statue recessed into the wall was created at the turn of the century and is hand-painted over cast metal. Mr. Nethercutt thought the image was reminiscent of the fabled times of Ali Baba, so he named the Statue Sali Baba - sister of Ali. *Plate 53, 54, & 55.*

Plate 48.

make the restored instrument all new and almost double the size of what it had been. Although the organ was "up and playing" a few ranks for the reopening of the tours, work progressed under the direction of Nethercutt Collection Vice President, Gordon Belt, and organ technician Jerry McCoy. Everyone performed many tasks so that this tremendous rebuild was accomplished in-house. The organ now boasts 74 ranks--over 5,000 pipes--and is capable of playing any and all musical styles and compositions. A digital system was originally built into the organ in 1972, and has been updated and upgraded over the years to capture over 2000 hours of live performances including works conducted by the late Carmine Coppola, and the world's leading organists. Hearing the great organ has become the finale of every San Sylmar tour, making this enchanted music yet another wondrous element to the unique charm of The Nethercutt Collection. *Plate 48 & 49.*

LOUIS XV DINING ROOM

The elegant Louis XV dining room, part of Cloud 99, contains the oldest item in the entire Nethercutt Collection, an exquisite crystal chandelier which dates from the 18th century.

Plate 49.

grand theater organ. Many pipes were damaged beyond repair, some repairable, others unscathed. The console was spared any damage, but the organ as we knew it was no more. A complete rebuild was needed. Our friend, organist-consultant Lyn Larsen drew up new specifications for the organ chambers so as to

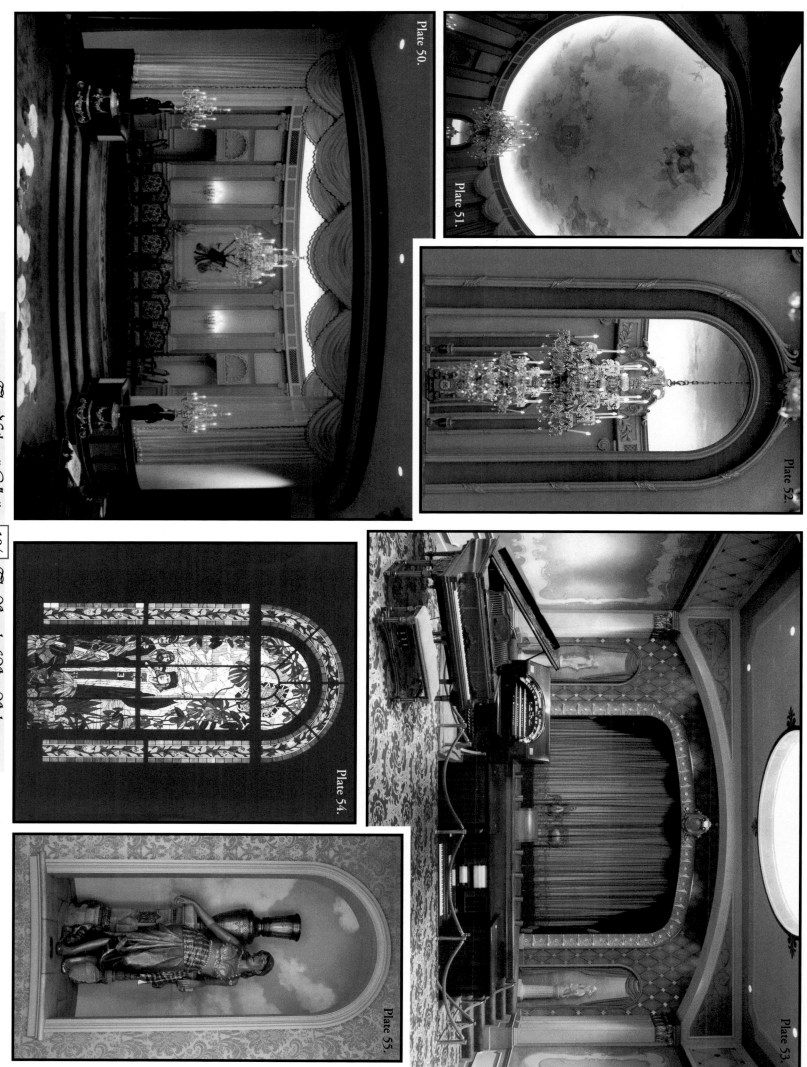

Plate 50.

Plate 51.

Plate 52.

Plate 54.

Plate 55.

Plate 53.

THE NETHERCUTT COLLECTION
MUSICAL COLLECTIONS
(NOT PICTURED)

AUTOMATANS

Item	Model	Date
Reuge: French Girl Pouring Tea		c. 1875
Reuge: French Oriental		c. 1875
Reuge: French Soldierette		c. 1875
Reuge: Girl Sitting on Wicker Basket		c. 1875
Reuge: Lady Harpist		c. 1875
Reuge: Mozart Playing the Piano		c. 1875
Reuge: Oriental Smoking his Hookah		c. 1875
Reuge: Turkish Magician		c. 1875
Magician in Gazebo with Clock		c. 1875
Miniature Bird Music Box		c. 1825
Reuge: Singing Birds		c. 1960
Fortissimo Piccolo Music Box	Musical Stage	c. 1890
Junod: Harmoniphone Music Box	Table Model	c. 1880
Mermod: Jaccard Music Box	Table Model	19th Century
Mermod: Music Box	Table Model	19th Century
Mermod: Music Box	Table Model	19th Century
Miniature Furrniture	Table, Sofa, and Chairs	c. 1968
Miniature Wooden Music Box	Dancing Dolls/Slides	c. 1880
Musical Stereopticon	Table Model	c. 1882
Nicole Freres: Music Box	Gloria Table Model	c. 1890
Paillard: Sublime Harmonie Music Box	Table Model	c. 1885
Paillard: Mandolin-Piccolo Music Box	Interchangeable Cylinders	19th Century
Paillard: Music Box	Table Model	19th Century
Paillard: Music Box	Musical Stage	c. 1890
Paillard: Orchestra Music Box	Telescopic Cylinders	c. 1880
Paillard: Plerodienique Music Box	Sublime	c. 1890
Paillard: Sublime Harmonie Music Box	Tremelo Zither	c. 1890
Paillard: Tremelo Zither Music Box	Ballerina and Bells	c. 1890
Reuge: Jewel Music Box	Rosewood Case	c. 1980
Reuge: Music Box	41 Note Reed Organ	20th Century
Rivenc/Bremond: Music Box	Eroull	c. 1875
Swiss Keywind Music Box		c. 1850

BARREL ORGANS

Item	Model	Date
British Chamber Organ	Hand Crank	c. 1850
Molinari: Street Barrel Organ	6 Tune Cylinder	c. 1900
Popper: Barrell Orchestrion	Othello	c. 1910
Strausberg: Castle Orchestrion	Style 2	c. 1868
Wurlitzer: Barrell Piano	Tonophone	c. 1900

ROLLER ORGANS

Item	Model	Date
Chantangua: Roller Organ	Concert Model	c. 1880
Gem: Roller Organ	Small Table Model	c. 1880
Melodia Organette	Small Table Model	c. 1900
Orguinette	Cabinet Model	c. 1880

CLOCKS

Item	Model	Date
Barometer and matching Cartell Clock	Red Chinese	c. 1760
Boulle: Clock		
Framed Musical Wall Clock	Square Gilt Frame	19th Century
Framed Musical Wall Clock	Square Gilt Frame	19th Century
Framed Musical Wall Clock	Round Gilt Frame	19th Century
Framed Musical Wall Clock	Round Gilt Frame	19th Century
French Wall Clock	Bronze and Green Marble with Matching Urns	19th Century
Marble and Bronze Clock	Red Enamel and Gilded	19th Century
Miniature Chair Clock		
Musical Clock Statue		
Ormolu Musical Clock	Gilded Ships	19th Century
Rocking Ship Automaton Clock	Style 18	c. 1876
Seth Thomas Clock	Franklin Mint Replica	
Steeple Clock		
Weight Wall Clock		
Wood Carved Wall Clock		
Bird Pavilion Clock	Sectional Comb Movement	c. 1820
Bird Pavilion Clock		19th Century
Symphonion Musical Clocks (2)	Disc Music Box	c. 1900
Neuchatel Carillon Bracket Clock	Louis XV Musical	c. 1815

CYLINDER MUSIC BOXES

Item	Model	Date
Alexandra: Music Box	Table Model	c. 1890
American: Music Box	Table Model	c. 1890
Bremond: Music Box	Table Model	c. 1870
Cuendet: Oriental Music Box	Table Model	c. 1850

DISC MUSIC BOXES

Item	Model	Date
Capital Cuff: Music Box	Style F	c. 1896
Criterion: Music Box	Upright Model	c. 1905
Faudels: Music Box	Table Model	c. 1900
German Music Box		19th Century
Imperial Symphonion: Music Box	Style 1oGI	c. 1899
Mira: Console Music Box	Console	c. 1890
Mira: Music Box	Table Model	c. 1890
New Century: Disc-Shifting Music Box	Duplex Table Model	c. 1900
Olympia: Music Box	Matching Table	c. 1898
Phoenix: Orchestrion Music Box	Floor Model	20th Century
Polyphon: Automatic Disc Changer	Large Upright	20th Century
Polyphon: Music Box	Serpentine Case	20th Century
Polyphon: Music Box	Standard Case	
Polyphon: Music Box	Style 105S with Base	
Regina: Automatic Concerto Music Box	Style 300 Console	
Regina: Automatic Disc Changer	Style 38 Round Front	
Regina: Automatic Disc Changer	Style 34 Gallery	
Regina: Doll Music Box		
Regina: Music Box	Floor Model	c. 1890
Regina: Music Box	Floor Model	20th Century
Regina: Music Box	Floor Model	
Regina: Music Box	Floor Model	
Roepke: Orchestral Music Box	Orchestral	c. 1895
Symphonion: Music Box	Eroica	c. 1893
Thorens: Platter Player	Platter Player	

NICKELODEONS

Item	Model	Date
Mills: Double Violano Virtuoso	Violano Virtuoso	c. 1925
Pneumatic Player Accordian		19th Century
Regina: Piano & Mandolin Orchestra	Style 303	c. 1910
Seeburg: Nickelodeon Piano	Style L Junior-Cabinet	c. 1920
Seeburg: Automatic Orchestra	Style L	c. 1917
Wurlitzer: Mandolin Quartet	Mandolin Quartet	c. 1906

ORCHESTRIONS

Item	Model	Date
Aeolian: Solo Orchestrelle	Style F	c. 1906
Hupfeld: Orchestrion	Helios	c. 1920

	Style 3 Keyboard	c.1925
Phillips: Violin Piano Orchestrion	Style 3 Keyboard	c.1925
Popper: Orchestrion	Iduna	c.1920
Popper: Orchestrion	Salon-Style 1	c.1920
Popper: Jazz Band Orchestrion	Swanee Flute	c.1920
Seeburg: Photoplayer Orchestra	Style R	c.1920
Weber: Orchestrion	Brabo-Model 2	c.1905
Welte: Philharmonic Pipe Orchestrion	Philharmonic I or II	c.1913
Wurlitzer-Phillips: Orchestrion	Paganini-Style 3	c.1925

ORGANS

Mason & Hamlin: Reed Organ	Parlor Organ	19th Century
Wurlitzer: 2 Manual Console	Hope-Jones Unit	
Wurlitzer: 3 Manual Console	Hope-Jones Unit	
Hammond: Aeolian Player		c.1926
Hammond: Novachord		

ORGAN PLAYERS

Aeolian: Duo-Art: Concertola	Multi-Roll Changer	c.1930
Aeolian: Pipe Organ Roll Player	Single Roll Style	c.1930
Moller: Artiste Pipe Organ Roll Player	2 Manual	c.1932
Moller: Pipe Organ Roll Player	4 Manual	c.1930
Wurlitzer: 165 Note Organ Player	Style R	c.1930
Wurlitzer: Concert Organ Player	97 Note Concert	c.1930

PHONOGRAPH PLAYERS

Capehart: Changer	Adam Case - 78 RPM	c.1947
Columbia: Graphaphone Graphanola	Opera Cylinders	c.1897
Columbia: Phonograph Cylinder Player	Graphanola	c.1905
Columbia: 78 RPM Record Player	Graphophone	c.1905
Edison: Diamond Disc Phonograph	Floor Model	c.1910
Edison: Cylinder Phonograph	Gem	c.1905
Edison: Cylinder Phonograph Player	Triumph	c.1905
Multiphone: Cylinder Changer		c.1905
Sonora: 78 RPM Record Player	Credenza	c.1920
Victor: 78 RPM Record Player	Gramophone	c.1920
Mira Columbia: Reginaphone	Phonograph/Music Box	c.1920
Regina: Reginaphone	Style 240 Console	c.1897

PIANOS

Baldwin Grand Piano	Style 225	19th Century
Schiep Giraff Tremelo Piano	Upright	19th Century

PIANO PLAYERS

Duo-Arr: Concertola	Cabinet Unit Piano	c.1920
Duo-Arr: Concertola	Cabinet Unit Piano	c.1920
Dynavoice: Piano Player Unit	Sits to Keyboard	c.1963
Hupfeld: Meisterspiel Vorsetzer	Dea	c.1907
Hupfeld: Meisterspiel Vorsetzer	Dea	c.1907
Welte Mignon: Cabinet Vorsetzer	Licensee	c.1910
Welte Mignon: Vorsetzer	Red Roll	c.1906
Welte: Vorsetzer	Red Roll	c.1905
Tel-Electric * Telektra Unit		c.1920

REPRODUCING & PLAYER PIANOS

Apollo: Grand Piano	Grand	c.1920
Broadwood: Ampico Piano	Upright	c.1926
Bush & Lane: Multi-control Welte	Welte Licensee	c.1926
Chickering: Ampico Piano	Grand	c.1929
Ellington: Arrio-Angelus Piano	Grand	c.1920
Gulbranson - 88-Note Player Piano	Upright	c.1912
Ivers & Pond: 88-Note Player Piano	Upright	
Marshall & Wendell: Ampico Piano	Grand/Ampicron Clock	
Marshall & Wendell: Ampico Piano	Spinet	
Phillips Ducai: Piano	Grand	c.1932
Steinway: Duo-Art Piano	Grand	c.1937
Steinway: Kellog Duo-Art Piano	Grand	c.1920
Steinway: Themodist Piano	Grand	c.1910
Steinway: Welte Licensee Piano	Upright	c.1920
Steinway: Welte Piano	Upright	c.1910
Welte: Artistic Krakauer Piano	Upright-Green Roll	c.1910
Welte: Cabinet Original Piano	Cabinet	c.1910
Weser: Cabinet Player Piano	Grand	c.1910

WATCHES

Benedict-Breguet: Watch	Closed Face	c.1860
Black Repeat Striker Watch	Open Face	c.1860
Blue Musical Watch	Closed Face	19th Century
Breguet: Automaton Repeat Striker	Open Face	c.1820
Breguet: Liberline Watch	Open Face	c.1820
C. Piquette: Watch	Closed Face	c.1820
Carnograph Repeat Striker Watch	Open Face	c.1820
Chaude: Musical Watch	Closed Face	c.1810
Colibri: Watch	Open Face	c.1810
Cylinder Watch	Open Face	c.1810
Duboise & Son: Musical Watch	Open Face	c.1810
Edward Prior: Watch	Open Face	c.1820
Elgin National: Watch	Open Face	c.1890
Elgin National: Watch	Open Face	c.1887
Elgin National: Watch	Open Face	c.1890
Elgin National: Watch	Open Face	c.1890
George Prior: Watch	Open Face	c.1890
Gold Crest Automaton Repeat Striker	Closed Case	c.1810
Gold Repeat Striker Watch	Closed Case	c.1805
Gold Repeat Striker Watch	Open Face	c.1890
Hamilton: Watch	Open Face	c.1890
J. Hicks: Borometer	Open Face	c.1810
John Casemore: Watch	Open Face	c.1910
Ladies Gold Musical Watch	Open Face	c.1880
Ladies Gold Watch	Open Face	c.1817
Ladies Musical Watch	Ladies Watch	c.1860
Longines: Watch	Open Face	c.1860
Marlboro: Watch	Open Face	c.1910
Meylan: Watch	Open Face	c.1810
Packard: Watch	Open Face	c.1900
Rockford: Watch	Open Face	c.1903
South Bend: Watch	Open Face	c.1906
Star of David Watch	Closed Case	c.1890
Tiffany & Co.: Watch	Closed Case	19th Century
Tschiefeli: Musical Watch	Open Face	c.1905
Waltham: Watch	Closed Case	c.1810
Waltham: Watch	Open Face	c.1906
Waltham: Watch	Open Face	c.1906
Waltham: Watch	Closed Case	c.1900
Waltham: Watch	Closed Case	c.1910
Waltham: Watch	Open Face	c.1890

Chapter Eight

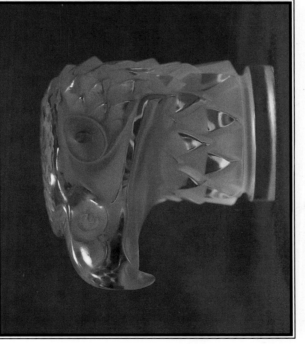

The Grand Salon, Mezzanine, Restoration Shops,

Mascots & Artifacts

The Grand Salon

Chapter Eight

Collecting is a verb. Throughout their life together, J.B. and Dorothy Nethercutt have collected automobiles, automotive artifacts, the world's grandest musical instruments, and fine antique furniture. The Nethercutt Collection spans not only decades, but centuries, with some of the most exquisite Grandfather clocks, artwork, and curios ever combined in a collection that is open to the public free of charge.

Many of these fine pieces are displayed in the collection's Grand Salon, its polished marble floor and three-story tall French mirrored walls, a tribute to the magnificent automobile showrooms of the 1920s and 1930s created by such legendary figures as Earl C. Anthony, J.S. Inskip, and Errett Lobban Cord. The Grand Salon at San Sylmar was designed by Mr. Nethercutt and renowned interior designer Anthony Heinsbergen, Jr. It is in this breathtaking room that visitors are permitted a close-up look at some of the most famous automobiles of the 20th century: the 1933 Duesenberg "Twenty Grand" built for the Chicago World's Fair, Rudolph Valentino's 1923 Avions Voisin Sporting Victoria, Roscoe "Fatty" Arbuckle's outrageous 1923 McFarlan Knickerbocker Cabriolet, and more than 25 other antique, vintage, and classic automobiles.

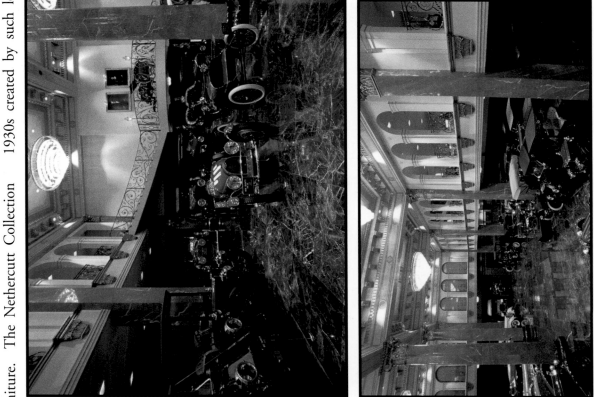

King Louis XV Desk

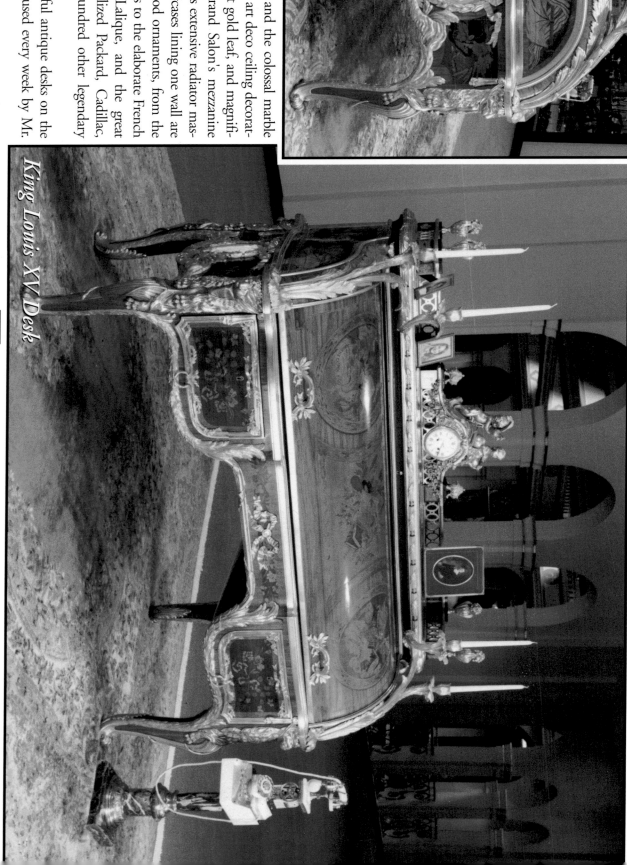

Nethercutt and his secretary when they are at San Sylmar.

The larger desk is one of five copies (made in Paris in the 1860s) of a special desk designed and manufactured for King Louis XV, in the 1760s. The illustrations are done with 15 different types of inlaid wood in an art form known as marquetry. The gleaming metal work on the desks, known as ormolu, is solid cast bronze plated with 24 carat gold so that it will not tarnish.

The plaques on each side of the desk are Sevre porcelain, depicting Adam and Eve and the Arch Angel on one side, and The Three Graces on the other.

The smaller cylinder-style desk is decorated with ormolu, and also with parquetry, an art form similar to marquetry, except that the inlaid wood forms mosaics and designs rather than scenes. The Danish cradle telephones used by Mr. Nethercutt date back to 1902.

Overlooking the main floor and the colossal marble pillars which support the ornate art deco ceiling decorated with fleur-de-lis and 24 carat gold leaf, and magnificent crystal chandeliers, the Grand Salon's mezzanine level is home to the Nethercutt's extensive radiator mascot collection. Eight glass showcases lining one wall are home to nearly a century of hood ornaments, from the earliest motometers of the 1900s to the elaborate French crystal masterpieces of René Lalique, and the great chromed figurines that symbolized Packard, Cadillac, Lincoln, Rolls-Royce, and a hundred other legendary automotive names.

There are also several beautiful antique desks on the mezzanine level which are still used every week by Mr.

Cylinder Desk

long, five feet in height and weighs 659 pounds of what the company called "pure silver, pure gold, and other precious metals." For many years it reposed in the famous Cliff House Museum in San Francisco, and came to the collection where it was superbly restored and to this day still dazzels spectators as it did more than eighty years ago.

The third piece of furniture in this grouping, an authentic butler's desk by Jean Henri Reisner, was made in the 1790s. It has no chair, as the busy butler stood at his desk to take care of his daily household accounts.

At the far end of the mezzanine level is the beautiful spiral "Stairway to the Stars" which leads to the fourth floor and the Nethercutt's grand music room.

The hand-painted musical notes which decorate the stairwell are from the Nethercutt's favorite song, Stairway to the Stars, which has been adopted as the theme song for San Sylmar. To the right of the stairway is a huge silver piece created by International Silver in 1915 for the Panama Pacific International Exposition held in San Francisco to celebrate the opening of the Panama Canal. It is nearly eight feet

Butler's Desk

The Mascot Collection

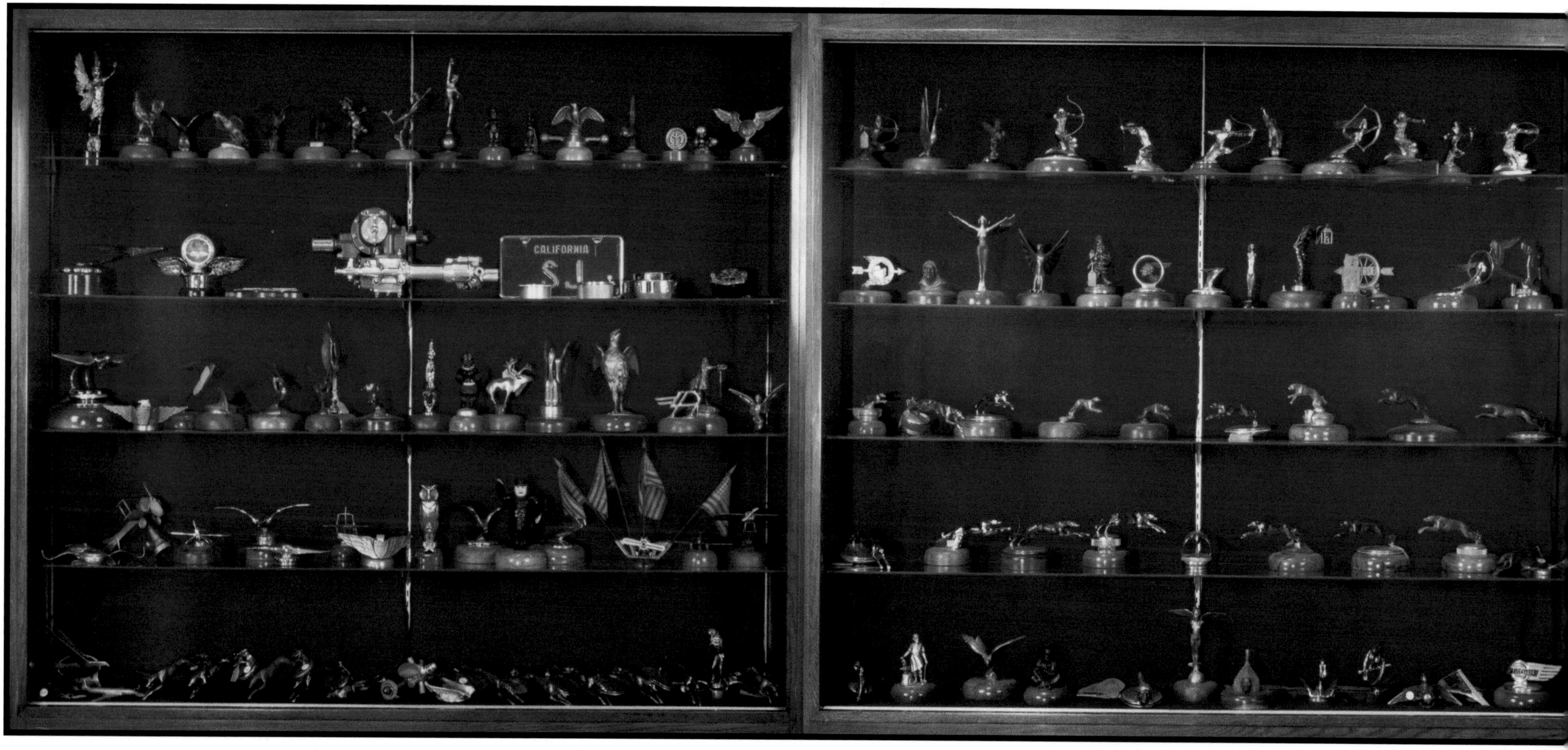

The Mascot Collection

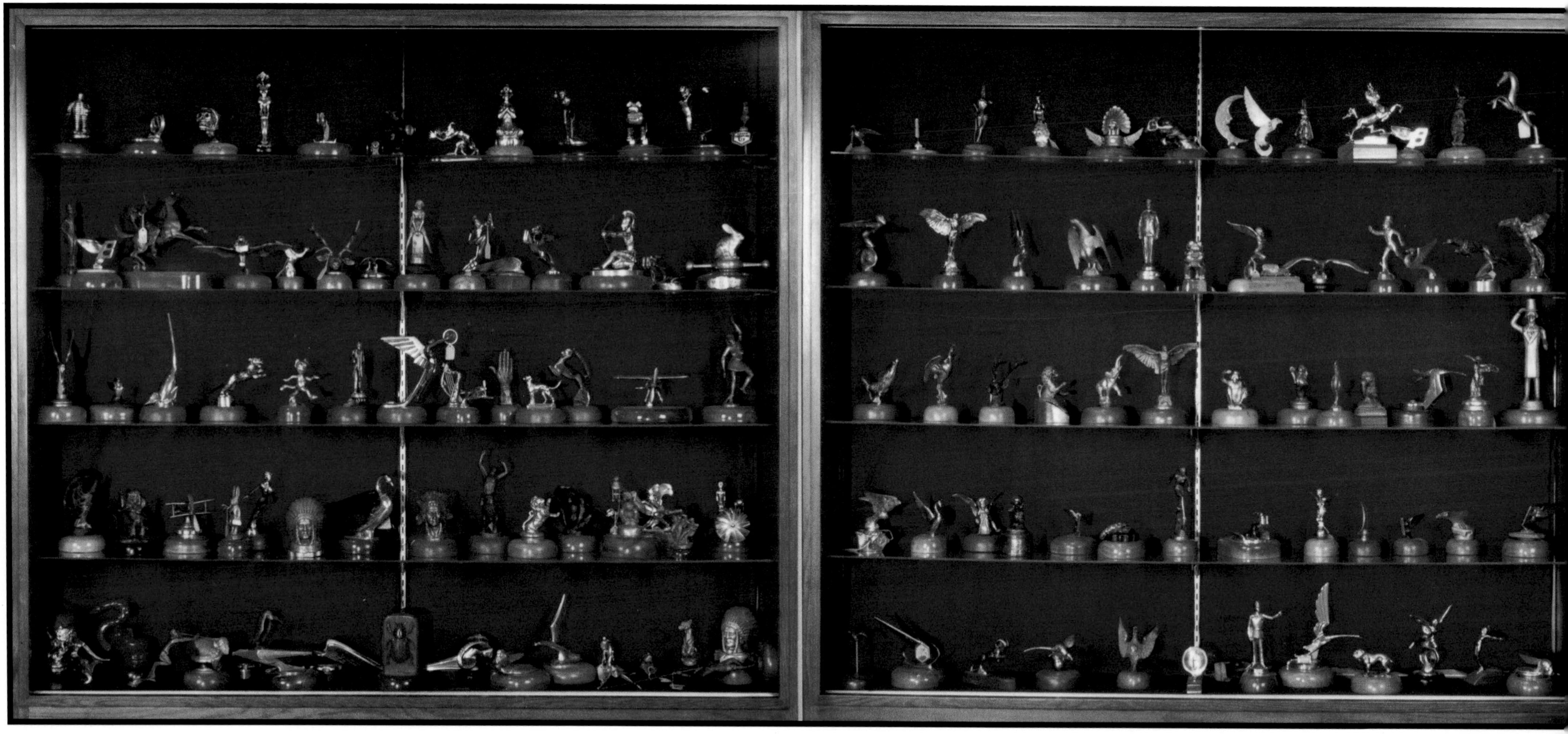

The Mascot Collection

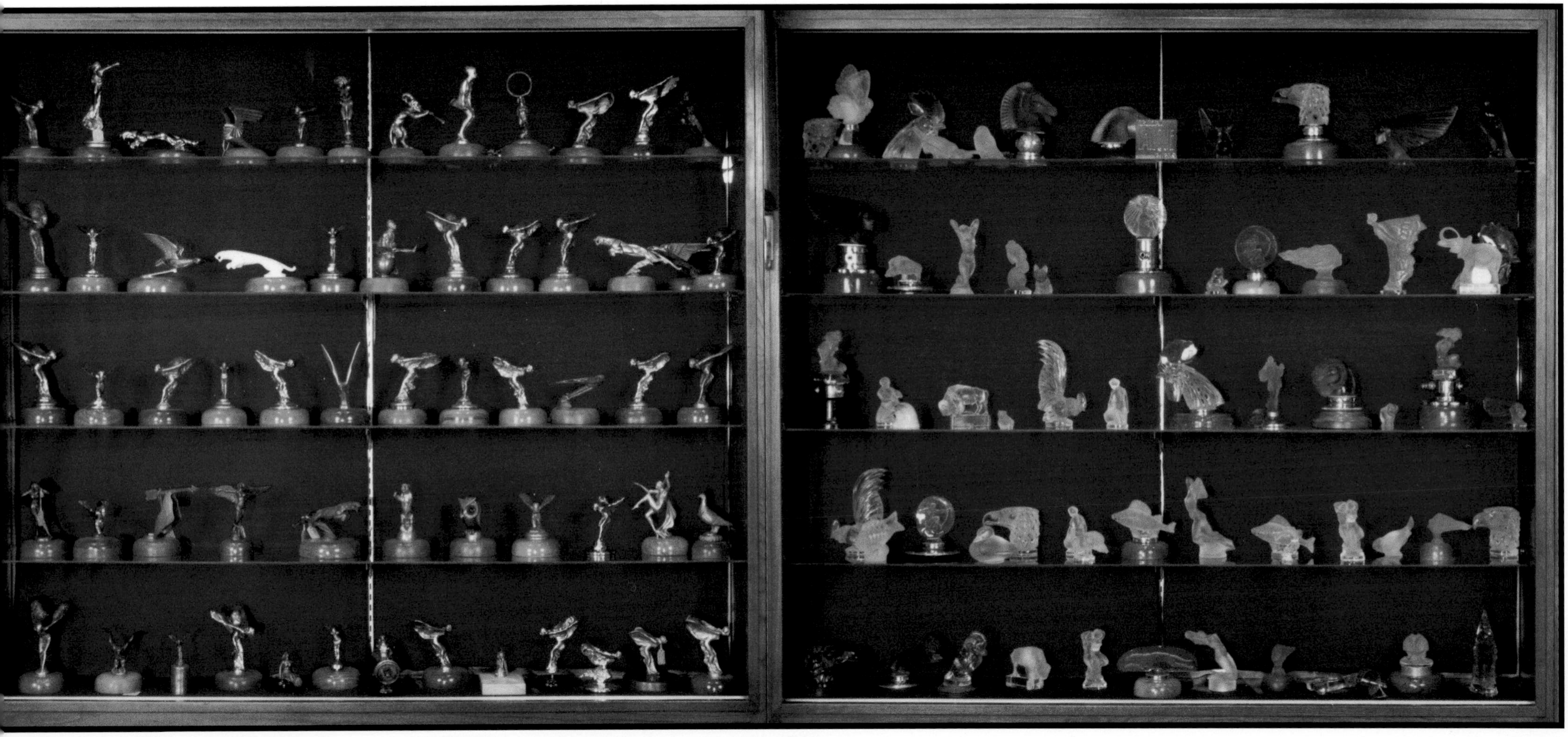

Like every other art form at San Sylmar, hood ornaments once served a function, albeit a somewhat aesthetic one. In the early automobiles, the caps for radiators were used to measure water temperature and included a thermometer in their design, which was most often a wreathed medallion with wings.

Cadillac was one of the first American automakers to create a distinctive hood ornament. The original was known as The Herald, a royal trumpeter with the Cadillac crest on his tunic. It was followed in later years by a variety of ornaments known as The Goddess.

With the advent of the dashboard temperature gauge, the winged motometer gave way to hood ornaments, which were usually an identifying logo or symbol of the manufacturer, the most famous of which being the Rolls-Royce Spirit of Ecstacy, better known as the "Flying Lady." Designed in 1911 by English sculptor Charles Sykes, there have been a number of variations on the design over the years and the San Sylmar collection has representative examples of each.

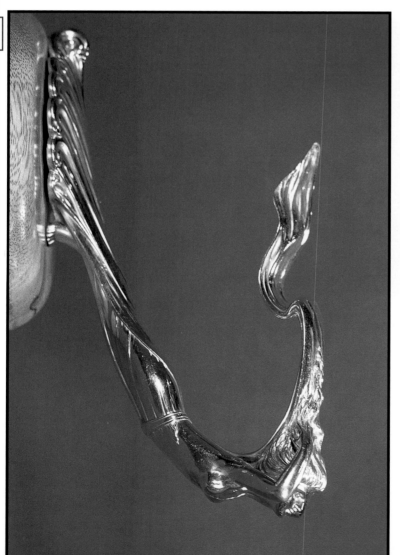

Pierce Arrow was recognized throughout the late 1920s and 1930s by the famous Archer, which was done in a few variations, but this is the most common.

Lincolns were best known by a silver greyhound, a symbol of grace and speed, designed for Edsel Ford by Gorham.

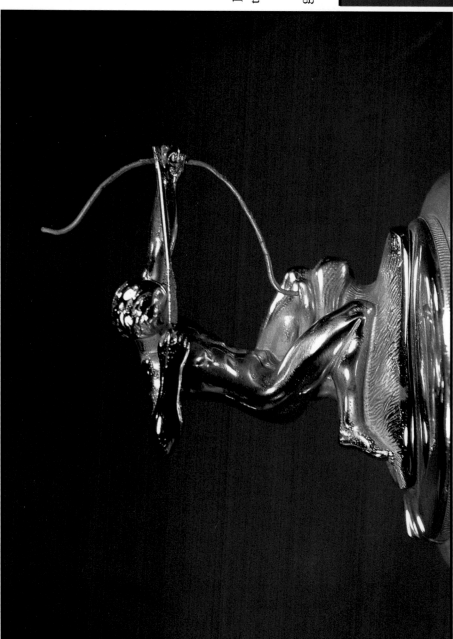

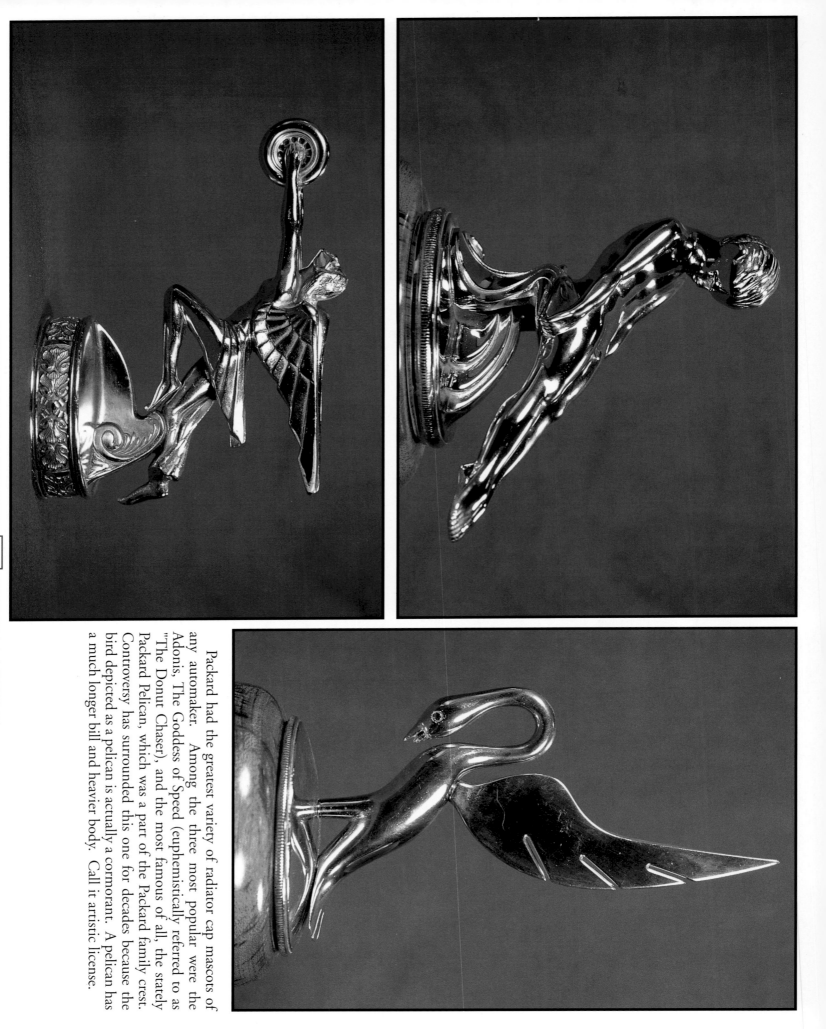

Packard had the greatest variety of radiator cap mascots of any automaker. Among the three most popular were the Adonis, The Goddess of Speed (euphemistically referred to as "The Donut Chaser), and the most famous of all, the stately Packard Pelican, which was a part of the Packard family crest. Controversy has surrounded this one for decades because the bird depicted as a pelican is actually a cormorant. A pelican has a much longer bill and heavier body. Call it artistic license.

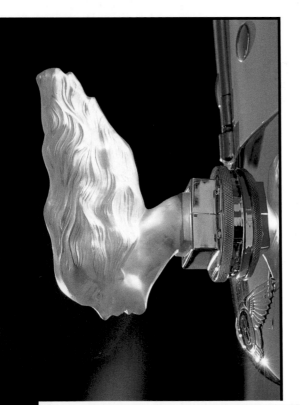

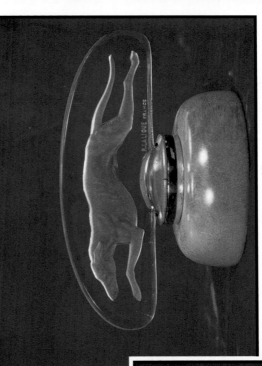

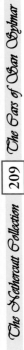

from the 1920s and 1930s, such as those displayed in
The Nethercutt Collection, are among the most valuable
of early automobilia.

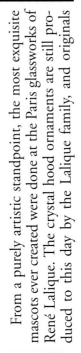

From a purely artistic standpoint, the most exquisite
mascots ever created were done at the Paris glassworks of
René Lalique. The crystal hood ornaments are still produced to this day by the Lalique family, and originals

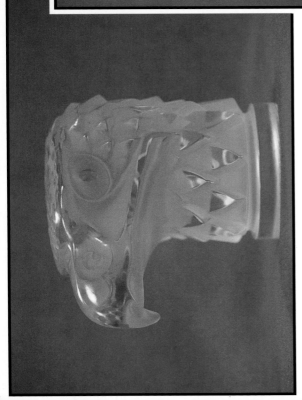

BEHIND CLOSED DOORS—THE RESTORATION SHOPS

The Nethercutt Collection has one of the world's finest restoration shops, staffed by master craftsmen skilled in chassis, engine, and body construction; electrical, upholstery, and paint. There are several different departments on the grounds of San Sylmar, located in different buildings; the body shop, engine shop, restoration shop and the paint shop.

This is one part of the tour few people have the opportunity to see up close. The new museum, opening in the year 2000, will have a restoration department located below the main display floor, that will allow visitors to peer through an opening overlooking the work area. This will be an exciting addition to the self-guided tour in the new Nethercutt Collection building across from the existing museum.

The present main shop is where routine repairs, engine work, upholstery, and general maintenance is performed. From the second floor storage area one can see the different types of cars that are being worked on at any one time. As many as eight different projects are usually ongoing in this very busy department.

The back room is where restored chassis are prepared for paint, such as this 1911 Pope-Hartford. The collection also has two complete spray booths to handle any type of painting process necessary in the restoration of a car. With everything in-house, The Nethercutt Collection is able to keep all of its cars in top shape and ready for the road.

W. EVERETT MILLER COLLECTION OF AUTOMOTIVE LITERATURE

Among the Nethercutt Collection's recent acquisitions is the W. Everett Miller Library, one of the finest collections of automotive literature in the world. Compiled by the late automotive designer and historian Wellington Everett Miller, the collection is housed in the new Nethercutt Collection Museum adjacent to San Sylmar, located in the foothills of the San Gabriel Mountains.

J.B. Nethercutt, founder of the Nethercutt Collection says that, "The library/archive will help us to continue our goal of educating the public on the first 100 years of automotive history through our exhibit of accurate and fully functional restorations of our automotive collection."

The Miller library contains literally thousands of original automotive manufacturer's catalogs, sales brochures, repair manuals, factory photographs and early motoring publications. Combined with the Nethercutt Collection's existing reference library, and the Jules M. and Sally Heumann Hispano-Suiza Library to be housed at San Sylmar, the Miller collection forms the basis for one of the nation's most complete and authoritative automotive reference libraries.

The new facility will also feature a lecture hall with lectures conducted by Nethercutt Collection curator/archivist Skip Marketti, as well as special guest lecturers covering a variety of historic and educational automotive topics.

Chapter Nine

THE CARS OF SAN SYLMAR

A Catalog of Grand Automobiles

1898 Eisenach Runabout
Manufacturer: Fahrzeugfabrik Eisenach
Coachbuilder: Fahrzeugfabrik Eisenach
Engine: Vertical Twin 2-cylinder
Bore x Stroke: 2.59x2.75 inches
Displacement: 28.9 cubic inches
Horsepower: 10

1903 Winton Runabout
Manufacturer: Winton Motor Carriage Co., Cleveland, OH
Coachbuilder: Winton Motor Carriage Co.
Engine: Horizontal 2-cylinder
Displacement: 200 cubic inches
Horsepower: 20
Price when new: $2,500

1904 Cameron Experimental J Light Touring
Manufacturer: United Motor Corp., Pawtucket, RI
Coachbuilder: Cameron
Engine: Air-cooled, 3-cylinder
Bore x Stroke: 3-5/8x3-3/4 inches
Displacement: 116.1 cubic inches
Horsepower: 12-15
Price when new: $800

1905 Buick Model C Touring
Manufacturer: Buick Motor Car Company, Jackson, MI
Coachbuilder: Buick Motor Car Company
Engine: OHV, Twin 2-cylinder
Bore x Stroke: 4-1/2x5 inches
Displacement: 159.0 cubic inches
Horsepower: 22
Price when new: $1,200

1906 Franklin Model G Light Touring
Manufacturer: H. H. Franklin Manufacturing Co., Syracuse, NY
Coachbuilder: H. H. Franklin Manufacturing Co.
Engine: Air-cooled, 4-cylinder
Bore x Stroke: 3-1/4x3-1/4 inches
Displacement: 107.8 cubic inches
Horsepower: 12
Price when new: $1,800

1906 Pope-Toledo Type XII Touring
Manufacturer: Pope Motor Car Company, Toledo, OH
Coachbuilder: Pope-Toledo
Engine: OHV, 4-cylinder
Bore x Stroke: 4-5/8x5-1/4 inches
Displacement: 352.8 cubic inches
Horsepower: 44
Price when new: $3,500

1907 Westinghouse Model 40 Demi-Limousine
Manufacturer: Ste des Automobiles Westinghouse, Le Havre, France
Coachbuilder: A. T. Demarest & Co., NY
Engine: T-head, 4-cylinder
Bore x Stroke: 4.7x5.5 inches
Displacement: 381.6 cubic inches
Horsepower: 40

1908 Northern Model C Touring
Manufacturer: Northern Motor Car Company, Detroit, MI
Coachbuilder: Northern Motor Car Company
Engine: Horizontal Opp., 2-cylinder
Bore x Stroke: 5-1/2x5-1/4 inches
Displacement: 249.4 cubic inches
Horsepower: 24
Price when new: $1,800

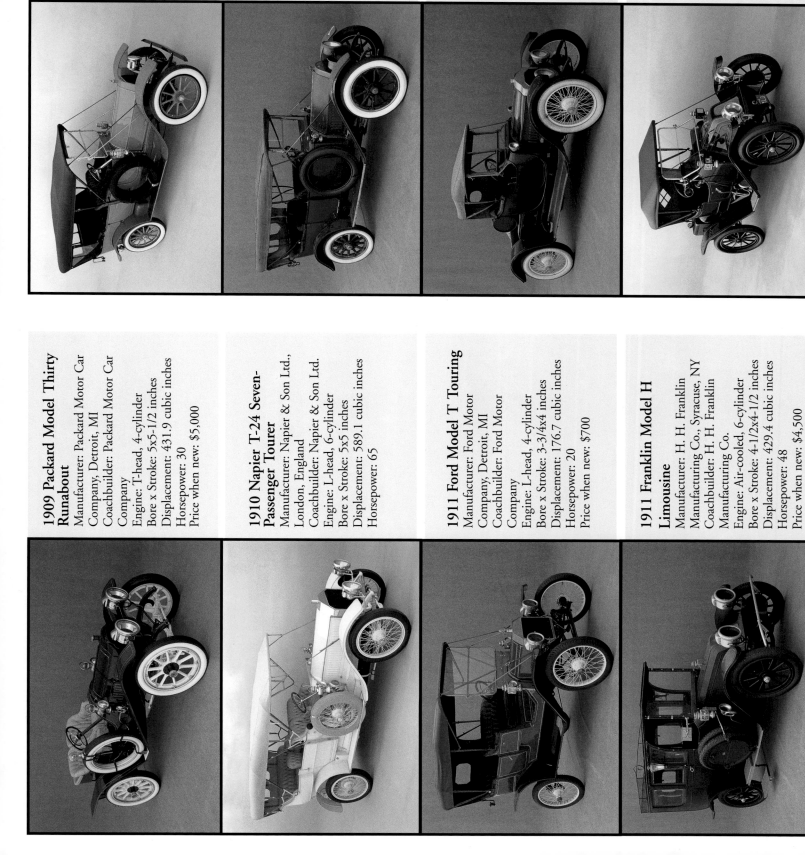

1911 Matheson Model 18 Silent Six Touring

Manufacturer: Matheson Automobile Company, Wilkes-Barre, PA
Coachbuilder: Quinby, New York, NY
Engine: OHV, 6-cylinder
Bore x Stroke: 4-1/2x5 inches
Displacement: 477.1 cubic inches
Horsepower: 50
Price when new: $4,000

1912 Chalmers Model 18, Six Touring

Manufacturer: Chalmers Motor Company, Detroit, MI
Coachbuilder: Chalmers Motor Company
Engine: F-head, 6-cylinder
Bore x Stroke: 4-1/4x5-1/4 inches
Displacement: 446.8 cubic inches
Horsepower: 54
Price when new: $3,250

1912 De Dion Bouton Model DM Roadster

Manufacturer: De Dion, Bouton et Cie, Puteaux, Seine, France
Coachbuilder: Flandrau & Co.
Engine: L-head, V-type, 8-cylinder
Bore x Stroke: 2.75x5.1 inches
Displacement: 242.3 cubic inches
Horsepower: 26

1912 Franklin Model G Series 1 Runabout

Manufacturer: H. H. Franklin Manufacturing Co., Syracuse, NY
Coachbuilder: H. H. Franklin Manufacturing Co.
Engine: Air-cooled, 4-cylinder
Bore x Stroke: 3-3/8x4 inches
Displacement: 143.1 cubic inches
Horsepower: 18
Price when new: $1,650

1909 Packard Model Thirty Runabout

Manufacturer: Packard Motor Car Company, Detroit, MI
Coachbuilder: Packard Motor Car Company
Engine: T-head, 4-cylinder
Bore x Stroke: 5x5-1/2 inches
Displacement: 431.9 cubic inches
Horsepower: 30
Price when new: $5,000

1910 Napier T-24 Seven-Passenger Tourer

Manufacturer: Napier & Son Ltd., London, England
Coachbuilder: Napier & Son Ltd.
Engine: L-head, 6-cylinder
Bore x Stroke: 5x5 inches
Displacement: 589.1 cubic inches
Horsepower: 65

1911 Ford Model T Touring

Manufacturer: Ford Motor Company, Detroit, MI
Coachbuilder: Ford Motor Company
Engine: L-head, 4-cylinder
Bore x Stroke: 3-3/4x4 inches
Displacement: 176.7 cubic inches
Horsepower: 20
Price when new: $700

1911 Franklin Model H Limousine

Manufacturer: H. H. Franklin Manufacturing Co., Syracuse, NY
Coachbuilder: H. H. Franklin Manufacturing Co.
Engine: Air-cooled, 6-cylinder
Bore x Stroke: 4-1/2x4-1/2 inches
Displacement: 429.4 cubic inches
Horsepower: 48
Price when new: $4,500

1912 Premier Model 6-60 Roadster
Manufacturer: Premier Motor
Manufacturing Co., Indianapolis,
IN
Coachbuilder: Premier Motor
Manufacturing Co.
Engine: T-head, 6-cylinder
Bore x Stroke: 4-1/2x5-1/4 inches
Displacement: 500.9 cubic inches
Horsepower: 60
Price when new: $4,000

1913 Hudson Model 6-54 Touring
Manufacturer: Hudson Motor Car
Co., Detroit, MI
Coachbuilder: Hudson Motor Car
Co.
Engine: L-head, 6-cylinder
Bore x Stroke: 4-1/8x5-1/4 inches
Displacement: 420.9 cubic inches
Horsepower: 54
Price when new: $2,600

1913 Lozier Type 72 Lakewood Torpedo
Manufacturer: Lozier Motor
Company, Detroit, MI
Coachbuilder: Lozier Motor
Company
Engine: T-head, 6-cylinder
Bore x Stroke: 4-5/8x5-1/2 inches
Displacement: 554.4 cubic inches
Horsepower: 80
Price when new: $5,000

1914 De Dion Bouton Type EY Limousine
Manufacturer: De Dion, Bouton et
Cie, Puteaux, Seine, France
Coachbuilder: De Dion, Bouton et
Cie
Engine: L-head, V-type, 8-cylinder
Bore x Stroke: 3-11/16x5-1/2 inches
Displacement: 474.3 cubic inches
Horsepower: 69
Price when new: $8,000

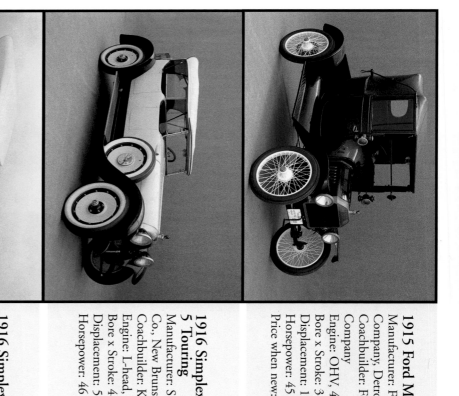

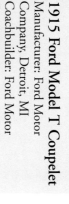

1915 Ford Model T Coupelet
Manufacturer: Ford Motor
Company, Detroit, MI
Coachbuilder: Ford Motor
Company
Engine: OHV, 4-cylinder
Bore x Stroke: 3-3/4x4 inches
Displacement: 176.7 cubic inches
Horsepower: 45 (with
modifications)
Price when new: $750

1916 Simplex, Crane, Model 5 Touring
Manufacturer: Simplex Automobile
Co., New Brunswick, NJ
Coachbuilder: Kimball
Engine: L-head, 6-cylinder
Bore x Stroke: 4-3/8x6-1/4 inches
Displacement: 563.7 cubic inches
Horsepower: 46

1916 Simplex, Crane, Model 5 Touring
Manufacturer: Simplex Automobile
Co., New Brunswick, NJ
Coachbuilder: Larkin Co.
Engine: L-head, 6-cylinder
Bore x Stroke: 4-3/8x6-1/4 inches
Displacement: 563.7 cubic inches
Horsepower: 46

1917 Chandler Type 17 Touring
Manufacturer: Chandler Motor Car
Co., Cleveland, OH
Coachbuilder: Chandler Motor Car
Co.
Engine: L-head, 6-cylinder
Bore x Stroke: 3-3/8x5 inches
Displacement: 268.3 cubic inches
Horsepower: 27
Price when new: $1,595

1918 Marmon Model 34 Four-Passenger Roadster
Manufacturer: Nordyke & Marmon Car Co., Indianapolis, IN
Coachbuilder: Nordyke & Marmon Car Co.
Engine: OHV, 6-cylinder
Bore x Stroke: 3-3/4x5-1/8 inches
Displacement: 339.63 cubic inches
Horsepower: 74
Price when new: $3,750

1918 Rauch & Lang, Electric, Brougham
Manufacturer: Rauch & Lang Carriage Co.
Coachbuilder: Rauch & Lang Carriage Co.
Engine: Electric
Horsepower: 80 volts

1919 Cunningham Series V-3 Limousine
Manufacturer: James Cunningham Son & Co., Inc., Rochester, NY
Coachbuilder: James Cunningham Son & Co., Inc.
Engine: L-head, V-type, 8-cylinder
Bore x Stroke: 3-3/4x5 inches
Displacement: 441.8 cubic inches
Horsepower: 45
Price when new: $8,100

1920 Kenworthy Model 4-80 Seven-Passenger Touring
Manufacturer: Kenworthy Motors, Mishawaka, IN
Coachbuilder: Kenworthy Motors
Engine: Duesenberg, 4-cylinder
Bore x Stroke: 4x6 inches
Displacement: 301.59 cubic inches
Horsepower: 100
Price when new: $5,000

1917 Owen Magnetic M-25 Touring
Manufacturer: Baker R & L Co., Cleveland, OH
Engine: L-head, 6-cylinder
Bore x Stroke: 3-1/2x5-1/4 inches
Displacement: 303.1 cubic inches
Horsepower: 29.4
Price when new: $3,300

1917 Packard 2-35 Twin Six Landaulet, 7-Passenger
Manufacturer: Packard Motor Car Co., Detroit, MI
Coachbuilder: Packard Motor Car Co.
Engine: L-head, V-type, 12-cylinder
Bore x Stroke: 3x5 inches
Displacement: 424.1 cubic inches
Horsepower: 88
Price when new: $4,000

1917 Pierce-Arrow Model 66A-4 Seven-Passenger Touring
Manufacturer: George N. Pierce Co., Buffalo, NY
Coachbuilder: Pierce-Arrow
Engine: T-head, 6-cylinder
Bore x Stroke: 5x7 inches
Displacement: 824.7 cubic inches
Horsepower: 66
Price when new: $8,000

1917 Simplex, Crane, Model 5 Limousine
Manufacturer: Simplex Automobile Co., New Brunswick, NJ
Coachbuilder: Brewster
Engine: 6-cylinder
Bore x Stroke: 4-3/8x6-1/4 inches
Displacement: 563.7 cubic inches
Horsepower: 46

1920 Packard Model 3-35 Twin Six Seven-Passenger Sedan
Manufacturer: Packard Motor Car Company
Coachbuilder: Fleetwood
Engine: L-Head V-Type 12-cylinder
Bore x Stroke: 3x5 inches
Displacement: 424.1 cubic inches
Horsepower: 75
Price when new $5,500

1921 Colonial Prototype Sedan (California Top Style)
Manufacturer: Colonial Motors Co., San Francisco, CA
Coachbuilder: Colonial Motors Co.
Engine: 8-cylinder
Horsepower: 60
Price when new: $1,800

1921 Lincoln Model L Phaeton
Manufacturer: Lincoln Motor Co., Detroit, MI
Coachbuilder: Brunn & Co.
Engine: L-head, V-type, 8-cylinder
Bore x Stroke: 3-3/8x5 inches
Displacement: 357.8 cubic inches
Horsepower: 81
Price when new: $4,300

1924 Cadillac Model V-63 Seven-Passenger Touring
Manufacturer: Cadillac Motor Car Co., Detroit, MI
Coachbuilder: Fisher Body Co.
Engine: L-head, V-type, 8-cylinder
Bore x Stroke: 3-1/8x5-1/8 inches
Displacement: 314.5 cubic inches
Horsepower: 80
Price when new: $2,985

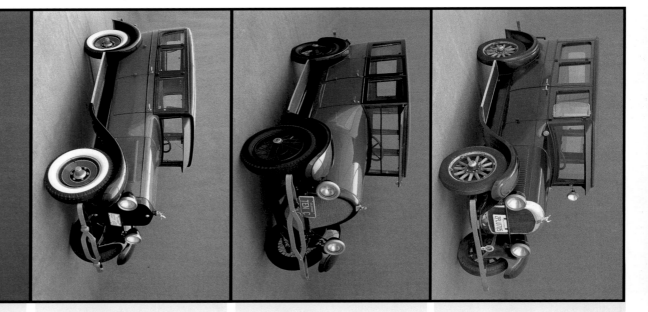

1924 Chrysler Model B70 Sedan
Manufacturer: Chrysler Corp., Detroit, MI
Coachbuilder: Fisher Body Corp.
Engine: L-head, 6-cylinder
Bore x Stroke: 3x4-3/4 inches
Displacement: 201.0 cubic inches
Horsepower: 68
Price when new: $1,625

1925 Franklin Model 10 C Sedan
Manufacturer: Franklin Automobile Co., Syracuse, NY
Coachbuilder: Franklin Automobile Co.
Engine: Air-cooled, 6-cylinder
Bore x Stroke: 3-1/4x4 inches
Displacement: 199.0 cubic inches
Horsepower: 32
Price when new: $2,850

1926 Wills Sainte Claire Model T-6 Sedan
Manufacturer: Wills Sainte Claire Co., Marysville, MI
Coachbuilder: American
Engine: SOHC, 6-cylinder
Bore x Stroke: 3-1/4x5-1/2 inches
Displacement: 273.0 cubic inches
Horsepower: 66

1926 Pierce-Arrow Model 33/34 Roadster
Manufacturer: Pierce-Arrow Co., Buffalo, NY
Coachbuilder: Pierce-Arrow
Engine: Dual Valve, T-Head, 6-cylinder
Bore x Stroke: 4x5-1/2 inches
Displacement: 414.69 cubic inches
Price when new: $5,250

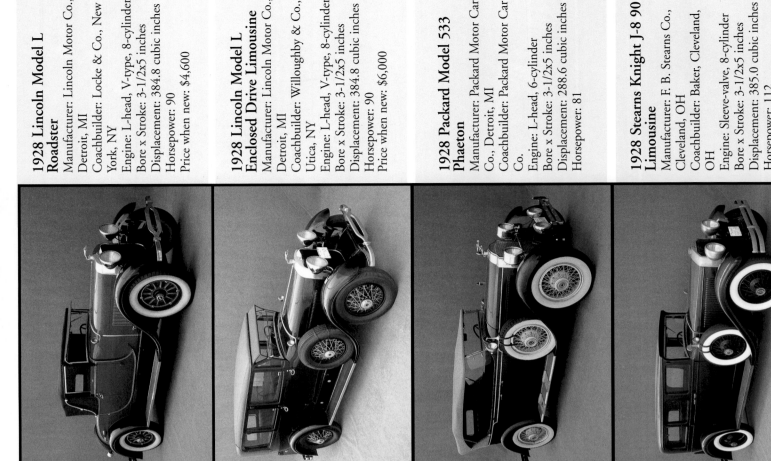

1928 Lincoln Model L Roadster
Manufacturer: Lincoln Motor Co., Detroit, MI
Coachbuilder: Locke & Co., New York, NY
Engine: L-head, V-type, 8-cylinder
Bore x Stroke: 3-1/2x5 inches
Displacement: 384.8 cubic inches
Horsepower: 90
Price when new: $4,600

1928 Lincoln Model L Enclosed Drive Limousine
Manufacturer: Lincoln Motor Co., Detroit, MI
Coachbuilder: Willoughby & Co., Utica, NY
Engine: L-head, V-type, 8-cylinder
Bore x Stroke: 3-1/2x5 inches
Displacement: 384.8 cubic inches
Horsepower: 90
Price when new: $6,000

1928 Packard Model 533 Phaeton
Manufacturer: Packard Motor Car Co., Detroit, MI
Coachbuilder: Packard Motor Car Co.
Engine: L-head, 6-cylinder
Bore x Stroke: 3-1/2x5 inches
Displacement: 288.6 cubic inches
Horsepower: 81

1928 Stearns Knight J-8 90 Limousine
Manufacturer: F. B. Stearns Co., Cleveland, OH
Coachbuilder: Baker, Cleveland, OH
Engine: Sleeve-valve, 8-cylinder
Bore x Stroke: 3-1/2x5 inches
Displacement: 385.0 cubic inches
Horsepower: 112
Price when new: $5,600

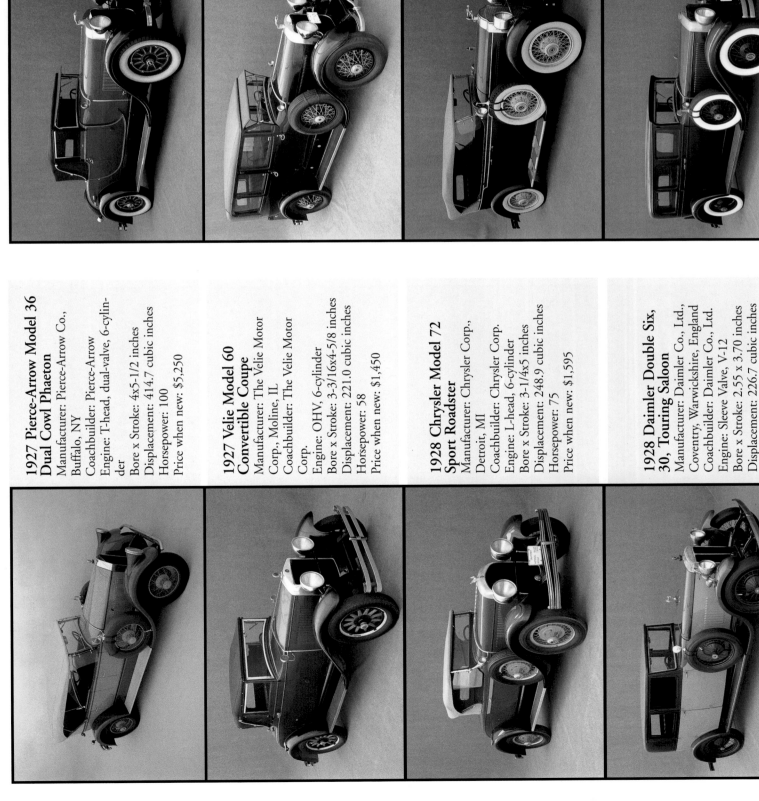

1927 Pierce-Arrow Model 36 Dual Cowl Phaeton
Manufacturer: Pierce-Arrow Co., Buffalo, NY
Coachbuilder: Pierce-Arrow
Engine: T-head, dual-valve, 6-cylinder
Bore x Stroke: 4x5-1/2 inches
Displacement: 414.7 cubic inches
Horsepower: 100
Price when new: $5,250

1927 Velie Model 60 Convertible Coupe
Manufacturer: The Velie Motor Corp., Moline, IL
Coachbuilder: The Velie Motor Corp.
Engine: OHV, 6-cylinder
Bore x Stroke: 3-3/16x4-5/8 inches
Displacement: 221.0 cubic inches
Horsepower: 58
Price when new: $1,450

1928 Chrysler Model 72 Sport Roadster
Manufacturer: Chrysler Corp., Detroit, MI
Coachbuilder: Chrysler Corp.
Engine: L-head, 6-cylinder
Bore x Stroke: 3-1/4x5 inches
Displacement: 248.9 cubic inches
Horsepower: 75
Price when new: $1,595

1928 Daimler Double Six, 30, Touring Saloon
Manufacturer: Daimler Co., Ltd., Coventry, Warwickshire, England
Coachbuilder: Daimler Co., Ltd.
Engine: Sleeve Valve, V-12
Bore x Stroke: 2.55 x 3.70 inches
Displacement: 226.7 cubic inches

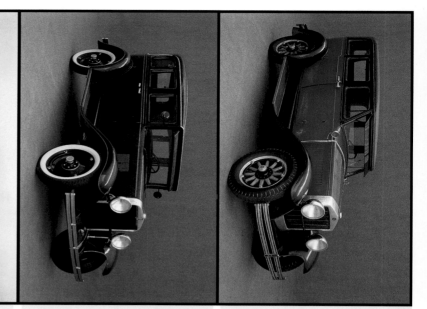

1928 Velie Model 77 Five-Passenger Sedan

Manufacturer: The Velie Motor Corp., Moline, IL
Coachbuilder: The Velie Motor Corp.
Engine: OHV, 6-cylinder
Bore x Stroke: 3-3/16x4-5/8 inches
Displacement: 221.0 cubic inches
Horsepower: 60
Price when new: $1,480

1929 Chevrolet AC, International Sedan (9AC)

Manufacturer: Chevrolet Div., General Motors Corp., Detroit, MI
Coachbuilder: Fisher, Detroit, MI
Engine: OHV, Inline, 6-cylinder
Bore x Stroke: 3-5/16x3-3/4 inches
Displacement: 194 cubic inches
Horsepower: 46
Price when new: $675

1929 Kissel Model 8-126 White Eagle Speedster

Manufacturer: Kissel Motor Car Co., Hartford, WI
Coachbuilder: Kissel Motor Car Co.
Engine: L-head, Inline, 8-cylinder
Bore x Stroke: 3-1/4x4-1/2 inches
Displacement: 298.6 cubic inches
Horsepower: 126
Price when new: $3,275

1930 Cadillac V-16 Model 452A Dual Cowl Phaeton

Manufacturer: Cadillac Motor Car Co., Detroit, MI
Coachbuilder: Fisher, Detroit, MI
Engine: OHV, V-type, V-16
Bore x Stroke: 3x4 inches
Displacement: 452 cubic inches
Horsepower: 175
Price when new: $6,500

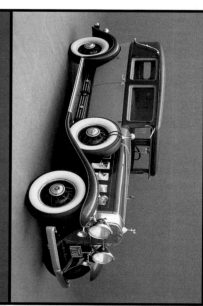

1930 Cadillac V-16 Model 452A Imperial Cabriolet

Manufacturer: Cadillac Motor Car Co., Detroit, MI
Coachbuilder: Fleetwood, Detroit, MI
Engine: OHV, V-type, V-16
Bore x Stroke: 3x4 inches
Displacement: 452 cubic inches
Horsepower: 175
Price when new: $6,125

1930 Ford Model A Sport Coupe

Manufacturer: Ford Motor Co., Detroit, MI
Coachbuilder: Ford Motor Co.
Engine: L-head, 4-cylinder
Bore x Stroke: 3-7/8x4-1/4 inches
Displacement: 200.5 cubic inches
Horsepower: 40
Price when new: $530

1930 Marmon Big Eight, 112 Sedan

Manufacturer: Marmon Motor Car Co., Indianapolis, IN
Coachbuilder: Hayes Body Corp., Cleveland, OH
Engine: L-head, straight eight
Bore x Stroke: 3-1/4x4-3/4 inches
Displacement: 315.2 cubic inches
Horsepower: 125
Price when new: $3,000

1930 Packard Model 734 Speedster Eight Victoria

Manufacturer: Packard Motor Car Co., Detroit, MI
Coachbuilder: Packard Custom, Detroit, MI
Engine: L-head, straight eight
Bore x Stroke: 3-1/2x5 inches
Displacement: 384.8 cubic inches
Horsepower: 145
Price when new: $6,000

1930 Packard Model 745 Deluxe Eight Imperial Sport Landaulet

Manufacturer: Packard Motor Car Co., Detroit, MI
Coachbuilder: Murphy Coach Builders, Pasadena, CA
Engine: L-head, straight eight
Bore x Stroke: 3-1/2x5 inches
Displacement: 384.8 cubic inches
Horsepower: 106

1931 Cadillac V-12 Model 370A Convertible Coupe

Manufacturer: Cadillac Motor Car Co., Detroit, MI
Coachbuilder: Fleetwood, Detroit, MI
Engine: OHV, V-12
Bore x Stroke: 3-1/8x4 inches
Displacement: 368 cubic inches
Horsepower: 135
Price when new: $4,895

1931 Packard Model 845 Deluxe Eight Dietrich Sport Sedan

Manufacturer: Packard Motor Car Co., Detroit, MI
Coachbuilder: Dietrich Inc., Detroit, MI
Engine: L-head, 8-cylinder
Bore x Stroke: 3-1/2x5 inches
Displacement: 384.8 cubic inches
Horsepower: 120
Price when new: $4,000

1931 REO Royale, Model 35 Sedan

Manufacturer: REO Motor Car Co., Lansing, MI
Coachbuilder: Murray Body Co., Detroit, MI
Engine: L-head, 8-cylinder
Bore x Stroke: 3-3/8x5 inches
Displacement: 356.0 cubic inches
Horsepower: 125
Price when new: $2,485

1931 Studebaker President, Series 80, Four Seasons Roadster

Manufacturer: Studebaker Corp., South Bend, IN
Coachbuilder: Studebaker Corp., South Bend, IN
Engine: L-head, 8-cylinder
Bore x Stroke: 3-1/2x4-3/8 inches
Displacement: 337 cubic inches
Horsepower: 122
Price when new: $1,900

1932 Auburn Model 12-161A Convertible Coupe

Manufacturer: Auburn Automobile Co., Auburn, IN
Coachbuilder: Central Mfg. Co., Connersville, IN
Engine: V-12 Lycoming
Bore x Stroke: 3-1/8x4-1/4 inches
Displacement: 391.16 cubic inches
Horsepower: 160

1932 Cadillac Model 355B Deluxe Sport Coupe

Manufacturer: Cadillac Motor Car Co., Detroit, MI
Coachbuilder: Fisher, Detroit, MI
Engine: L-head, V-type, 8-cylinder
Bore x Stroke: 3-3/8x4-15/16 inches
Displacement: 353.0 cubic inches
Horsepower: 115
Price when new: $2,795

1932 Chevrolet Confederate Series BA Deluxe Coupe

Manufacturer: Chevrolet Motor Car Co., Detroit, MI
Coachbuilder: Fisher Body Co., Detroit, MI
Engine: OHV, 6-cylinder
Bore x Stroke: 3-5/16x3-3/4 inches
Displacement: 196.0 cubic inches
Horsepower: 60
Price when new: $575

220

1933 Pierce-Arrow Model 1242 Seven-Passenger Touring
Manufacturer: Pierce-Arrow Motor Car Co., Buffalo, NY
Coachbuilder: Pierce-Arrow, Buffalo, NY
Engine: L-head, V-type, 12-cylinder
Bore x Stroke: 3-1/2x4 inches
Displacement: 462 cubic inches
Horsepower: 175
Price when new: $4,250

1933 Cadillac V-16 Model 452C Imperial Limousine
Manufacturer: Cadillac Motor Car Co., Detroit, MI
Coachbuilder: Fleetwood Inc., Detroit, MI
Engine: OHV, V-type, 16-cylinder
Bore x Stroke: 3x4 inches
Displacement: 452 cubic inches
Horsepower: 175
Price when new: $6,400

1932 Pierce-Arrow Model 53 Sedan
Manufacturer: Pierce-Arrow Motor Car Co., Buffalo, NY
Coachbuilder: Pierce-Arrow Motor Car Co.
Engine: L-head, V-type, 12-cylinder
Bore x Stroke: 3-3/8x4 inches
Displacement: 398.0 cubic inches
Horsepower: 140
Price when new: $3,650

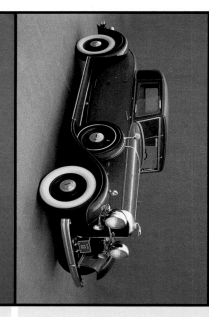

1932 Lincoln Series 231, KB Coupe
Manufacturer: Lincoln Motor Co., Detroit, MI
Coachbuilder: Judkins, Merrimac, MA
Engine: L-head, V-type, 12-cylinder
Bore x Stroke: 3-1/4x4-1/2 inches
Displacement: 447.9 cubic inches
Horsepower: 150
Price when new: $6,500

1937 Pierce-Arrow Model 1702 Enclosed Drive Limousine
Manufacturer: Pierce-Arrow Motor Car Co., Buffalo, NY
Coachbuilder: Pierce-Arrow Motor Car Co.
Engine: L-head, V-type, 12-cylinder
Bore x Stroke: 3-1/2x5 inches
Displacement: 462 cubic inches
Horsepower: 185
Price when new: $4,953

1937 Packard Twelve Model 1507 Club Sedan
Manufacturer: Packard Motor Car Co., Detroit, MI
Coachbuilder: Packard Motor Car Co.
Engine: L-head, V-type, 12-cylinder
Bore x Stroke: 3-7/16x4-1/4 inches
Displacement: 473.3 cubic inches
Horsepower: 175
Price when new: $4,860

1937 Cord 812 Supercharged Phaeton Sedan
Manufacturer: Auburn Automobile Co., Auburn, IN
Coachbuilder: Central Manufacturing Co., Connersville, IN
Engine: L-head, Lycoming, 8-cylinder
Bore x Stroke: 3-1/2x3-3/4 inches
Displacement: 288.6 cubic inches
Horsepower: 175
Price when new: $2,645

1936 Ford Model 68 Deluxe Roadster
Manufacturer: Ford Motor Co., Dearborn, MI
Coachbuilder: Ford Motor Co.
Engine: L-head, V-type, 8-cylinder
Bore x Stroke: 3-1/16x3-3/4 inches
Displacement: 221.0 cubic inches
Horsepower: 85
Price when new: $560

1939 Packard Twelve Model 1707 Formal Sedan

Manufacturer: Packard Motor Car Co., Detroit, MI
Coachbuilder: Budd, Detroit, MI
Engine: L-head, V-type, 12-cylinder
Bore x Stroke: 3-7/16x4-1/4 inches
Displacement: 473.0 cubic inches
Horsepower: 175
Price when new: $5,000

1947 Ford Super Deluxe 79A Station Wagon

Manufacturer: Ford Motor Co., Detroit, MI
Coachbuilder: Ford Motor Co., Detroit, MI
Engine: L-head, V-type, 8-cylinder
Bore x Stroke: 3.187x3.75 inches
Displacement: 239 cubic inches
Horsepower: 100
Price when new: $1,975

1948 MG TC Roadster

Manufacturer: M. G. Car Co., Ltd., Abingdon-on-Thames, England
Coachbuilder: M. G. Car Co., Ltd.
Engine: OHV, 4-cylinder
Bore x Stroke: 2.62x3.54 inches
Displacement: 76.3 cubic inches
Horsepower: 70
Price when new: $2,238

1948 Tucker, Model 48 Sedan

Manufacturer: The Tucker Corp., Chicago, IL
Coachbuilder: The Tucker Corp.
Engine: Horizontal-Opp., 6-cylinder
Bore x Stroke: 4.5x3.5 inches
Displacement: 334.1 cubic inches
Horsepower: 166
Price when new: $2,450

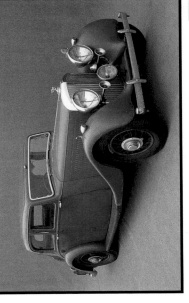

1938 Bentley 4-1/4 Liter Convertible Sedan

Manufacturer: Bentley Motors Ltd., Derby, England
Coachbuilder: Hooper & Co., London, England
Engine: OHV, 6-cylinder
Bore x Stroke: 3-1/2x4-1/2 inches
Displacement: 259.7 cubic inches
Horsepower: 126

1938 Cadillac Series 75 Convertible Coupe

Manufacturer: Cadillac Motor Car Co., Detroit, MI
Coachbuilder: Fleetwood, Detroit, MI
Engine: L-head, V-type, 8-cylinder
Bore x Stroke: 3-1/2x4-1/2 inches
Displacement: 346 cubic inches
Horsepower: 140
Price when new: $3,380

1938 Lincoln K, Twelve Touring Coupe/Limousine

Manufacturer: Lincoln Motor Co., Detroit, MI
Coachbuilder: Judkins, Merrimac, MA
Engine: L-head, V-type, 12-cylinder
Bore x Stroke: 3-1/8x4-1/2 inches
Displacement: 414.0 cubic inches
Horsepower: 150
Price when new: $7,000

1939 Bentley 4-1/4 Liter Saloon

Manufacturer: Bentley Motors Ltd., Derby, England
Coachbuilder: Park Ward, London, England
Engine: OHV, 6-cylinder
Bore x Stroke: 3-1/2x4-1/2 inches
Displacement: 259.7 cubic inches
Horsepower: 126

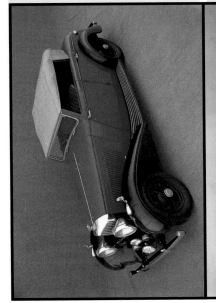

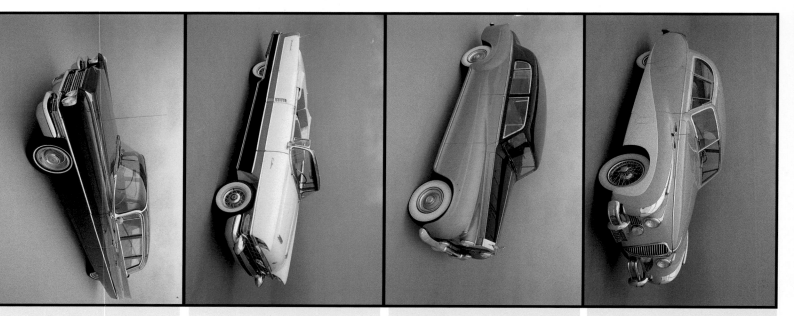

1949 Delahaye Type 175 Coupe de Ville
Manufacturer: Automobile Delahaye, Tours, Paris, France
Coachbuilder: Carrossier Saoutchik, Paris, France
Engine: OHV, 6-cylinder
Bore x Stroke: 3.70x4.21 inches
Displacement: 271.6 cubic inches
Horsepower: 185
Price when new: $20,000

1955 Rolls-Royce Silver Wraith Touring Limousine
Manufacturer: Rolls-Royce Ltd., Crewe, Cheshire, England
Coachbuilder: James Young Ltd., London, England
Engine: F-head, 6-cylinder
Bore x Stroke: 3.62x4.50 inches
Displacement: 278.5 cubic inches
Horsepower: 150
Price when new: $11,000

1956 Packard Caribbean, 56th Series, Convertible
Manufacturer: Studebaker-Packard Corp., Detroit, MI
Coachbuilder: Packard, Detroit, MI
Engine: OHV, V-type, 8-cylinder
Bore x Stroke: 4-1/8x3-1/2 inches
Displacement: 374 cubic inches
Horsepower: 310
Price when new: $5,995

1963 Cadillac Model 75 Eight-Passenger Sedan
Manufacturer: Cadillac Motor Car Co., Detroit, MI
Coachbuilder: Fleetwood, Detroit, MI
Engine: OHV, 8-cylinder
Bore x Stroke: 4.0x3.8 inches
Displacement: 390 cubic inches
Horsepower: 325
Price when new: $9,724

1963 Rolls-Royce Silver Cloud III Saloon
Manufacturer: Rolls-Royce Ltd., Crewe, Cheshire, England
Coachbuilder: James Young Ltd., London, England
Engine: OHV, V-type, 8-cylinder
Bore x Stroke: 4.1x3.6 inches
Displacement: 380 cubic inches
Horsepower: 200

1976 Cadillac Castillion Station Wagon
Manufacturer: Cadillac Motor Car Co., Detroit, MI
Engine: OHV, 8-cylinder
Bore x Stroke: 4.30x4.304 inches
Displacement: 500 cubic inches
Horsepower: 190

1979 Rolls-Royce Silver Wraith II Saloon
Manufacturer: Rolls-Royce Ltd., Crewe, Cheshire, England
Engine: OHV, V-type, 8-cylinder

1983 DeLorean Series DMC 12 Coupe
Manufacturer: De Lorean, Dunmurry, Ireland
Coachbuilder: De Lorean
Engine: SOHC, V-type, 6-cylinder
Bore x Stroke: 3.58x2.87 inches
Displacement: 174 cubic inches
Horsepower: 130
Price when new: $25,000

Index